THIS PROGRAM IS SUPPORTED BY THE ARKANSAS ARTS COUNCIL, AN AGENCY OF THE DEPARTMENT OF ARKANSAS HERITAGE, THE NATIONAL ENDOWMENT FOR THE ARTS, AND THE ARKANSAS HUMANITIES COUNCIL.

MARY LEWIS

THE GOLDEN HAIRED
BEAUTY
WITH THE GOLDEN
VOICE

Also by
Alice Fitch Zeman
Wabansi: Fiend or Friend?
1981

MARY LEWIS

THE GOLDEN HAIRED BEAUTY WITH THE GOLDEN VOICE

ALICE FITCH ZEMAN

ROSE PUBLISHING
LITTLE ROCK

Published by
Rose Publishing Company, Inc.
Little Rock, Arkansas

Library of Congress Cataloging-in-Publication Data
Zeman, Alice Fitch
Mary Lewis: the golden haired beauty with the golden voice / Alice Fitch Zeman
p. cm.
ISBN 0-914546-99-6
1. Lewis, Mary.
1. Singers - United States - Biography.
I. Title
ML420.L39Z35 2000
784.092
LC card number - 134985

Printed in the United States of America
January 2001

To my family -

to those who have gone before

and

to those who will come after

TABLE OF CONTENTS

List of Illustrations

Acknowledgments

Thanks are due for the generous cooperation of my parents, Blanche and Finley Fitch, of Yorkville, Illinois; my step-grandmother, Mildred Fitch; to my grandfather the Rev. Frank F. Fitch of Earlville, Illinois; to my great grandparents, the Reverend William and Anna Fitch, for the wealth of information they left; and to my sons, Joe, Mike, Andy, and Allyn. I am grateful to Jeff Politsch for computer programming and support; Connie Avery, former Paw Paw (Illinois) Librarian, for research and encouragement; David Duncan Larson, Combined Arts and Charles F. Martin of Paw Paw, for consultation and design; Maxwell Silverman, research in the New York Public Library archives; and John Pennino, archivist at the Metropolitan Opera Association; and Laura Nitanda, research at Chicago Public Library; and the archivists at the Little Rock Public Library. Translation suggestions were provided in French by Karen Lyons, Paw Paw High School French teacher; Italian by Valerio Paduanelli of Brindisi, Italy; and German by Christoph Galle of Weiden, Germany.

Three large (16" x 17") scrapbooks, which were the personal property of Mary Lewis, were generously loaned for research for the biography by Lawrence F. Holdridge of New York. The scrapbooks, filled with newspaper clippings and memorabilia, were invaluable in providing material for the latter part of the biography. Holdridge explained that the scrapbooks were among the musical memorabilia he purchased from the estate of Frederic Langford, a tenor and pupil of Seneca Pierce, who had been a friend and accompanist of Mary Lewis. Pierce, born in Milwaukee, studied piano in Chicago with Glenn Dillard Gunn and accompanying in New York with Frank LaForge. Several of his songs were in the concert repertoire of singers active in the late ’teens and early ’20s. In addition to accompanying, Pierce studied voice and made his debut as a baritone in Paris, 1926, touring Europe in 1926-27. He later became a voice teacher and coach.

I appreciate permission given by W. R. Moran and Michael Quinn for use of their listings and the valuable information concerning the recordings of Mary Lewis.

Recognition for the impetus to motivate undertaking of this biography belongs to the 1982 Paw Paw Centennial. Thanks to Dr. Wayne and Doris Brown, who headed the Centennial committee, and all those who helped with the Centennial. Credit must be given to Joan Mercer, who organized the Centennial Style Show that featured the Mary Lewis dress. It was her interest that inspired the initial research.

Special thanks go to Prof. Michael Dougan and Carol Dougan, of Jonesboro, Arkansas, for contributions and editing. Thanks to Carol Griffee, Editorial Services, Inc., for editing and suggestions.

Deepest gratitude goes to Gale Stewart, of Little Rock, Arkansas, for believing the Mary Lewis story should be told. I am especially grateful most of all to my friends and family for listening to me as I unraveled and wove together the Mary Lewis story.

AUTHOR'S NOTE: This work was begun about 18 years ago, first by typewriter, then upgraded to basic computer text program. Final work is on Corel Suite 8. Reference for style has been *A Manual for Writers* by Kate L. Turabian, 4th edition. The material has been gathered from numerous sources, causing variations in listing of titles, and writing style. An effort has been made for uniformity by choosing a single spelling or title to be coordinated throughout while material used in quotations follows as it appears in the original. Therefore, possessive of Mary Lewis's name is used according to the style manual in the text, except when Lewis' is used in the original quotation. The same is true for series appearing in sentences. Text use is with a comma between elements and before a conjunction separating the last two (i.e., Mary Lewis sang in America, England, and Europe); whereas, the quotation from material of the time period in the early 1900s was to omit the last comma. Names of foreign places are not italicized (i.e., as Casa Del Mare), although foreign words which appear in the text are italicized (i.e., *mise-en-scene*). Works, books, periodicals, plays, motion pictures, and operas are italicized. Arias and songs are set in quotation marks and regular font.

Introduction

In searching the family trunks and attics for old clothes to be worn in a 1982 Paw Paw, Illinois, Centennial style show, I came across the ragged little "Mary Lewis" dress packed away with my great grandmother's silken memory quilt. Along with the mementoes was a collection of family history and packets of Mary Lewis clippings. Intrigued by her adventures, I began research to compile the information into a biography and, as I attempted to glean further resources, I found my assortment was much more complete than any other data and contained some highly unusual, untold material concerning Mary Lewis. Her story has been aptly described as an "enigma"—something puzzling, a riddle. Faded into the past is the period of time in America when such a story could take place.

Mary's life is a part of the history of the development of our nation with such milestones as:

> **From spirituals, jazz and "mammy" era songs, and Broadway hits, to classical concerts and Grand Opera. Mary sang them all!**
>
> **From rail and ship to the newest and fastest planes and even a dirigible, Mary traveled them all!**
>
> **From silent movies and early radio to the talkies, Mary Lewis was at one point the most publicized personality of the 1920s!**

During Lewis's heyday, newspaper readers were greeted by her name and picture splashed across their papers in glowing headlines such as:

> **Chorus Girl Lewis in Opera Triumph, Given Greatest Welcome, Slips in on the *Aquitania*, Sings at the Met, Sings on Radio, Sings as Recitalist, Romance Not Suspected, Postpones Honeymoon, Wed By Mayor Walker, Snaring a Song Bird with Sound, Is Accused, To Sail, Toast of Paris in Title Role, Wed to Oil Man, Aids Trade Recovery, Successful in Efforts to Evade Press, Fails in Flight Record Fighting Heavy Winds, Boards Air Ship, Opera Star Dead.**

Mary's story is best told by direct quotations taken from newspaper reports of the day. Some of these were saved in scrapbooks. Others were found by original research. An effort was made to be as accurate as possible and therefore sometimes contradictory reports were included.

Who was Mary Lewis?

Mary Lewis received five curtain calls on her first appearance in January 1926, at the Metropolitan Opera House in New York. Unidentified newspaper clipping. Fitch album.

Tinted publicity photo of Mary Lewis, an American Cinderella. Undated, unidentified. Fitch album.

ABOUT THE AUTHOR

For the research and writing the biography on Mary Lewis, Alice Fitch Zeman used skills and tools she has learned in her work as a secretary, journalist, photographer, and historian.

Zeman previously published a biography, *Wabansi: Fiend or Friend?*—a research work on Wabansi, a Potawatomi Indian leader who sometimes made his home at the Paw Paw Grove in Illinois. She also designed and published a map/brochure, *Chief Shabbona's Path of Peace*, which highlights sites linked with the Potawatomi leader.

For each of these publications Zeman received recognition from the Illinois State Historical Society for her work in preserving information related to the state's heritage.

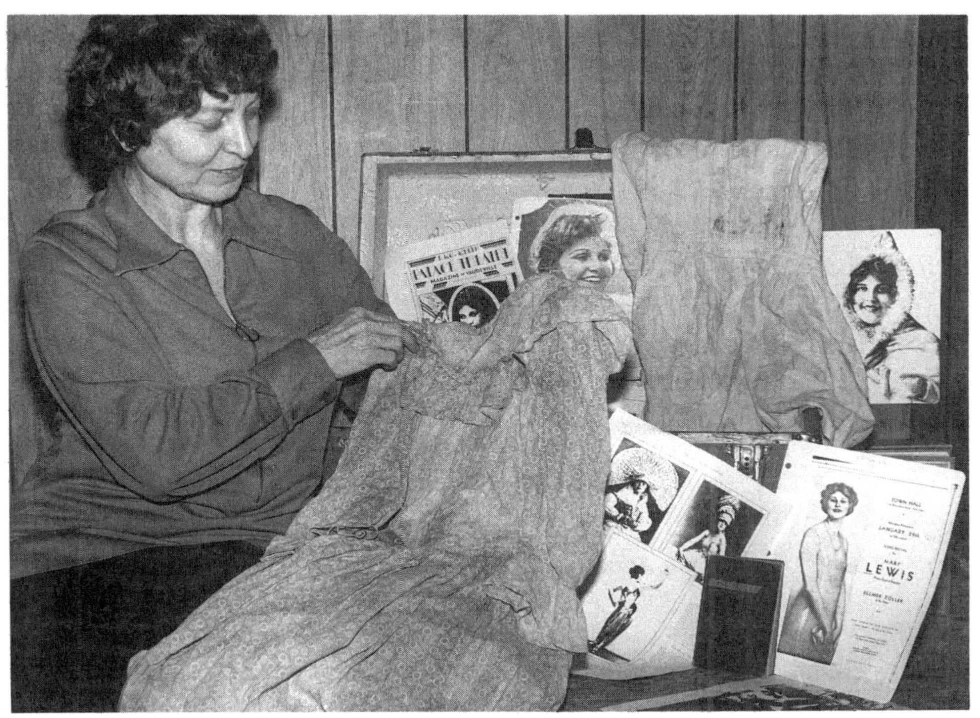

The riddle of "Who was Mary Lewis?" began to be solved when a look into the family trunks and attics revealed some unusual, unknown information regarding the woman who captured the hearts of the international press and the world during the 1920s. Photo by Alice Zeman.

1

Mary

Although one of the first events (or so it seemed) at the turn of the twentieth century was the birth of a child,[1] the world took little notice. But within twenty-five years, flashbulbs were popping and her every move was recorded by the press and broadcast over the radio. The public loved the rags-to-riches story of Mary Lewis which had all the ingredients of a fairy tale. A starving waif, rescued from the gutter, became, in succession a movie star, a Ziegfeld prima donna, and a diva at the Metropolitan Opera. All of this was climaxed with a marriage to a wealthy oil shipping tycoon. This was a tale of the American dream that leads to a life of happiness ever after—or so it might have seemed.

Scrutiny reveals that actually our heroine made her appearance a little earlier than the January 7, 1900, birth date given to the public.[2] Vanity may have been the reason for subtracting several years from her age, or possibly it was simply an easier date to remember. It made small difference, because even Mary knew little surrounding the circumstances of her birth.

A certificate indicates the child, Mary, was born January 29, 1897, in Hot Springs, Arkansas, to Hattie and Charles Kidd. Her father was formerly of Chicago, Illinois,[3] and apparently of German ancestry.[4] Her mother had been born Hattie Lewis in Louisville, Kentucky.[5] The child was named for her maternal grandmother,[6] her middle name was Sybil,[7] and she was christened August 29 of the same year at St. Mary's Catholic Church in Hot Springs.[8]

Mary later recalled she first remembered her family as her mother, grandmother, and a younger brother, Joe Kidd. She said her father died when she was less than two years old, a few weeks before the birth of her brother.[9] Another version of the story makes no mention of the father, and says her grandmother, upon whom the family depended for a tiny income, died when Mary was two.[10] Her mother gathered up her two babies to migrate first to Little Rock, then to Dallas, Texas, to eke out a living. She was unsuccessful in this attempt and the babies were starving.[11]

Mary grew thin and rickety with big hollows under her blue eyes. Freckles took over the snub-nosed, pinched face, and her voice became frail and weak. Her makeshift clothing was ragged and dirty, as her poor mother had neither time nor money to launder clothes. Mary's feet were bare in the summer and covered with worn-out, discarded shoes in the winter. She was plagued with a head cold and sniffles at the first cold blast of winter, and the thin skin of her hands and face was chapped. Mary later described herself as "just a scrawny, freckle-faced little brat, full of honest intentions and joyousness, and with an infinite capacity for puppylike misadventure."[12]

The desperate mother entrusted her two little ones into the care of an orphan asylum. Mary later said, "The first day in this refuge I was visited with a great and heartbreaking humiliation. My one claim to loveliness, long curls—neither red nor yellow, but honest gold—were shorn from my outraged scalp," and kerosene was rubbed into the remaining stubble to cure the lice infestation. Her mother was horrified when, on her first visit, "a bald-headed terror with a face that was all one freckle" hurled herself into her mother's arms, causing the overtired, lamenting woman to weep.[13]

Mary's memories of the orphanage can bring tears to the eyes of even the most hard-hearted. According to one interview, within a few weeks Mary was convinced it was better to starve in the shelter of her mother's warm love than to die of filth and poor food which characterized the institution.[14] According to another even more heartbreaking narration, "Mary knew dreary days as alike as the inevitable peas in the inevitable pod. Days when she wore gray dresses and ate gray porridge and looked out on a gray world, peopled with an unending monotony of gray days."[15] Mary thought she was perhaps four years old, although she probably was a little older.[16]

Mary recalled, "I slept in a dormitory with a mob of other children of the poor, a place where even the most elementary of sanitation never entered. It was not long before it seemed that I was always ailing. It was the food, perhaps, or the filthiness of the dormitory, or the fact that I missed my mother and her quick warm love."[17]

Her brother was the first to make his escape from the orphanage with its high, unscalable walls, and he found his way back to their mother, who hurried to retrieve Mary when she learned of the child's wretched condition. The situation came to the attention of a family who agreed to take Mary into their home.[18] Hope glimmered.

Mary was taken to a two-story house, which overwhelmed her with its magnificence, with even an attic and a basement. The unkempt ward was bathed, provided with new clothes, and fed before being instructed in her new tasks. Mary was to assist the single servant by drying the dishes, dusting, sweeping and other small chores. That evening after the dishes were finished, which seemed like an endless chore to the tiny servant, she was taken to her quarters. There in the basement she lay trembling, sleepless, throughout the dark night, listening to the rats scurrying about. Mary managed for several agonizing days. During the nights she hid under the thin coverlet to protect herself from the dark horror and scampering rodents.[19]

On a Sunday morning, while the family was at mass, Mary recalled, she gathered up her clothing, castoff toys, and trinkets, tied her meager possessions into a handkerchief, and left. She followed endless streets from the affluent neighborhood to make her way back to the slums and the arms of her mother. Years later she remembered the day had "blurred into a sensation of trudging, aching feet which felt the shock of each footstep on the hot pavement." Mary's mother had found employment, and was torn between yearning to keep the child with her, but in despair as to how she could care for her.[20] No further mention is made of the little boy, Joe, who may have been sent to live with his father's people in Chicago.

So Mary, near the age of six, became a child of the streets. She remembered it as a time of happy-go-lucky days, when she played with the children of the Italians, Spanish, Portuguese, and Negroes, as well as the Irish, like herself. All had a heritage of gaiety, dancing, singing and joyousness. She "danced to the hurdy-gurdies" and learned "jig steps, and the gayly insolent darky songs." Together they danced and sang at religious festivals, united in a very true democracy by the common cause of poverty, giving them a great tolerance of both race and religion. Mary joined the lifestyle and sang with abandon.[21]

Two of her playmates were children of Italian parentage who lived behind the family's fruit shop. About a block away was a saloon to which the grocer's wife was reluctant to send her own children on an undignified errand, so Mary was sent instead with a bucket for beer. She felt important to be selected for the task, even though she realized it was demeaning. She carefully performed her duty giving up the entrusted nickel for the foaming broth, and retraced her steps smoothly, not spilling a drop. Mission completed, Mary was given an overripe banana as her reward. The unsalable, blackened fruit was relished by the happy urchin. Later she could not abide what was considered an edible banana, because she had learned to love the rotten blobs. Several years were spent in this tramp-like existence.[22]

Mary's other playmates included Sylvia, a haughty Spanish beauty. Mary said, "I worshiped this arrogance and bitterly envied her ivory satin skin, her dark, bold eyes and magnificent black hair." Others were also attracted by Sylvia's good looks, and Mary watched with envy as Sylvia was adored. Sylvia wore simple, cheap dresses made marvelous by her mother's needlework. And Sylvia herself was kept clean and sweet- smelling, something that Mary was not.[23] Imitating her idol, Mary would preen, strut, and toss her head about, only to be taken aback when she caught a reflection in a window of the scrawny, freckle-faced clown grimacing in return. Mary's smile revealed an early lost baby tooth, making her look even more like a hoodlum. Mary knew she was the ugly duckling; not only was she told, she could see. Mary became Sylvia's shadow. While the little ragamuffin watched, Sylvia was groomed, brushed, combed, and curled before being dispatched to the Settlement Sunday School. Mary went, too, as far as the door. Her peers had let her know, she says, "that I was a dirty brat and my clothes were a disgrace to even the Dallas slums." Mary did not dare enter the sanctuary in her rags and tangled hair.[24]

"One memorable Wednesday evening," Mary recalled, "I followed Sylvia and her escort of Settlement workers who had called for her to prayer meeting and settled myself to wait for her on the church steps. I stared sleepily at a streak of light escaping from the church and yawned prodigiously with boredom. The night air was like a drugged wine, and my eyelids drooped and I stretched myself along the step. A great foot crushed me presently and I woke with a yell." Mary fled across the street, where she was found cowering and whimpering behind a tree. The congregation streamed from the little church, with the preacher following and demanding to know what had disrupted the vesper service. The story was told and Sylvia acknowledged it was her friend, Mary, who always waited for her.[25]

The preacher's wife hurried to the side of the frightened, hurt child, sympathetically asking, "But why didn't you come in?" Mary told of her shame. "If your mother will let me give you a new dress, will you come in?" the preacher's wife questioned. Mary was speechless. The following day the pastor's wife appeared with a complete outfit, which Mary tried on with much preening. Mary says, "How vain I was of it! And how I cherished it! It was dedicated to the Sabbath. I would not have dreamed of wearing it on a mere week day. But on Sunday morning I would take it out of its newspapers and put it on and walk carefully to church, avoiding all dust and mud puddles. Upon my return home, it was instantly removed and restored to its protecting newspaper."[26]

A new life unfolded for the untended, unsupervised child. Mary displaced Sylvia as the protégée of the preacher's wife. Sylvia had not been properly appreciative, Mary remembered, for all the clothing and gifts given her by the preacher's wife. The haughty Sylvia had accepted all things as her due, while Mary, having had nothing up to this point of her life, was overcome with gratefulness.[27] During a Methodist revival series, Mary appeared every day at the mission tent. Intrigued, her fingers ran over the organ keys. The child had an inborn sense of music which had been unfettered and freely given to the songs of the international street people.[28]

The couple, always eager to bring a lost soul into the fold, had found one in need. A willing pupil, Mary was taught the familiar childhood favorite, "Jesus Wants Me For a Sunbeam." Before she was allowed to sing, Mary chanted the words until the pastor's wife could hear every syllable distinctly:[29]

> Jesus wants me for a sunbeam, to shine for Him each day;
> In every way try to please Him, at home, at school, at play.
> A sunbeam, a sunbeam, Jesus wants me for a sunbeam;
> A sunbeam, a sunbeam, I'll be a sunbeam for Him.[30]

Mary said, "And thus, before I was ten years old, I acquired the rare art of singing as clearly as I would speak, and I have never ceased to be grateful to her." After her diction was pronounced acceptable, the musical debut of the pupil was scheduled and her newly learned song presented with gusto during a Settlement program. Applause and adoration were her reward, and Mary recalled, "The triumph brought my patroness to a decision. She had been pondering whether to adopt Sylvia or me, and my success decided her." Mary's mother was consulted, and she agreed she was only too happy to be assured of proper care and training for her daughter.[31]

This is the way Mary told the story. Actually, it is doubtful the minister and his wife were actively seeking to adopt a child, let alone such an impossibly raw, unfinished product. Rev. William S. Fitch and his wife, Anna, were sixty years old at the time![32]

Endnotes Chapter 1 Mary

1. *Who's Who in America*, 1932-33, p. 1413.
2. Ibid.
3. Baptismal records, St. Mary's Catholic Church, Arkansas.
4. RKO-Keith Palace Theatre Magazine of Vaudeville, 22 Nov. 1930.
5. Obituary, n.p., n.d., file Pinecrest Memorial Park, Alexander, Hot Springs, Arkansas.
6. Ibid.
7. *Who's Who*, 1932-33, p. 1413.
8. Baptismal records.
9. Mary Lewis, "From the Slums, to the Follies, to Grand Opera," *Ladies' Home Journal*, (May 1927), p. 3.
10. Michael B. Dougan, "Mary Lewis, An Arkansas Girl in Grand Opera," *The Record Collector* 23, Dec. 1976, p. 172.
11. Lewis, "From the Slums," *LHJ*, (May 1927), p. 3.
12. Ibid.
13. Ibid.
14. Ibid.
15. Gladys Hall, "She Obeyed that Impulse," *Motion Picture*, n.d., p. 50.
16. Her Little Rock High School records give her birth as 1897 as well as her first marriage license, cited by Michael B. Dougan, "A Touching Enigma.: The Opera Career of Mary Lewis," *Arkansas Historical Quarterly* (1975), p. 259. Also, Dougan refers in notes, p. 259, Mary Lewis, in a letter to her mother, n.p., n.d., says, "Having up until two years ago always believed I was born in 1898."
17. Lewis, "From the Slums," *LHJ*, (May 1927), p. 3.
18. Ibid.
19. Ibid.
20. Ibid.

21. Ibid.
22. Ibid., p. 4.
23. Ibid.
24. Ibid.
25. Ibid.
26. Ibid.
27. Ibid.
28. W.E. Orr, *That's Judsonia*. (Judsonia: White Company Printing, 1957), p. 290.
29. Lewis, "From the Slums," *LHJ*, (May 1927), p. 5.
30. Nellie Talbot, *Praises* (E.O. Excell, n.p., n.d.).
31. Lewis, "From the Slums," *LHJ*, (May 1927), p. 5.
32. Fitch family file, author's collection.

The Hope Methodist Church in Dallas, Texas, where Rev. William Fitch served as pastor when Mary appeared to make her home with the pastor and his wife. From the Fitch album, 1905.

Mary liked to come to the pastor's revival tent and run her fingers over the organ keys. One day she announced, "My mother says you can have me." The little tattered blue-gray gown she wore was cleaned and packed away by the pastor's wife—a remembrance of Mary's former existence. Model Alicia Slaughterback. Photo by Zeman.

Anna and Rev. William Fitch as they appeared in 1903, the year before Mary entered their lives. From the Fitch album.

2

William and Anna

It was into no ordinary frontier home that Mary had made her way. There existed not only a generation gap, but a cultural gap as well! Rev. William Strickland Fitch left a "record far more than an ordinary one," his obituary reads. He was born in Perry County, Ohio, in 1845, the son of a Methodist minister, Rev. John Fitch. The elder Fitch served several pastorates in Ohio until 1865.[1]

William enlisted in 1861 as a drummer in Company A, 60th Ohio Volunteer Infantry, and was sent home after two months because his father protested he was only sixteen years old. In January 1862, shortly before he turned seventeen years old, William enlisted as a bugler in the 60th Ohio Volunteer Infantry. After being involved in several battles in Virginia, the young Fitch was among those of the garrison that surrendered at the Battle of Harper's Ferry. The captives were later sent north by the Confederates for parole after a promise was coerced that they would not take up arms again against the Southern States. The South had no facilities or funding to retain the prisoners-of-war and the release offered an expedient solution to the problem.[2] William, forsaking his promise, re-enlisted as a bugler and was among the 9th Ohio Cavalry taking part in Sherman's "March to the Sea." He was mustered out as Bugler, Co. K., 9th Ohio Cavalry in 1865.[3]

The young musician returned to Ohio, where his father served as a Presbyterian supply minister around Delaware, Ohio. Earlier, his maternal uncle, Rev. William Peter Strickland,[4] had been one of a committee of three appointed by the Ohio Methodist Conference Committee to select a site for a university. The committee selected a sulphur spa, Elliot Hotel, Delaware, as their recommendation to be purchased to establish the university, Ohio Wesleyan. It was founded in 1844.[5] William chose to attend Ohio Wesleyan and received his degree in 1870. He then continued his schooling at Garrett Biblical Institute in Evanston, Illinois.[6]

Anna's childhood days were comfortable compared to those of many during those early pioneer days. She was born at Holmesville, Holmes County, Ohio, Nov. 16, 1846, at her parent's farm in Prairie Township. She was the daughter of Thomas and Anna (Kendall) Lecky. At a time when even elementary education for women was a rarity, Anna Lecky was sent to Ohio Wesleyan Female Academy, also at Delaware, Ohio. The Female Academy, founded in 1853, was set high on a hill about six blocks from the site of the all-male university. There were some coeducational activities, but contacts between the opposite sexes were carefully monitored.[7]

The couple's courtship survived "the walking rule," the academy guideline which specifically stated: "No female was allowed to walk with a gentleman at any time." The rule required "if a gentleman wished to call upon a lady, he first sent a note of the Preceptress who accepted or rejected the invitation for the girl. If he was morally and otherwise acceptable, on the appointed Saturday night, the couple could sit in the parlor or walk back and forth in the Main Hall of Monnett," the women's dormitory. All this was under the watchful eyes of the chaperons.[8]

Following Anna's graduation with a degree in English Literature in 1869, she taught public school while waiting for her young beau to complete his education. The couple married in 1872, after William completed requirements for his Master's Degree from Ohio Wesleyan, and the young pastor was assigned to serve several churches in the Ohio Conference in 1873.[9]

Their only son, Francis (Frank), was born in 1873 in Ohio. His early remembrances record the couple visited the Centennial Exposition at Philadelphia, Pennsylvania. Several important events in 1881 shaped the future. On June 2, 1881, William was among those invited to attend the dedication ceremony of Thomas Edison's first electric light plant in Akron, Ohio. Years later the still-rankled Anna wrote to her son "<u>no women</u> invited, but I've been at the home and all over the grounds of Lewis Miller," the father of Edison's second wife.[10]

Also in 1881 the family was among those attending the funeral of President James Garfield in Cleveland, Ohio. The president had been felled by an assassin's bullet soon after his election and inauguration. Following the funeral, the family went on to Lakeside, Ohio, to attend a camp meeting. The Methodist retreat was located at Indian Lake.[11] There Rev. William Fitch met John Baldwin, Sr., a wealthy, eccentric philanthropist. Baldwin was formerly of Berea, Ohio, location of Baldwin-Wallace College. He had made his fortune selling his farm near Berea after sandstone was discovered on his land. He then purchased 17,000 acres consisting of deserted plantations in St. Mary's Parish in southern Louisiana and founded the town of Baldwin.[12]

Baldwin desired to establish a mission and school for the poor white people who still remained in that bayou section of Louisiana. With this thought in mind, he returned to his native state and sought, among the many preachers who spent their summers at Lakeside, someone who could undertake the planning of this mission. As a result of the meeting, Rev. William Fitch agreed to move to Baldwin to organize the mission and school.[13]

Following the session of the North Ohio Conference in September, 1881, the Fitch family visited relatives before moving. They arrived in Baldwin on October 22, 1881, the eighth birthday of their son. The home proved to be in a delightful semi-tropical country, comprised of thirty acres of land bordering on the historic Bayou Teche made famous by Longfellow's immortal "Evangeline."[14] In the poem Longfellow had the young French Acadian lovers reunited under a live oak tree on the banks of the Teche. The Fitches found that the French culture had merged with the Spanish to form the Creole. Even the Negro population spoke in a French dialect.

The Fitches' Baldwin home, which was called "The Mansion," had been occupied by wealthy plantation owners. The cabins for the former slaves were nearby, many of them abandoned. The living rooms of The Mansion were on the second floor, while the first floor served as kitchen, dining room and cellar. The Mansion had been used by Union General Nathaniel P. Banks as his headquarters during the Civil War. There were many remaining marks of their occupation, including the feathers and droppings of the poultry which had been kept in the large attic out of the reach of midnight prowlers.[15] Other buildings of the former plantation were used for chapel, school, and servant's quarters, etc. The thirty acres of semi-tropical scenery, dominated by large trees, so different from that of the North, created constant surprises for the new arrivals.[16]

There were about 500 Negroes to each white person in the area. Because he had a degree as a Doctor of Divinity, Rev. Fitch was often called "Doctor." He was sometimes called to minister to the physical needs of the natives as well as to their spiritual needs. During the sultry evenings the drums of the voodoo worshipers drifted across the bayou.[17]

Set in the midst of the predominantly Catholic parish, Baldwin Seminary, under the auspices of the Methodist Church, flourished with more than eight boarding students and several local pupils by 1884. While William was organizing the Seminary, Anna taught religion, classes, and served as the school's first preceptress. Anna, a talented artist, also instructed the pupils in drawing and painting. She then had her turn at total control over the lives of her young charges, as once her life had been dominated by her overseer. William, besides supervising the Seminary, preached and directed the music. From the beginning, education started as a religious concept and was regarded as a part of religion. The main purpose of education was to enable the child to read the Bible.[18]

At the close of the Seminary year in May, 1885, the captain of the river steamer, *New Iberia*, invited the family to be his guests on a round trip from Baldwin to St. Martinsville and New Orleans, a trip which covered more than 450 miles of magnificent tropical river scenery. The basking alligators were disturbed by the steamer. The family saw the sugar, lumber, and salt industries at work.[19]

The school's success attracted attention and Rev. Fitch was soon appointed to organize the St. John's River Conference College to be located at Mt. Dora, Orange County, Florida. Gathering their belongings and their son, the family journeyed by steamer, by narrow gauge railway through a pine woods fire, and finally, by sailing sloop to their new home. There was no railway at that time to Mt. Dora, which was situated on the east end of a lake. Entertainment on the sloop was "the weird and enchanting singing of the roustabouts," remembered the young Frank.[20]

The family made its new home among the cotton plantations, the stronghold of the Spanish priests. School and church work was at once begun by William, while Anna engaged in teaching. A printing press was purchased and the St. John's River Conference Paper publication begun, but Anna remembered later, "I made the living teaching school." William promptly organized a brass band and gave young Frank lessons in brass, woodwind, and percussion.[21]

A vacation trip north found the family celebrating Frank's thirteenth birthday in New York City at the dedication of the magnificent Statue of Liberty. President Grover Cleveland was the master of ceremonies at the 1886 celebration. The following year the family moved to a home among the citrus groves at Orange City, Colusia County, Florida, where there was a better opportunity for operating the conference college. William was elected the first president, and Anna, Preceptress.[22]

In 1888 William answered a call to serve a church at St. Augustine, a new resort area.[23] A member of their church, the commanding colonel of the military post of the U.S. troop, often entertained the family. In 1889 Yellow Fever raged, and a strict quarantine was established around the city by a cordon of three hundred guards. Proof of health certificates was needed even to hold the annual Sunday School picnic.[24]

After nine years in the South, William decided in February of 1890 it was time to return to the North for the education of their son. Anna had served as his teacher for most of his early years. The move took them to Harriman, Tennessee, where coal had recently been discovered. The newly developing industrial nation was demanding fuel. A great rush of people descended upon the town, which was just being platted. A hotel was hurriedly built, and young Frank served as the first clerk while William was busy organizing a Methodist Church.[25] For the rest of her life Anna remembered with horror the men burrowing beneath the hills for the black fuel.[26]

During the move to their next appointment in Fairfield, Maine, the family journeyed by train and ocean steamship. Bobsled parties with the church members were organized, and they slid over snows six feet deep. Anna embroidered blocks for her silken memory quilt. One of the blocks Anna embroidered read: "Mt. Dora, Florida, April 1890—orange blossoms. Fairfield, Maine, April 1891—no blossoms—snowballs."[27]

From that temporary appointment in Fairfield, the Fitches moved to a new charge at Wellfleet, Massachusetts, on Cape Cod. That church had been struck by lightning and had to be rebuilt As Frank remembers, the congregation held its Sunday School picnic in the lighthouse as guests of the captain in charge of the lifesaving crew. Frank remembered all of these exciting events.[28]

Frank graduated from high school at Wellfleet. He then enrolled in Colorado Preparatory school, Denver, Colorado, in 1893, where he studied a year before he entered his parent's alma mater, Ohio Wesleyan University, at Delaware, Ohio. After his graduation, he was ordained into the ministry, and he married a classmate,[29] the lovely Bertha Clark.[30] Following his father's and grandfather's footsteps, he began crisscrossing the United States carrying the gospel message. He and Bertha had three children. All were about the same age as Mary. The children were Francis William, born in Boston, Massachusetts, in 1897; Finley Thomas, born in Keene, Ohio, in 1900; and Margaret E., born in Kentucky, in 1903.[31]

At Silver City, New Mexico Territory, in 1893 and 1894, William and Anna found themselves missionaries—not to the recently subdued Indians, but to the Chinese. The hapless, impoverished Oriental males were imported to mine the silver deposits. This alternative to starvation and poverty in their homeland was exchanged for indentured service. At Silver City, the Fitches set up school to teach the illiterate servants to read and write, along with converting them to Christianity. There are faded photographs of Anna and William and their class of Oriental students, who were garbed in traditional kimonos, their heads shaved except for the cap left at the crown, and the long black strands gathered into braids hanging down their backs.[32]

After three years serving the Mission Conference in the untamed West, the next appointment was to return to the East—this time to the mountains of tenements erupting in Brooklyn in the heart of New York City where the couple ministered to and taught the newly arriving immigrants in 1897 and 1898.[33]

A move to North Carolina brought three stops in quick succession. The pair traversed the state from Elizabeth City on the coast in 1899, then on to Greensboro in 1901, and westward to Gastonia in 1902. Here they found the state's economy centered around the cotton mills. From the Appalachian Mountains the couple moved to the wide, open plains of Texas at Friberg Church, Wichita Falls, in 1904.[34]

Anna became acquainted with frontier pioneers in yet another category—the woman's movement. Among the pages of her autograph book are messages from Carry A. Nation and Frances Willard. Nation felt she was preordained by her name for responsibility. She declared war on the saloons of the west. This tall, strong woman took up an axe and literally chopped the saloon to pieces. Using the Bible as her text, Nation eloquently inspired others to join her in the battle against immoral vices: liquor, tobacco and immodesty in women's dress. In Guthrie, Oklahoma Territory, she penned in Anna's book, "Live to live." Frances Willard was a social reformer and organizer of the Women's Christian Temperance Union, a national organization. Along with the battle for prohibition of alcohol, Willard crusaded for women's right to vote. To Anna she penned, "Yours for God and Home and Native Land."[35]

From Wichita Falls the Fitches were sent to Hope Church, Dallas, Texas, in 1905, where Mary entered their lives presenting challenges never encountered before in their varied experiences! They plunged wholeheartedly into the saving of Mary—her mind and body, and most of all, her soul![36]

Endnotes Chapter 2 William & Anna

1. Rev. John Fitch served as itinerant pastor of the Methodist denomination from 1827 to 1865. He then united with the Presbyterian Church in order to have a settled pastorate and accepted a call as pastor of the Presbyterian Church, Bridgehampton, Long Island. Fitch family scrapbooks.
2. At this time of the war, William's parole was a promise not to fight only until he was exchanged for a Confederate captive. Since exchanges continued, he may not have been illegally serving when he re-enlisted. If he was not exchanged for a prisoner, the Confederates lawfully could have had him shot if he was captured again. Notes to author from Dougan, Oct. 1999.
3. Fitch family scrapbooks. Civil War record of William S. Fitch, 1862-1865, Department of the Army, Office of the Adjutant General, Washington, D.C., Pension Certificate No. 998,732.
4. William Peter Strickland, D.D., was born 1909 in Pittsburgh, Pennsylvania. He wrote and also edited a number of publications, was five years as agent of the American Bible Society, and served as author and Associate Editor, *The Christian Advocate*, a Methodist publication. Strickland died in Ocean Grove, New Jersey, 1884. Fitch family scrapbooks.
5. E.T. Nelson, Fifty Years of History of the Ohio Wesleyan University, 1844-1894. (Cleveland, Ohio: The Cleveland Printing & Publishing Co., 1895), introduction.

6. *Focus* #38 (Delaware, Ohio: Ohio Wesleyan University, Nov. 1977). *Focus* was a newsletter published by Ohio Wesleyan University.
7. Ibid. Holmesville is located about 60 miles southwest of Massillon, Ohio, in Holmes County.
8. Fitch family scrapbooks.
9. Ibid.
10. Ibid.
11. Lakeview, Ohio, is located about 30 miles southeast of Lima, Ohio.
12. Fitch family scrapbooks.
13. Ibid.
14. Ibid. Baldwin is located about 10 miles inland from the Gulf of Mexico about midway between the western Texas/Louisiana border and the city of New Orleans.
15. Ibid. An historic landmark, the plantation home is currently known as "Darby House," on the lower level is located a branch office of St. Mary Bank and Trust Co., *Daughters of the American Revolution Magazine* (Washington, D.C.), May 1974, p. 468.
16. Ibid.
17. Ibid.
18. Ibid.
19. Ibid.
20. Ibid.
21. Ibid.
22. Ibid.
23. Ibid. The frequent moves can be explained from information from the Rev. William Fitch's obituary, *Christian Advocate*, Oct. 1918, that he stayed "on each charge the then limit of two years." The Methodist Conference met every six months to make the new appointments. According to newspaper clippings in family scrapbooks, Rev. William Fitch received high commendations on his assignment to a new charge and again as he left for a new appointment. He was recognized for the quality of his preaching and dedication and for his musical talents as well. Many of the appointments the Rev. Fitch and his wife, Anna, served were in the mission field.
24. Ibid.
25. Ibid.
26. Anna Lecky Fitch, personal letters written to her son, Rev. Frank Fitch, 1934-36.
27. Memory quilt is in family collection.
28. Fitch family scrapbooks.
29. The Ohio Wesleyan Female Academy was merged with Ohio Wesleyan University by a resolution in 1877. Nelson, *Fifty Years of History of the Ohio Wesleyan University, 1844-1894.* (Cleveland, Ohio: The Cleveland Printing & Publishing Co., 1895), p. 56.
30. Ibid. Bertha Clark was born in Caledonia, Ohio, in 1874. They were married, 1896, in Rockland, Massachusetts.
31. Ibid.
32. Ibid.
33. Ibid.

34. Ibid.
35. Ibid.
36. Ibid.

MONDAY EVENING, JULY 2, 1906.

National Sunday at M. E. Church

The Patriotic Service at the First M. E. church yesterday was well attended and proved to be very interesting and satisfactory.

The special features of the service were the fine organ voluntary by Mrs. B. F. Gambell; the beautiful song, "The Banner and Beauty of Glory," sung by the sweet-voiced child, Mary Maynard, and the sermon by Rev. Fitch, the pastor.

We present to our readers a synopsis of the sermon: The text was Psalm 100:1. "Make a joyful noise unto the Lord."

Clipping, *Daily Times-Echo*,
Eureka Springs, Arkansas.
Fitch scrapbooks.

While Mary's scalp was being shaved and treated for disease, she wore bonnets fashioned by Anna. *LHJ*, May 1927.

3

A Home

It is unclear just when and how Mary made her arrival into the Fitch family. It must have been at least in the first half of the pastor's six-month stay in Dallas in 1905. Contrary to Mary's version, Anna remembered she began feeding Mary as one would a stray puppy, until, tummy full, the child would curl up under the table for a nap. One day Mary appeared and announced, "My mother says you can have me." Taken aback, the elderly Anna gently told her, "I'm not sure Mr. Fitch would like a little girl just now." But take her, they did.[1]

Mary's mother must have married Ed Maynard about this time, as Mary Kidd goes forth with a new surname.[2] Perhaps the new marriage could not cope with the added vexation of a sickly, unsightly child. Mary leaves a trail of misinformation concerning her childhood. Ed Maynard is never mentioned in Mary's accounts. An explanation is never given of her use of the surname of Maynard.

The first step of Mary's induction into the family was to rid her head of its tenacious tenants. What hair had not fallen out in patches of mange was shorn off and the scaly scalp soothed by Anna with cream.[3] The faded and torn blue-gray gown and slip were removed, cleaned, and packed away among sentimental trivia as remnants of Mary's former being.[4]

The memory of the first evening in her new home was embedded in Mary's mind, and Mary remained unforgiving. "A soap box had been set under my feet to add to my stature and bring me level with the dish pan. After I had washed and dried a huge stack of dishes, I encircled the pile, balancing it, and anxiously reached a foot down from the box. And stumbled! The dishes crashed to the floor, and a dozen plates were broken. I picked myself up and regarded the havoc with stunned horror. My new mother came running, and I was introduced for the first time to Solomon's admirable precept concerning the rod and the child."[5]

Mary explained that Anna had "but one argument for all childish sinfulness, and that was a sound thrashing. She found her justification for this method in the Bible, and often used to chant between blows 'Spare the rod and spoil the child. He that spareth his rod hateth his son.'" Mary said, "She always concluded dramatically with the ironic moldy phrase, 'I'm only doing this for your own good.'"[6] Mary never seemed to sense the disaster of annihilating the family's china in one major attack. At any rate, she must have learned her lesson well, as she never mentioned having trouble with the dishes again and little mention was made of household tasks.

Rev. Fitch and his wife, Anna, had a unique station, moving freely and interchangeably throughout the communities, and were equally at ease and welcome in the homes of the wealthy and the poor. Maintaining their own dignity was no small task, considering the puny salary donated to the learned couple. Salary negotiations, contracts, benefits, or housing were never the subject of bargaining. The concept was not even considered. The pastor and his family simply made do with receipts of the weekly collections, which paid the preacher as well as bills for upkeep of the church. The more fiery the oratory, the more full the offering plate. William records an average of $16.85, monthly with weekly income ranging from a low of $2.05 to a high of $5.40. Not to be discounted were the many extra benevolences, produce and food, clothing, furnishings, and courtesies all so willingly shared by their Christian communities. All were gratefully and graciously received, whether or not they suited the recipients' needs or tastes.[7]

According to Mary's version, while the family was still in Dallas, "someone suggested to the minister that he must see to having my voice trained and he flew into a rage. He told them 'that I sang as naturally as a bird, with a talent that was God-given. It would be an offense to Divine Majesty,' he informed them, 'to tamper with my gift.'"[8] William's sharp retort may have been influenced by the major concern during that period in Dallas—the nurturing of Mary's health, training in manners, and schooling, of which she had none up to that point. Voice lessons were not in the financial budget; William and Anna felt quite capable of training their little songbird. Piano lessons were soon begun, along with instruction on the violin. Strangely, in any of her later accounts, Mary rarely mentioned the influence of William on her early musical training, although she said he spanked her when she would not practice her lessons on the piano or the violin. Possibly this was overshadowed by her frequent, stinging clashes with Anna.

"My new mother," Mary remembered, "had been a school-teacher before her marriage and was possessed of all the virtues except those of understanding and tolerance. She shrank with horror from dancing as the most potent invention of the devil. Music she countenanced only in hymn form. And she looked upon this life only as a preparation for the life after death."[9] Mary was disciplined for life and the hereafter much as Anna had been in the mid-1800s.

On a more positive note, Mary remembered, "Occasionally I have marveled at the mental attitude of that otherwise intelligent woman. She took me into her household, a half-starved little wretch, suffering from all the symptoms of pernicious anemia, my hair falling out in patches, my body emaciated—a child altogether so ailing that the doctors told her that it would be best for me to be taught privately and not attend the public schools until I was well."[10] During the first year, while Mary's head was shaved and treated, Anna labored endlessly, making poke bonnets filled in about the face with frills to hide the denuded state of Mary's scalp. Mary was fed wholesome, body-building food; she was well-clothed, and hours were spent shampooing and brushing the new growth of hair. In adulthood, Mary said, "The pile of wavy hair I knot on my neck today I owe to her unceasing care."[11]

"She cheerfully added the task of being my governess to her already burdened shoulders and divided my day into well-balanced periods of study and recitation, homely tasks and play. She won my speech from the patois common to the slums and taught me the wisdom of self-control and of curbing my impulsive temper." Mary added, "She took me into her household as her own daughter, a child without health, doomed to die before she was ten, without loveliness, without manners or training. In her tight-lipped, relentless way she loved me. A curious, curious woman. She was ever alert to exorcize the 'devil' in me. I had picked up dancing—the jig, the two-step and the waltz—in the tenements. Boisterous songs, heady with the beat of ragtime, had been learned to gratify my instinct for melody and rhythm. And I could not quite put away such childish ecstasies even in my new surroundings of bleak piety."[12]

In August of 1906 Rev. Fitch was transferred to serve the First Methodist Episcopal Church at Eureka Springs, Arkansas, near the northern border of the state. The elderly couple moved from Dallas taking their new child with them. Mary had no records of any kind, so the Fitches guessed she was seven-years-old when she joined the family in 1905. Because the church at Eureka Springs was located on the mountain's brow, one of William's first acts of aggressive evangelism was to rent a room to be used as a downtown annex to the church, reaching out to those who did not live in the upper class neighborhoods.[13]

Meanwhile, work with Mary continued, healing and teaching. Anna served as her private tutor and governess, and William directed the musical education. A year later, the July 2, 1906, Eureka Springs *Daily Times-Echo* reported: "The Patriotic Service at the First M.E. Church yesterday was well attended and proved to be very interesting and satisfactory. The special features of the service were the beautiful song 'The Banner and Beauty of Glory,' sung by the sweet-voiced child, Mary Maynard, and the sermon by Rev. Fitch, the pastor." Under the couple's tutelage the eight-year-old child was receiving top billing.[14]

Mary recalled that her public appearances then began with a song every Sunday in church—a new song for each week. "I was an important member of the choir and had excited much favorable comment," she recalled, "...by the time I had become something of a mainstay in the choir, my father was called to Little Rock and its environs."[15]

Rev. William Fitch was remembered in Eureka Springs as "a scholarly man, and his methods have won the esteem, not only of his congregation, but of the citizens as well." At the semi-annual church conference, he was assigned a six-month stint to serve the Frank Lynn Memorial M.E. Church in Little Rock. This was followed by an appointment in Judsonia, Arkansas. The press of Judsonia reported in February, 1907, "Rev. W.S. Fitch, who was appointed pastor of Trinity M.E. Church comes to us from the Frank Lynn Church in Little Rock. He has the reputation of being a preacher of no mean ability. We have often seen him highly spoken of in the Little Rock dailies, and a number of times these papers have published his sermons in full. During the recent session of Conference, he was highly complimented by Bishop Warren on a paper which he read. Judsonia is indeed fortunate in getting such a strong preacher. He will be here next Sunday, and expects to move his family, which consists of his wife and little girl, here the latter part of next week."[16]

Mary's progress can be noted in the move some thirty miles northeast of Little Rock. She was remembered in Judsonia in a 1957 publication:[17]

> ...the very plain little eight-year-old girl who had sung her solos so frequently in the local Methodist Episcopal Church.... The adopted daughter of the new Methodist preacher attracted very little attention when she arrived here.... Those who did give her a glance saw a chunky, blue-eyed girl with high cheek bones and an exceedingly demure personality.[18] The eyes were matched almost every day by a prim little hair ribbon.
>
> Mrs. Fitch insisted upon long sleeves for her dresses, which met with Mary's disfavor. Probably deciding that in hiding her plump arms she was masking a single redeeming feature, she would pause on her errand after rounding the Elliott Hotel corner to roll the hated sleeves up as far as they would go. On the return trip, before coming within sight of the parsonage, she would roll them down again. Temptation also troubled her if she tried the short way to town past Dr. Eastland's house. There was the big lawn swing which completely fascinated her. To linger was to risk her foster mother's anger. She solved this problem by running to town in order that the time saved might be used for extra minutes in the swing.
>
> It is to be feared that her early audiences did not receive her efforts with as much appreciation as did those of later years. Rev. Fitch had quite a knowledge of music, and in his desire for perfection the child was sometimes almost mechanical in her singing. This, added to the frequency of her appearance, began to cause whispers among the sisters in the choir before many months had gone by.
>
> Once, however, a traveling salesman, who was a music lover, stood outside the crowded church during a program. Suddenly Mary's voice came to him, full and clear on the evening air. 'Who is that kid?' he excitedly inquired of those around him. 'I tell you she's going places.'

"Life is Like a Mountain Railroad" was one of the hymns the child often sang. While at Judsonia Mary received an invitation to return to Little Rock to perform in a benefit concert. The eleven-year-old was gaining attention. Mary later recalled:[19]

> The benefit concert was arranged to aid a certain girl dangerously ill with tuberculosis. One of the church deacons, [H.F. Auten], who had heard me and had been impressed by my accomplishments was in charge of the program. I was asked to come to Little Rock, with all my expenses paid, to sing. I was stunned that anyone should be willing to pay good money to hear me sing. Then this first touch of being a prima donna went to my head and I allowed myself a few airs. My foster mother, fortunately, was so delighted that she overlooked this sudden access of worldly pride and set herself to training me in some new songs, including 'The Holy City,'[20].... The program was arranged to glorify my songs and the crowd was enthused over my voice to the point of contributing most generously when the collection was taken up after the concert. This triumphant event was a turning point in my ambitions. Hitherto I had yearned to be a missionary in China or Japan and help convert the heathen. I had calculated that, with my musical training, I could play and sing and be generally useful all round. An earlier adopted daughter of my foster parents had achieved glory as a deaconess in the Methodist church and had been held up to me as a shining example and her virtues extolled endlessly. I felt that to follow in her footsteps and receive such praise would be an admirable thing to do. I was, no doubt, prompted to this altruism by an inborn desire for globetrotting. Like the sailor, I had some idea of joining the missionaries and seeing the world. But now a more worldly goal presented itself vaguely to me.

In Judsonia Rev. Fitch's musical talents were not unnoticed either. A clipping reports: "...the orchestra music was resumed at the M.E. Church last Sunday morning and there was quite an increase in attendance. The music was fine. This feature of the service will be kept up from that time on. It is the desire of the pastor to make even greater improvement along this line."[21]

The orchestra of the Methodist Church presented a concert with special mention of the songs by Mary Maynard.[22] Under the auspices of the Epworth League of the Methodist Church in Judsonia, a surprise donation party was given to William and his family. The clipping noted: "While the surprise was not as great as had been anticipated (owing to someone's uncontrollable tongue [it must have been Mary]), the evening was an enjoyable one for all who were present. There were vocal solos, piano solos, and recitations by Mary Fitch." This seems to be the only time she was referred to with the Fitch family name.[23]

Here, at Judsonia, a staggering situation faced the family unit—the dynamic William's health was failing. At the winter conference, he was forced to take superannuated status, or pensioned. William recorded Monday, January 25, 1909: "Conference adjourned, my appointment for next year is Little Rock Mission."[24]

In a farewell tribute, a Judsonia paper printed: "Rev. W.S. Fitch, who has been pastor of the M.E. Church at this place for the past two years, leaves this week for Little Rock.... Rev. Fitch is a man of ability as a preacher, he has always used the greatest care in preparing and delivering his sermons, nothing he has said has been in a haphazard way. He is not only a preacher but a musician of many years of experience and has been associated with some of the best musical talent in the country, and is known as an able composer of music."[25]

While in Judsonia, Mary found a wild holly bush which was transplanted in the parsonage yard. Mary's little holly bush was dug and potted for the move, as she could not bear to leave her very own possession.[26]

The outlook was bleak. The superannuation was debilitating, not only psychologically, but financially as well. After thirty-eight years of ministering to God's flocks no matter where he was sent, the family had no home or savings and very little anticipated income. Since Rev. Fitch was not assigned as pastor to a church, a parsonage would not be provided. On March 18, William wrote: "Moved from Judsonia to Little Rock, entertained at H.F. Auten's." On March 20 he wrote: "attended the Union Sunday School and rested" and the following day he began unpacking.[27]

The next entries in the family scrapbooks are puzzling. Plans for a home were drawn on paper with the H.F. Auten letterhead. A contract on June 18, 1909, was an agreement for a cottage to be built on Hillcrest for Mrs. Anna M. Fitch on her lot in Hillcrest Addition to the City of Little Rock, as shown by an attached sketch. The price completed was to be $1,000.[28] Anna did not have $1,000 or money for a lot in the new Hillcrest addition! Nevertheless, the house was built and occupied, one of the first homes in the subdivision. Mary's holly bush was planted in the corner of the lot.

The home and lot, mortgaged in Anna's name, were paid off. How? Anna had an "ace up her sleeve!" In a letter written to her son in 1936, shortly before her death, Anna revealed her secret: "My father owned four hundred acres of the best land in Ohio and made lots of money, sent us to college and before he died [in 1910] he gave me, also my sister, three thousand dollars in gold. I invested here. I carried my sister's share down to her."[29] Anna had visited her home in Ohio in 1909, before her father's death and returned with a carpetbag full of gold! How Mary's eyes must have popped when she saw it. Mary seems oblivious to the family's financial need whose income was William's small pension.

Mary later recalled visiting Ohio with Anna when she was about twelve-years-old spending the summer near Plain City, where Anna's sister, Rhoda (Lecky) and her husband, Dr. Francis Mattoon, lived. Mary said later, "And, oh, how I did love the haystacks! I learned to milk the cows and gather eggs, 'n everything." When they returned to Little Rock they moved into their new home.[30]

Mary also seemed oblivious that her metamorphosis from the "ugly duckling into a swan" was taking place. On September 29 the Little Rock papers give descriptive accounts of a "house warming"—a unique surprise of the season:[31]

> Mr. Fitch, formerly pastor of the M.E. church of Little Rock and now in charge of Little Rock Mission, has just completed and moved into a new house—a beautiful home in a beautiful place—more wonderful because of its being the first real home he and his wife have ever owned....
>
> Since their stay in our midst, while building, they have aided with willing hand and heart in the work of the Pulaski Heights

> Union Sunday School of which Rev. W. S. Fitch is leader and organizer of the Sunday school orchestra, which speaks for itself at each service. He also conducted a popular service every Sunday night.
>
> So appreciative of his efforts were the people that they turned out 'en masse' in good old donation style to show their gratitude and joy for two who had given their lives for others.
>
> All was quiet along the Arkansas; lights gleamed from the overlooking fort, when with a rush at front and rear of house came a crowd with baskets and parcels and a noise of vocal artillery.
>
> The home was besieged and the inmates gracefully surrendered and turned the house over to the crowd. As if by magic the lights went on—no one knew how.
>
> Every one got busy—some made coffee, some popped corn, others interspersed music in variety from old-time love songs, Negro melodies, hymns along with innocent jokes and pranks. The sound of merry-making floated out upon the evening air....
>
> The Sunday School superintendent, H.F. Auten, gave a fitting closing, the subject, 'Home, the pride of every true American, the center of affection and patriotism.' He voiced the sentiments of the crowd by saying we had come to congratulate this family; that a home had come and in the midst of pleasant views, pure air and a host of friends, he spoke with a pathos that touched alike the hearts of guests and host and hostess....
>
> 'May Mr. and Mrs. Fitch and their beautiful daughter, whose voice in song is ever charming, live with us many years, and may their final homecoming to the Father's house be the climax of this evening's pleasure and a life of service.'

Mary recalled the times in Hillcrest addition, the gay songs of her childhood still in her mind, "...but intuition warned me to be secretive about these outbursts, even in the very beginning. How well I remember my first indulgence. Our cottage was small and my room, a sweet, clean little chamber with rugs on the floor, was on the second story." Mary was assigned the nearly sixteen by sixteen foot dormer room. "No one but I ever went up there, because my new mother was not young enough to enjoy climbing stairs." This seems to be her only reference to the elderly age of her parents, who were by then in their mid-sixties. "And, knowing this, that room came to represent refuge to me—a place in which I might work off my excess spirits, let myself run riot for the moment without fear of detection. I had heard a new song that afternoon—'Down on Mississippi Bay'—and its throbbing phrases tempted me. Before my mirror I began to hum it and my treacherous feet began to tap. Suddenly the door at the foot of the stairs creaked and my breath stopped. It had never dawned on me that she could hear me."[32]

"Mary," Anna called sharply. "What are you doing?"

"N-nothing."

"Yes, you were. What were you doing with your feet? Dancing?"

"Well," Mary stammered. "I was dancing a little."

"You come right down here this minute," Anna reprimanded.[33]

Mary obeyed and was told the dancing steps were the devil in her feet. To get rid of that bad influence, Mary received a thrashing. Mary said, "It was not the last time. For I could not always remember that I would come to no good end if my voice strayed from hymns and my feet from sedateness." Mary had an older friend who "could beat a piano blue with jazz." Mary loved it and managed to set her own piano throbbing when she was alone. Since jazz in printed form was not allowed in the household, Mary played by ear. Sometimes, she admitted, she was caught and thoroughly whipped. The secret disobediences were proof to Anna that Mary was incorrigible and would, in spite of all of Anna's care and diligence, come to no good end.[34]

In Little Rock Mary's life under the relentless discipline continued. Someone later told her that she had no childhood. Mary said, "I can only answer that mine was no worse than the lot of most adopted children; and at least my new father and mother were sincere in their desire to make me praiseworthy in the sight of God. Unfortunately for me, they worshiped a cruel God, a relentless God."[35]

Mary remembered that Anna never allowed her to forget her deplorable early upbringing and, because Mary refused to give up singing and dancing, she was "possessed of the devil.... I shall never forget, however, one scathing phrase with which she accounted for all my shortcomings. Should I not dry the dishes quite thoroughly, or sweep the last atom of dust from the corners, or blunder in my table manners or speech, it was because I was 'shanty Irish!'"[36]

Anna had found a key to motivate Mary, who understood that it was not her foster parent's intention to be cruel. Mary said, "They took a sickly hoodlum and brought her to health and politeness—no puny or pleasant task. They denied her neither excellent clothes nor wholesome food, a comfortable room, sound musical training and the best education to be had in their community."[37]

Anna and William looked down from their perch high above the Arkansas Capitol and defied the 1909 state mandate—public education for all. They continued the home-study course, with their young apprentice advancing beyond her peers. Mary never attended grammar school.[38]

Mary was aware that the absence of understanding and demonstrative love was not the fault of the Fitch's hearts, but of their era. "Although I was too intensely individual, too much of a rebel to be cowed or demoralized or to have my spirit broken or my instinct for happiness and laughter annihilated by their punishments, this understanding of their sincerity saved me from bitterness, or the twisted psychology that usually is the result of such a childhood. In their ignorance, they feared for me and clutched at the only method known to them to save my soul." Mary remembered that the beatings were an almost daily occurrence until she was fifteen years old.[39] Some journalists made Mary's story harsh and unrelenting. However, in her own version appearing in the *Ladies' Home Journal*, Mary provided a more compassionate picture. William's influence and her musical training in voice, piano, organ, and violin is generally omitted, while Anna's reputation suffered in the varying descriptions as a cruel foster mother.

Besides the almost daily thrashing, Mary's life was filled with the routine of schooling, tasks about the house, practicing and weekly solos in church. Mary's little holly bush grew and blossomed, as did Mary herself. Anna later remembered long walks taken with Mary, teaching her of the wild flowers that grew in abundance in the wilderness of the new subdivision high on a bluff overlooking the Arkansas River.[40]

As Mary grew older she refused to accept that the frequent disciplinary measures were justified. She said, "One day my foster mother punished me again without cause or explanation." Mary did have a way of bending the rules in her favor. "After the familiar tirade and prophecy of my ultimate bad end with which she always concluded these sessions, I climbed to my room and put on two suits of underwear, two pairs of stockings and two dresses. I stuffed trinkets and sundry other trifles into my blouse until I looked as fat as any Kewpie. My savings amounted to two dollars in nickels and dimes, and with this wealth I walked out of the house forever."[41]

It was a good move. William, at 68, was failing in health and near death. Anna had her hands full. Anna, who grew up in the days before the Civil War, was holding tightly onto the reins of her adopted daughter—precocious, beautiful, and talented, straining at the leash to become a part of the "ragtime era" with her peers. Anna had received the unwelcome news that her son was on his way and would be depositing his wife and three teenage children, all about the same age as Mary. They would remain for an extended stay as he sought out a new pastoral appointment. Anna had four more mouths to feed and three more inquiring young minds to educate. During their six-month stay in the summer and fall, Anna's grandchildren did not attend school. The three teenagers, two boys and a girl, shared Mary's upper dormer bedroom, completely unaware of its previous occupant.[42]

Mary wisely turned to the deacon, H.F. Auten, for help. She says, "He was a man of considerable means and standing as a lawyer of brilliance, and should, I thought, know of some simple employment to which my experience and years would be adapted. I went to him and stated my need and attempted vainly to withhold my reasons for leaving my foster parents. For, in spite of a childhood and upbringing that would have tended to destroy such traits, I possessed a painful pride and a dreadful sensitiveness. I was going to get a job, support myself and keep straight. I'd show my foster mother! When I asked him [the deacon] if he would be willing to use his influence to place me as a pianist in some motion-picture theater or as clerk in some store, he told me I was much too young and too gifted for either."[43]

Mary had found another benefactor.

Endnotes Chapter 3 A Home

1. Oral interview, 1983, Mildred McCausland Fitch, (1896-1992), 2nd wife of Rev. Frank F. Fitch, (1873-1952), son of Rev. William and Anna Fitch. Rev. Frank Fitch married Mildred, a young woman who nursed Bertha in her final illness. Mildred was close in age to Mary and to Rev. Fitch's own children.
2. *Daily Times-Echo*, (Eureka Springs, Ark.) 2 July 1906, Fitch scrapbooks.
3. Lewis, "From the Slums," *LHJ*, May, 1927, p. 5.
4. Fitch collection.
5. Lewis, "From the Slums," *LHJ*, May, 1927, p. 5.
6. Ibid.
7. Fitch scrapbooks.
8. Lewis, "From the Slums," *LHJ*, May, 1927, p. 49.
9. Ibid.
10. Ibid., p. 5. Research by Janice Guthrie, *The Health Resource*, Conway, Arkansas, long term effects of malnutrition in childhood are not fully understood, but cause problems which can include greater susceptibility to infections.
11. Lewis, "From the Slums," *LHJ*, May, 1927, p. 5.
12. Ibid., pp 5, 49.
13. Fitch scrapbooks.
14. *Daily Times-Echo*, (Eureka Springs, Ark.) 2 July 1906. Fitch scrapbooks.
15. Lewis, "From the Slums," *LHJ*, May, 1927, p. 49.
16. Fitch scrapbooks.
17. Orr, *Judsonia*, pp. 289-290.
18. This seems to be the only notation describing Mary as "demure," or anything close to that adjective!
19. Lewis, "From the Slums," *LHJ*, May, 1927, p. 49.
20. A difficult piece for a child so young!
21. Fitch scrapbook, Judsonia clippings, n.p., 25 Jan. 1906.
22. Fitch scrapbook, Judsonia clipping, n.p., n.d.
23. Ibid.
24. Fitch scrapbooks. Only some of Rev. William Fitch's written notes remain in a scrapbook with the samples pertaining mostly to his career. No personal mention is made of Mary.
25. Fitch scrapbooks. Judsonia clippings, n.p., 25 Jan. 1906. None of Rev. William Fitch's compositions seem to have been published and no record of any remain. The compositions were instrumental in nature. Therefore, it is doubtful Mary sang any of Fitch's work.
26. Fitch scrapbooks, n.p., Dec. 1936.
27. Fitch scrapbooks.
28. Ibid.
29. Anna Lecky Fitch, letters to her son, Rev. Frank Fitch, 1934-36.

30. Mary Lewis's scrapbooks #2, n.d., n.p. (Columbus, Ohio, circa 4 May 1926) courtesy of Lawrence Holdridge. Fitch family genealogy records. Plain City is about 20 miles west of Columbus, Ohio.
31. Fitch scrapbooks. Two clippings, n.p., n.d.
32. Lewis, "From the Slums," *LHJ*, May, 1927, p. 49.
33. Ibid.
34. Ibid.
35. Ibid.
36. Ibid.
37. Ibid.
38. *Arkansas Democrat*, Little Rock, Ark. 22 November 1931. Fitch scrapbooks.
39. Lewis, "From the Slums," *LHJ*, May, 1927, p. 49.
40. Fitch scrapbooks, n.p., Dec. 1936.
41. Lewis, "From the Slums," *LHJ*, May, 1927, p. 49.
42. Oral interview, 1983, F.T. Fitch, son of Rev. Frank Fitch. Mary was not living in the Fitch's home when Anna's daughter-in-law, Bertha, and grandchildren were there.
43. Lewis, "From the Slums," *LHJ*, May, 1927, p. 49.

Mary in front of the parsonage at Judsonia, Arkansas, in 1908. While the family lived at Judsonia, a stranger standing outside the church heard Mary singing and excitedly said, "Who is that kid? I tell you she's going places." From the Fitch album.

The Rev. William and Anna Fitch and Mary in Little Rock, Arkansas. The home was one of the first in Hillcrest Addition high up in Pulaski Heights. When destitution faced the family due to William's failing health, Anna appeared with a bag full of gold—$3,000! She bought the lot, built the house, and invested the rest. Mary received her musical and educational instruction from her elderly foster parents at home. From the Fitch album.

4

The New Patron

Henry Franklin Auten was well acquainted with the characters involved in the scenario. Mary found understanding and sympathy and someone interested in supporting her talent. Mary explained, "He was by way of being something of an art patron, the sort whose early artistic aspirations were thwarted and who gratified them in later life vicariously by helping others with talent to succeed."[1]

Auten was born February 4, 1861, the youngest of eight children of Henry and Anna Lantz Auten of St. Johns, Michigan. According to his obituary, he was himself orphaned at twelve. However this does not correspond to the Auten family genealogy, which states both of Henry's parents died within a year of each other, in 1878 and 1879, making him an orphan at the age of eighteen left to provide for five older unmarried sisters.[2] By determination he made his way through years of schooling. His goal of becoming a lawyer was reached when he graduated from University of Michigan Law Department in 1883. In about 1889 he moved to Little Rock to open his own law practice. Auten's move to Arkansas, like so much of his life, is shrouded in mystery.[3]

More confusion surrounds Auten's family. His first wife was Clara J. Auten. They had two sons, H. Clare and Harry. Henry and Clare were subsequently divorced, and on March 10, 1896, Auten married L. Carrie Carus, also a native of Michigan, who operated a private school in Little Rock. She was 34 and Auten 35. On December 31, 1896, Lawrence was born, and shortly after that a second son, Franko.[4] Lawrence and Franko were close to the age of Mary when she joined the household.

While the Northeast and Midwest underwent an economic and industrial change and growth in the years after the Civil War, the South, especially Arkansas, remained a state without industry, finance, and significant urban development. Without a class of native businessmen adventurous enough to take a chance on spurring economic growth, newly arrived Northern immigrants tried their hand at new projects during the Reconstruction period in Arkansas which ended in 1874. Auten was in this group of entrepreneurs. Auten's family papers and business archives did not survive, making it difficult for much research into this period of his life.[5]

A leader in Republican politics, Auten was soon candidate for governor of Arkansas.[6] Although Arkansas was traditionally a state tied heavily to the Democratic ticket, he conducted a spirited campaign promoting "Industrial and Commercial Improvement—A Policy Recommended which will Induce Capital and Enterprising Immigration." Auten received 22,524 votes, while the incumbent governor, Daniel W. Jones, received 75,362. William S. Morgan, Populist Party nominee, tallied 8,332 votes.[7]

Auten's wealth was accumulated by dealing in real estate. The development of Pulaski Heights was one of his greatest accomplishments. In connection with this, he promoted the building of the Pulaski Heights street car line which connected the bluff with the city below, and he established the wildlife preserve, Forest Park (originally called Mountain Park), which had walks, drives, flower gardens, a dancing pavilion and band stand, as well as a horse racing track. In 1908 Auten incorporated the New Capital Hotel Company, which then purchased the elegant Capital Hotel in downtown Little Rock.[8]

Auten was vitally interested in civic improvement. A charter member of the Little Rock Lions Club, he also was a leader in the organization of the Little Rock Chamber of Commerce, which later merged with the Board of Trade to become the Board of Commerce. Auten served as its president. He was a member of the Public Library Board. Since prime livestock was raised on his farm west of the city, he also served as president of the Arkansas Dairymen's Association.[9]

When Mary was taken into the Auten home she states, "He and his wife and their two sons, boys of about my own age, and an adopted son a little older, accepted me as one of the family."[10] Auten, probably remembering the difficulties of his early life, took in several orphans, as well as a foster child, Frank Myers.[11]

For three years Mary stayed in this home, accepted and loved. Arrangements were made for vocal lessons with Mrs. Alice Henniger.

"Already expert in the piano and sight reading, thanks to the stern training of my foster father, I was able to teach and soon was earning enough to pay for my own lessons on the pipe organ," Mary said. Along with these and general music study, Mary continued on the violin. "All in all, there is no saying that my musical foundation was not a sound one!" she said. Mary became a member of the choir and secured a position as organist at the Second Baptist Church.[12]

Mary was enrolled at the Little Rock High School, her first classroom experience. A search for her birth certificate resulted in the information which revealed Mary was really a year older than she thought! Her birth date was given as 1897 instead of 1898, as previously believed. She joined the Thalian Literary Society, and was made a member of the honor society as a sophomore in 1914 and enrolled in German as a foreign language.[13] Mary was a good student, but she retained her sensitivity, deeply wounded by the taunts of her classmates about her orphan status. Mary had adjustment problems. Nevertheless, she said, "I was becoming something of a celebrity as a singer. The society editors had admitted it with endless columns of generous praise and the pillars of the town recognized it by putting a premium on my services. No wedding, reception, church affair, private entertainment, funeral or social function seemed able to manage without my voice." She sang before President Theodore Roosevelt when he visited Little Rock.[14]

"I was given important roles in amateur performances of traditional operettas," Mary explained. "And succeeded somewhat sensationally," she added. With her patron, Auten, she was introduced to theater performances, something that would have been out-of-bounds to the Fitch budget and precepts. These entertainments were still condemned by church guidelines as Satan's territory. One memorable occasion was her introduction to opera, attending Giuseppe Verdi's *Rigoletto* presented by the San Carlos Company, a traveling cast. "Heaven flung itself wide for me with the lifting of the curtain on Verdi's undying opus." She had heard rumors of fabulous sums, maybe even a hundred dollars a week, paid to the prima donna. Mary fastened her heart and mind on being a star. She read in the newspaper of a teacher who had taken singer Rosa Ponselle from vaudeville and put her into opera. Mary clutched the hope inside. Unfortunately, the reporter failed to mention the name of the famous teacher. Undaunted, Mary made up her mind that someday she would study with that maestro.[15]

Auten was impressed with Mary's advancement and predicted international fame as a concert and opera singer. Auten laid down one firm admonition—"no puppy love!" If he was going to invest time and money into his young protégée, Auten wanted guarantee of results. Mary was warned "no girl amounted to anything who got 'boy crazy' and the moment he [Auten] found this hideous malady had attacked me he was 'through'!" The rules were loud and clear.[16] Mary seems to have wandered into another *Pygmalion* situation. Instead of being groomed for missionary work as the pastor and wife had attempted to do, Auten was determined to develop an artistic triumph.

Mary was used to bending the rules a bit and, according to her own account, "it was only a matter of months before the inevitable occurred." She became infatuated with a young man from New York. Her own version of the account says, "I fell quite madly in love with him at first sight. We saw each other at every opportunity, and away from him I mooned deliciously." Her musical study wandered, and the symptoms were obvious.[17]

Auten warned he "was not going to have any young cub hanging around the house and spoiling the career he had mapped out for me!" Mary admits, "The warning was futile. The boy and I merely transferred our meetings from the house to drug stores and street corners."[18] Mary was following the same evasive pattern which nearly exasperated Anna!

The eldest son of the household was drawn into the intrigue and persuaded to take Mary out to be exchanged for the idolized lover. When the couple returned from a dance, Mary said, "The house was dark when we arrived, no lights brightened the bedroom windows or streaked the moonless night. We were quite safe, I decided. The household was all safely in bed and asleep. We stole up on the porch and found the porch swing, that haven of small town courtship, where the first kiss is given and the first troth plighted. It was perhaps midnight. We sat there, two young things, murmuring delicious idiocies and ecstatically oblivious to all the world...."[19] Mary's feet, always getting her into trouble, rocked the swing into motion. The two young lovers were so entranced with each other that the noise caused by the rusty hinges was unnoticed. The door opened, Auten appeared, and sent Mary to bed. The ax fell the following morning.[20] A promised trip to Europe was off. It could not have been made at that time, anyway, for the German war machine was on the march.

Auten was through! He hit home with, "I've decided that you may as well settle down to being a small-town mediocrity now as ever." The phrase "small-town mediocrity" stung as much as Anna's "shanty Irish!" All the tears, promises, and theatrics Mary could muster were not enough to change his decision.[21]

Mary continued to be noticed by the local press for her successes, and found satisfaction by appearing in amateur theatricals. Then, one evening, enchanted by a dance performance in a local theater, Mary decided impulsively to ask for a job in the chorus. "It would mean escape," Mary thought. "And my instinct for self-preservation had been whispering to me for weeks."[22]

The next day Mary asked a friend for a letter of introduction to the head of the troupe. During the interview Mary confided her desire to make her way eventually to New York City to continue musical studies. "No, if you want my advice," the dancer said, "don't do any more studying. You've had enough of it. What you need now is experience." He gave Mary a letter of introduction to a theater down the street, where he said a couple of chorus girls were needed.[23]

Again with a note in her handbag, Mary approached the manager, showed her letter of introduction, and offered a resume of her appearances. "All right," the manager said. "I'll take you on at $25 a week." Mary gasped and was ready to beg him to repeat it. Taking her beaming face as acceptance of the offer, he continued, "But—you'll have to be ready to leave tonight at 8:30."[24]

That night at 8:30! Mary remembered it was just two weeks before Christmas and that would mean being in a strange town Christmas Eve—no presents, no Christmas tree, and none of the good times at home or at church. Preparations were already underway weaving baskets, making artificial flowers, shelling pecans, and stringing popcorn. Mary suddenly felt very forlorn and alone as she sat there in the manager's office.[25]

As she started to offer to join the show after the holiday, Auten's phrase, "a small-town mediocrity," echoed in her ears, and Mary promised she would be at the station. Hurrying home, she found the family gone, so she quickly packed and stole away. Sitting on the bench at the station, Mary mused what the lawyer and his wife would say when they found her gone. She decided it would probably be: "That's what you get when you pick up orphans and try to do something for them!"[26]

This is the way Mary told of her escape from Little Rock. Research reveals there is a different, more accurate, version of the story.

Endnotes Chapter 4 The New Patron

1. Lewis, "From the Slums," *LHJ*, May, 1927, p. 49.
2. Dillard, Tom W. "H.F. Auten: A Man Who Could Not Stand Still." *Pulaski County Historical Review*, XXIX (Spring 1981), p. 11-12.
3. Ibid., p. 12.
4. Ibid., p. 13. H. Clare was mentally retarded.
5. Ibid., p. 11.
6. Little Rock *Arkansas Gazette*, 24 May 1918, Fitch scrapbooks.
7. Dillard, "Auten."*Pulaski County Historical Review*, XXIX, p. 13.
8. Ibid., p. 15.
9. Little Rock *Arkansas Gazette*, 24 May 1918, Fitch scrapbooks.
10. Lewis, "From the Slums," *LHJ*, May, 1927. p. 49.
11. Dillard, "Auten."*Pulaski County Historical Review*, XXIX, p. 13.
12. Lewis, "From the Slums," *LHJ*, May, 1927, p. 50.
13. Dougan, "Enigma," p. 261.
14. Lewis, "From the Slums," *LHJ*, May 1927, p. 50. Roosevelt reference, Dougan, "Enigma," p. 262. Auten supported Theodore Roosevelt in his 1912 Democratic Bull Moose campaign for president. Dillard, "Auten."*Pulaski County Historical Review*, XXIX, p. 17, footnote 13.
15. Ibid.
16. Ibid.
17. Ibid.
18. Ibid.
19. Ibid.
20. Ibid.
21. Ibid.
22. Ibid.
23. Ibid.
24. Ibid.
25. Ibid.
26. Ibid.

5

Marriage: A Short Chapter

Mary's recollections seem to reflect an intentional amnesia lasting for several years. She was very protective of the privacy of those in her background. Instead of a young man from New York, the beau actually was J. Keene Lewis, who was also a member of the Second Baptist Church in Little Rock where Mary sang and accompanied the choir. Lewis had been permitted by Auten to escort Mary home from church and choir practice.[1]

Auten, with boys in his own household, was unaccustomed to the emotions of a teenage daughter. Possibly he had tired of the project. After a month of allowing the courtship, Auten heard Mary crying in her room and decided she must be in love. Keene Lewis received a call from Auten asking him what his plans were in regard to Mary. Although Keene replied that he had no plans, Auten suggested marriage. The lawyer had tried, judged, and passed sentence.[2]

The gallant young gentleman took his place at the altar on September 16, 1915, with the Second Baptist Church decorated with palms, greenery, and cut flowers. Wearing a gown of blue with a matching hat, the bride walked down the aisle accompanied by H.F. Auten. She carried a bridal bouquet of valley lilies and roses. Mary's attendant wore pink chiffon, a pink picture hat, and carried pink roses. The best man was Kenneth Lewis.[3]

The young honeymooners set up housekeeping in one of Auten's houses on North Ash Street in his Pulaski Heights subdivision. He had generously offered its use for a year. Keene Lewis was born in Owensboro, Kentucky; he was an avid lover of horses and listed hunting as a favorite hobby. Young Lewis was named the most handsome boy and most athletic boy of his 1911 Little Rock High School graduating class. He was captain of the basketball team in his senior year. He pitched for the school baseball team, as well as competing in football and track. Lewis was employed at Hollis and Company, a large industrial supply house.[4]

Mary had attended three years at Little Rock High School. She continued study with Mrs. Alice Henniger at the Henniger School of Music and she was continually in demand locally for her musical talents.

Auten was felled by a stroke at age fifty-eight. Laid to rest May 24, 1918, he was eulogized as "one of Little Rock's best known and wealthiest residents." His obituary listed survivors as his wife and four sons.[5]

The funeral service for Auten was held on the lawn of the Auten home at 520 North Elm Street. Although a Protestant clergyman [the Rev. S.E. Ryan, pastor of the Scott Street Methodist church] conducted the service, a Jewish rabbi, Louis Witt, gave the eulogy calling Auten "a builder, a pathfinder...not afraid to go where others had not gone before." Rabbi Witt called the deceased Auten "a man that could not stand still."[6]

In the eulogy Rabbi Witt acknowledged although Auten "has been charged by some with being irreligious and atheistic" he viewed Auten as "essentially a religious man."[7] This conflicts with the information that Auten was superintendent of the Pulaski Heights Sunday School and referred to as being a deacon in the Methodist Church.[8]

At the time of his death he was called one of the city's richest men. During the settling of his estate, the discovery was made, like many businessmen, Auten had financed many of his activities with loans. Although the assets of the estate were large, the debts against it were equally as large. By 1932 when the estate was settled, there was a balance of only $9.98. Apparently, through the efforts of Auten's son, Lawrence, the family managed to maintain possession of the Capital Hotel.[9]

Four months later another of Mary's props was removed when William Fitch died September 28, 1918, at the age of seventy-three after a long illness. He was laid to rest in National Cemetery at Little Rock by pallbearers, his comrades of the Grand Army of the Republic. William had served as chaplain of the McPherson Post #1 at Little Rock. Anna wrote to her son years later the post furnished the burial suit. Anna was alone.[10]

Long before it was fashionable, Mary was suffering an identity crises and longed for her biological roots. On Armistice Day, November 11, 1918, while the rest of the nation was celebrating the signing of the world-wide peace treaty, Mary coerced Lewis into taking her to Chicago hoping her brother, Joe Kidd, might be found there.[11]

A month later, two weeks before Christmas, restless Mary left town with the traveling troupe of *Restless Eve*.[12] It was her ticket to be something more than "a small-town mediocrity." Mary left with her husband's knowledge, but not his approval. Lewis, a devout Baptist, never forgave her for breaking her marriage vow. He remembered, "She had the most beautiful voice I have ever heard."[13]

The only thing permanent about the marriage was that Mary retained the name Lewis, her mother's maiden name. This made her name identical to the name of her deceased grandmother, Mary Lewis.

When Mary became famous and his name was mentioned Keene threatened a law suit. The result was that Mary agreed to keep his name out of future stories.[14]

Mary eliminates mention of this episode of her life by changing her birthday to January 7, 1900. The marriage was never mentioned. In this fictional world she thus becomes a naive eighteen-year-old, as she left her home in Little Rock to seek fame and fortune behind the footlights.

A divorce for J. Keene Lewis and Mary Lewis was granted in 1920.[15]

Endnotes Chapter 5 Marriage: A Short Chapter

1. Dougan, "Enigma," p. 262.
2. Ibid.
3. Little Rock *Arkansas Gazette*, 17 Sept. 1915, Fitch scrapbooks. The relationship of Kenneth Lewis to J. Keene Lewis is not available.
4. Letters to author from Mary Woodward Lewis, 3rd wife of J. Keene Lewis. *The Cage 1911*, yearbook, pp. 9, 27, 82, 91. Lewis was yearbook athletic editor. According to his obituary, he was once owner of Hollis Mill Company.
5. Little Rock *Arkansas Gazette*, 24 May 1918, Fitch scrapbooks.
6. Dillard, "Auten."*Pulaski County Historical Review*, XXIX, p. 16.
7. Ibid., footnote 28, p. 17.
8. Fitch scrapbooks.
9. Dillard, "Auten."*Pulaski County Historical Review*, XXIX, p. 16.
10. Fitch scrapbooks.

11. Dougan, "Arkansas Girl in Grand Opera," p. 176.
12. Lewis, "From the Slums," *LHJ*, May 1927, p. 50. A check by Dougan of the *Arkansas Gazette* found no mention of the show in question. It was referred to in a later press release as "Reckless Eve."
13. Letters to author from Mary Woodward Lewis.
14. Mary Woodward Lewis to Dougan.
15. *New York Times*, 15 April 1927.

Under his yearbook picture, Keene Lewis is noted to be the "Handsomest boy. Most athletic boy." *The Cage*, page 27, Little Rock High School.

6

On The Road

The train pulled away from Little Rock that night in December 1918, bound for Fort Worth, Texas, and Mary made tentative acquaintances before the train arrived the following morning. The next week was absorbed in training sessions for the chorus under the direction of the patient, hard-working chorus director, who struggled valiantly to teach Mary to dance to the count of "one-two-three." Mary could not master the technique and, after several disastrous days of tangled feet, she convinced him to let her dance to her own sense of rhythm and soon became adept at mastering the patterns.[1]

"Most of the girls were a hard lot and their manners frightened me," Mary said. "Profanity ruled their talk, fogging the air backstage." So ingrained was her training in the pious household where even "darn" was frowned upon, she could not disguise her discomfort. Although she attempted to evade the others, they found delight in tormenting the newcomer with filthy phrases. Mary found some protection with the *soubrette*, or leading lady and her husband, and the musical director and his wife, where she found advice and guidance to cope with her emergence into a new world. Unfortunately, her friendship with the management did not set well with the other chorus members.[2]

Christmas was celebrated in San Antonio the following week. Early and alone on the day after arrival, Mary found happiness touring the historic Alamo and was awed with the huge downtown office buildings. "But when the birthday of Our Lord arrived, it found me rather forlorn," Mary admitted, and, during a period of homesickness, she sent Christmas telegrams to her people back home. No one answered.[3]

Mary knew what they were thinking of the ungrateful runaway. "The citizens of my home town had decided that I was a lost soul," she imagined. "It was the old story, they pointed out with solemn head shaking, of the silk purse and the sow's ear. Here I had been given every advantage, intellectually and morally and spiritually. Look at my schooling and music; as for my religious training, hadn't I been 'brought up in a preacher's family and sung in the choir for years?' And instead of all this making a silken purse of me or a good, straight, womanly woman, hadn't it merely emphasized my commonness? What better proof of my low streak did anyone need than my joining a fifth-rate musical show where I could paint my face and kick and show my legs and go completely to the dogs to my heart's content?" Later, in telling her own story, Mary commented, "Only one woman in Little Rock ever wrote to me in my unknown years." It was Anna.[4] "But being cast off, as I was in these unknown years, did not bother me too much," she explained. "The footlights dazzled me nightly. The routine steps of the dance enchanted my feet, and the clatter of applause thrilled my ears. Too, new towns continually revealing themselves to me satisfied my inborn wanderlust." In spite of the scandal she had caused, Mary was having a beautiful time.[5]

From San Antonio they went to Oklahoma City and then to Tulsa where calamity overtook them. The show went on the rocks. "This was a disaster upon which I had not counted," Mary said. "It found me with perhaps $15—money accumulated, fifty cents at a time, by giving singing lessons to the *soubrette* and piano lessons to two of the chorus. The $25 a week salary, which had stunned me at first, had gone for hotel bills, traveling expenses and stockings."[6]

Her small accumulation of funds was gone in two weeks. After that Mary survived on beans, cheese and ham sandwiches, which she soon despised. When she could shake no more coins from her purse, she pleaded for a loan of fifty cents from the manager, but the other members from the troupe had already depleted his funds. After three weeks of unemployment, the manager pawned his negotiable security—his diamond ring—and the funds provided travel from Tulsa to Duluth, Minnesota, for an engagement. Mary, born and raised in the South, was introduced to frigid weather and almost died of the cold. She soon contracted the flu and missed two weeks of performances while suffering from the chills and fever. "This enforced vacation did not add to my prosperity," she said. "I found myself in need of heavy clothing to protect me from blizzard weather and with no money to buy it. What clothes I had were no longer presentable. Hard usage had scuffed out the toes of my shoes and rubbed my dresses thin and put holes, anxiously darned, in the elbows. Stiff pride held me from writing to Little Rock for aid. Gossip [from Anna] had reached me that my abject return on my knees was freely predicted by my well-wishers in Arkansas, and I had rather perished of bitter weather and influenza than have fulfilled that prophecy."[7]

In spite of the cold and inadequate wardrobe, Mary soon adapted and was having the time of her life as the troupe moved from Duluth on to Calgary, Canada, then east to Winnipeg and Montreal. She reveled in winter sports. Mary's first glimpse of the snow-capped Canadian Rockies struck her as the most magnificent sight of her life. She described them as "remote pinnacles of snow with great icicles hanging on them from huge boulders, glittering like eardrops of diamonds." The troupe moved westward to the Puget Sound where her first trip on a boat was almost as exciting as her first trip in the Pullman railway car. Passage by boat brought them back to the United States at Portland, Oregon.[8]

The season ended at San Francisco, California, at the Orpheum and Mary again found herself unemployed in May, a dead season for theatrical performers. Mary noted that some of the other troupers could afford to work the nine-month tours and take three months of vacation—but she needed a job—right away! Destitute, she discovered a mini-follies performing at Tait's Restaurant and, after an audition, she was hired at $50 a week.[9]

Although the audience was receptive, Mary explained, "...the joy of the program to them was the singing of a certain crippled girl. A special organ had been built for her which allowed her to remain in her invalid chair while playing, and the appeal of her handicap and pluckiness combined with two or three rather shrewd musical specialties brought her great success"—so much so that she left for better employment and Mary was asked to fill the role. In an attempt to develop her own act, Mary pulled out her own bag of tricks. One specialty she had was to begin the number by imitating a violin and ending by picking up a violin and playing an obbligato to her own song. The manager approved Mary's use of her own acts, but still insisted she fill the role as an invalid and pumping the organ.[10]

Mary attempted it, but she said, "...it was terrible. In the first place, pumping the organ took my breath away and I wheezed my songs. The crippled girl must have been a Samson to manage it or had some unusual muscular development. In the second place, trying to sing sitting down instead of standing upset me and made every move clumsy, and third, I was frightened to death. In addition, the clatter of the dishes and general confusion threw my voice off pitch. All told, I couldn't have been worse. After that fiasco I was allowed to abandon the wheel chair for the rest of the week." After the patrons voiced complaints about the show, an expert was hired to weed out the misfits, including Mary.[11]

For three weeks Mary plodded daily to a theatrical agency with hopeful anticipation. Finally she was sent "to a millionaire oil town in Southern California," where, for a salary of $35 a week, she found herself in the "wildest of the boom-towns." The girls in the show sat in a semi-circle on stage and took turns singing. If the men at the tables on the floor approved of a performer, they threw quarters, dimes, and half-dollars on stage for the girl to retrieve. The more inebriated the customer, the more money they would throw. Success was determined entirely on sex appeal rather than talent, and Mary reported, "Mine seemed negligible." While most of the girls made as much as $75 or $100 over their $35 a week salary, Mary said, "I never made more than $50."[12] After the second week the manager said to Mary, "You don't seem to make friends." Mary answered, "I don't get a chance. The girls are always going off to some party while I go home and go to bed. Why? Has any of them been saying anything? Have I done anything to make them sore at me?" The manager giggled and suggested she sell herself. Unemployment and starvation seemed a more attractive alternative and Mary quit the show. She was so unnerved she said, "I forgot to demand the final week's salary, which was due me under my guaranty from the agency."[13]

Slightly sickened by the experience, she returned to San Francisco the next day and ran into Marco, of the Fanchon and Marco vaudeville team, in the lobby of the hotel. While Mary had been salvaging quarters and dimes from the stage of the oil town resort, the manager of the show on Tait's Roof had been fired. Mary had become acquainted with Fanchon and Marco during her attempt as the invalid. "How would you like to come and work in our show?" Marco said.[14]

Flattered, Mary gratefully accepted. The show was smart and coordinated. Accustomed to a sense of inferiority, Mary felt she had neither the face or figure for such sophisticated showmanship. She described herself as "very tall and very thin and gawky, with the undevelopment of the teens, and it never occurred to me or anyone else that Nature had assembled me into anything like beauty. Even Fanchon despaired of my height for a time. The other girls were of the pony type—little quick things, who could look delightful in a couple of silk handkerchiefs and a few beads. I felt like an elephant among them."[15]

Fanchon designed all the costumes in an artful combination of colors and styling. "I don't know what I can do with you," she exclaimed wearily to Mary. "You are so much taller than the other girls." She tossed Mary a scanty bathing suit and liked what she saw. After consideration she said, "I see what's been wrong with you. You've been wearing too many clothes. Your street things make you look like a scarecrow. Now I know what to make for you." More of Mary was seen after that with scanty, short, very tight fitting, backless costumes. These were offset with impressive trains, supplemented with great fans and high headdresses to make Mary seem even more statuesque. Mary loved it![16]

With her added attraction, Fanchon saw even more possibilities and took Mary home with her. She gave Mary extra coaching in songs, teaching her tricks of accent, shading, dance steps, and knowledge of stage smartness. Mary's reputation as a jazz singer became impressive. She said, "The Coast was the stomping ground of jazz that was jazz and not just half-hearted syncopation." The songs written about the African-Americans, as the New York songwriters depicted them a generation away from slavery, were particularly popular. A good example is the familiar, "Won't You Come Home, Bill Bailey, Won't You Please Come Home?" The songs were sung with a guttural sound, "like clearing your throat," Mary explained.[17]

In response to the acclaim, Mary let out all the stops singing the style she knew so early in her childhood—the style that called for punishment as sinfulness when she tried it around Anna. Mary danced and pranced and sang the rhythms with abandon until one night, as she went into her act, she opened her mouth to sing—and found she had lost her voice! She made it through by talking her songs.[18]

"As I stood there, numb and heartsick, my mind kept conjuring up new horrors: 'What if I can't ever sing again? What will I do? How shall I ever earn my living without my voice? Please, God, help me!'" Back in her room, the despondent star flung herself onto her bed and sobbed. Fanchon and Marco consoled her with reassuring words that her young voice would return after rest. Fanchon planned personality stunts for the silent songbird. She was taught the vaudeville trick of reciting and acting a song to music and a new world opened up! "Hitherto I had always regarded a song merely as a piece of music and not as a latent bit of drama" in accord with the rigid vocal training of her youth. The audiences loved her rendition of "Mammy o' Mine," which she chanted with emotion.[19]

In spite of her new successes, Mary experienced days when she said, "I wanted to die. Days when I realized anew that the money I was hoarding to pay vocal teachers to restore my voice was being thrown away." Of the experience, she said, "…only a painter who has lost his sight, a pianist who has lamed his hand, an acrobat with maimed body can understand what I went through."[20]

After finishing the contract at Tait's, the company was organized to move and Mary went on the road with her act. She met Al Christie of Christie Comedies while on tour in Los Angeles, and Mary and another girl were invited to the studio for film testing. They were pronounced acceptable and given promise of a job in the movies when they were ready. The other girl immediately embarked on the new career, but Mary traveled on with the show to Denver. There trouble set in when the orchestra leader's wife, who was also a member of the chorus, became jealous of the favoritism shown to Mary by Fanchon and Marco. "She nagged her husband into making my life miserable," Mary remembered, so she contacted Christie by wire of her application for the movies and was invited to return at once to Los Angeles to begin.[21]

The next six months in the warm sun and climate of Los Angeles were good days for Mary. As a member of the Christie Stock Company, she was "on call" at any time when needed. Mary played in one picture with Colleen Moore, who later became a well known star. In another, Mary played a leading role in *The Ugly Duckling*, which she felt was perfect casting. "I was the ugly duckling," Mary remembered from her early childhood trauma. She played opposite the lead with her hair twisted up in a knot, age-lined face, and a blackened front tooth. "That was my debut as a screen comedian." Mary never saw the release, but heard reports it was quite good.[22]

Mary had arrived in Hollywood when the movie industry was emerging in a wacky, zany fashion. Peace may have been established following World War I, but Hollywood was involved in its own battle. The undeclared war over the use of Thomas A. Edison's invention of silent entertainment involved patent and copyright infringements, lawsuits, name-calling, and undercutting by hideaway studios. The public became a part of it by paying the admission price of a nickel. They were held captive at the nickelodeon as the piano maestros composed original background scores.

As box office attraction, New York's Broadway stars were imported to the west coast since it was easier to film the professional actors with stage savvy than to try to train the new recruits. *The Keystone Cops* is the epitome of early movie comedy with its bathing beauties and custard pies. Al Christie's comedies were the nearest competitor to Mack Sennett's "Cops." Mary was there. The silent movies were the perfect vehicle for the silenced singer.[23]

"One day, after I had hurled custard pies for Christie for about five months, I was shocked to find myself singing. My voice had come back to me!" Mary admitted she never was very accurate with the custard pies anyway. In another version, she said she tripped over shoes and fell downstairs, screamed, and discovered her voice was healed.[24]

What good was a beautiful voice in the silent flicks? Mary yearned for New York and further study. She interviewed everyone she met who came from New York or had been there. She gleaned information about the stage, theatrical managers, chorus girls' salaries, cost of living, and the standard of the musical and dramatic productions. She purchased a map and memorized the principal streets, studied post cards, and souvenir pictures. Mary was convinced New York held the opportunity for her.[25]

Raymond Hitchcock, actor, singer, and comedian, had brought his production of *Kitchy-Koo* to Los Angeles. Hearing from members of his troupe that chorus girls could make $40 a week in the East, Mary asked for a chance. "I haven't any place for you now. But—what can you do?"

Hitchcock questioned. "I can sing and dance," Mary answered, "and I am pretty good at jazz stunts." After some thought, Hitchcock said, "I'll tell you what I'll do. You go to New York along about August. We're going to put on a new show in the fall and if you come in to see me about then, I'll give you a job in the chorus."[26]

Mary couldn't wait!

Endnotes Chapter 6 On the Road

1. Lewis, "From the Slums," *LHJ*, June 1927, p. 26.
2. Ibid.
3. Ibid.
4. Ibid.
5. Ibid.
6. Ibid.
7. Ibid., pp. 26-27.
8. Ibid., p. 27.
9. Ibid.
10. Ibid.
11. Ibid.
12. Ibid.
13. Ibid., p. 64.
14. Ibid.
15. Ibid.
16. Ibid.
17. Ibid.
18. Ibid.
19. Ibid.
20. Ibid.
21. Ibid., pp. 64, 65.
22. Ibid., p. 66. Myrene Wentworth, "Who's An Ugly Duckling?" *Screenland*, July 1930, p. 83.
23. Daniel Blum, *A Pictorial History of the Silent Screen*. (New York: G. B. Putnam's Sons, 1953), pp. 107-171.
24. Lewis, "From the Slums," *LHJ*, June 1927, p. 66.
25. Ibid.
26. Ibid.

7

New York

Mary said, "I took what little money I had saved, settled up my affairs in Los Angeles, told the Christie people of my plans, bought a ticket, and set out for New York." By finding the cheapest hotel she could, Mary stretched her total cash of several hundred dollars, but she had other wealth—her youth, beauty, talent, training, and ambition.[1]

"For two or three days nothing happened," she said. "Then I was introduced to Stanton Leeds, a writer on *Variety*," a theatrical magazine. "Learning that I could sing and dance," Mary continued, "Leeds got up a party that included a woman who knew Barney [Bernard] Gallant." The group went to Gallant's night club, The Greenwich Village Inn, on MacDougal Street. The Inn advertised, "An unspoiled rendezvous where spontaneous entertainment frequently occurs among a talented and distinguished patronage."[2]

Mary was introduced to Gallant, who had an interest in the *Greenwich Village Follies*. He made arrangements for Mary to have an audition for director John Murray Anderson at the Greenwich Village Theater the following afternoon.[3]

Mary was taken to the Greenwich Village Theater the next day and introduced to director Anderson.[4] "I sang a ballad, danced to it a bit, and then jazzed the chorus," Mary said. "When I was finished, Mr. Anderson told me I'd do, and to go upstairs and get a contract. This contract gave me $40 a week, downtown, and $50 when the show moved uptown" to the Shubert Theater at West 44th Street. Mary was also told that if any new number was created, it would be hers.[5]

This took place during the month of June and rehearsals did not begin until the end of July. Mary sublet a small apartment and settled down to study and practice. Finally, the end of July rolled around. After ten days of rehearsals, Mary began to worry as no one had taken any notice of her. When small bit parts were added, they were given to the regular girls of the troupe. Mary found herself in the back row, with one exception, when she was on the end in a special chorus with twelve other girls.[6]

Mary thought to herself, "This isn't so good. This isn't what I wanted to do. I don't mind being a chorus girl, but if I am going to be a chorus girl, I want to be one of the leading ones." Shortly after this thought crossed her mind, designs for the costumes were sent in by Bobbie Locher and James Reynolds, who was a young Irishman. "Again the old girls got the more gorgeous ones and I was ignored," she pouted.[7]

Realizing that chances in this production were slim, Mary began to look around quietly for another job. She had rented her apartment from a man who had once been a jazz singer. Hearing her sing one day, he commented, "You ought to try for something better than a chorus job." "But I don't know how to go about it," Mary protested and received his advice. "For a week I made the round with 'Mammy' songs under one arm and straight music under the other. This tour brought me at last to Charles B. Dillingham."[8] This gentleman had earlier teamed with Florenz Ziegfeld[9] in a *Follies* production. Dillingham sent Mary to sing for Fred G. Latham, who was director for a show Dillingham was producing. Latham happened to be in a bad mood. "Well, what are you going to sing?" he demanded.[10]

Mary answered, "My Little Grey Home in the West." Latham groaned, "Anything but that. I don't care what it is, but not that." Mary sang it anyway. Then she sat at the piano and played and sang a jazz song. Latham made no comment, but asked for another, and then still another. He gave no word of criticism or praise, until at the end of the fourth song, he took Mary to Dillingham's office in the Globe Theater. A contract was offered, to be effective that autumn, of a job at $75 a week, with a two-year option for $100 a week. The agreement further stipulated Mary was to be under Latham's special supervision and was to receive a minor role. Mary was overwhelmed at her success.[11]

With renewed courage, Mary returned to the *Greenwich Follies* and announced, "If I'm not given something to do in the show, I'm going to leave." "What do you mean by going out and looking for another job when you are under contract to me?" Anderson demanded. "Well, you promised me a small part if one happened to turn up," Mary pointed out, "and while several have, someone else always got them. Besides, you haven't paid much attention to me since I've been coming around here and it began to look as though you never would." "Well, what can you do?" Anderson asked. "You've heard me in jazz songs," Mary answered. "But I have a prima donna who sings jazz," Anderson countered. "How about letting me sing a ballad then?" Mary countered. Anderson scowled. "I'll tell you what," he offered. "We have tryouts every afternoon and I'll give you one to see whether you'll do as understudy to the prima donna or not."[12]

Thinking to herself, "Understudy, your foot!" Mary left with the Dillingham contract crackling in her handbag, "However, I took my tryout, stubbornly making no effort to impress or please. They could like me or not, I told myself, I'd live through it either way." After a wait of four days, Mary was called by the musical director who asked to hear her highest notes. Mary reported boredom with all this maneuvering and returned to Gallant. She told him of her new contract offer from Dillingham and why she had signed it. "I have sung three or four times for Anderson and his crowd," she said, "and nothing has come of it. So, if I walk out on you some day, you'll know the reason why."[13] Soon after these encounters, Mary was given the principal song to sing at rehearsals, although no comment was made. "This made me the new prima donna," Mary said, "but everyone carefully avoided mentioning this obvious fact. I knew that I was under contract with the *Greenwich Village Follies* for 25 weeks more and I decided to have it out with Anderson. I went into his office one day after rehearsal and said, 'Then I am to be the prima donna after all?'" "You are," he answered abruptly. "But," Mary informed him pleasantly, "I have a contract with Mr. Dillingham." Anderson exploded with rage. Shaking his fists, raging about the room, he implored the heavens to observe this ungrateful creature. He had lain awake at night to plan special numbers for her, he said, and she had gone off and signed a contract with another manager while still contracted with him. As a result, Mary's contract was raised to $75 and the Dillingham contract canceled.[14]

The following five weeks were full of strain "with the last days before opening like a never-ending nightmare," Mary said. Rehearsals were from 10:30 a.m. until 5 or 6 a.m. the next morning. The cast members were allowed an hour for lunch and an hour for dinner before returning at 9 p.m. to rehearse through the night. "The pressure is ghastly, and by the time the show is ready to open you want to cut anyone's throat who even looks at you," Mary later said.[15]

Cast in an old-fashioned waltz number with four couples, Mary sang as well as danced. Instead of using an accompanist for rehearsals, Mary was required to sing "hour after hour through endless repetitions until those dancers pleased him. It nearly killed me," she said, but did not complain. Three days before opening, the strain had taken its toll. "Half dead, I started in the morning on the Valentine number," Mary explained. Halfway through the first verse, Murray started in. "Do you think you can sing that song that way and get away with it?" he squalled at Mary. "You'll ruin my show. Now do it again, and do it right." "I did it again. And again. And again. With Murray standing a foot from me, yelling," Mary said. "Everything was terrible—the way I used my hands, pronounced the words and walked. At last I broke." Mary shrieked at him, "Do you think I can sing with you screaming in my ear like that?" and ran sobbing to her dressing room.[16]

Murray followed and banged on the door. "At last, I've made you cry," he raved. "Now I know that you have a soul, some heart, some temperament. I was just about ready to give you up as hopeless. . . ." "Oh, get out of here," Mary cried. "Soul or no soul, I'm through. I'm going home." "Now, look here, Lewis," cajoled the director, "You know I like you. . . ." "I can't work with you screaming at me every minute," Mary told him. "I was doing the best I could." "All right, all right. I won't do it any more," promised Anderson. "Now, pull yourself together and come on back and let's get through this rehearsal."[17]

Like many of the other theatrical giants, Anderson was a genius, although difficult of temperament. Under his inspired guidance, the *Greenwich Village Follies* achieved success combining simplicity, wit, and taste. Greenwich Village was teeming with budding artists and Anderson was a master at casting. Of all the hopefuls that swarmed to the village, few survived. After the clash, friendship between Anderson and Mary grew.

In the fall of 1920, the second edition of the *Greenwich Village Follies* opened with Mary starring as prima donna. Besides the Valentine number, she sang in a skit, "The Pawn Broker," which begins in a pawnshop with singer Frank Crumit attempting to engage a cast for a musical production. He redeems the voice of a silvery-toned prima donna (Mary), which she has been forced to leave to get funds for food. He then adds the feet of a dancer and the laughs of a comedian, continuing until the show is complete.

Mary Lewis also appeared in a perfume allegory entitled, "Tsin," (pronounced "Sin"), in which an Oriental slave guarded a large reflector pool in the center stage with the show girls portraying various bottled scents arranged in tiered columns. As Mary Lewis sang the title song, "Perfume of Love," the girls moved toward the pool for a sexy bow as the slave proceeded to stir the heady mixture. Mary was coupled with Eugene Fosdicks in "The Golden Carnival." Royal red was used for contrast in the skit, imperial in effect. Four couples formed the background for Margaret Severn who fascinated the audience with her "Dance of the Benda Masks," in which she projected an entire roster of characters via switching of masks.[18]

Critic Leo Marsh wrote: "Mary Lewis was also among the most decorative portions of the show and her voice was quite up to the high standard set by her face. Miss Lewis can sing and she is easy to gaze at, which strikes us as a pretty fair combination to bring on success."[19]

The show played in New York for seven months followed by a short season in Philadelphia, Boston, and Pittsburgh. That winter Mary sat in the balcony of the Metropolitan Opera House for her initiation to grand opera at its finest. Mary reported, "I scarcely breathed at this beauty before me" watching Geraldine Farrar[20] perform in *Madama Butterfly,* an Italian tragic grand opera based on a story by American novelist, John Luther Long. The music was composed by Giacomo Puccini. The picturesque background of Japanese life, the pathetic story of the little bride, and the lovely harmonies of the score combine to give it unfailing popularity. "And," Mary said, "I promised myself, sitting there, that if it were humanly possible, I should be singing on that great stage one day. At least, I hitched my wagon to no modest ambition!"[21]

One day at rehearsal at the *Follies* Crumit told of being sent by a talking-machine company to study with a teacher so his voice might record better. "He's the guy who put [Rosa Melba] Ponselle in opera," Crumit said. "William Thorner!" Mary embraced the name. Her hopes were almost dashed when Crumit told of the fee, but Mary determined to someday earn the salary to be able to pay for lessons with that master.[22] In the spring of 1921, as the *Greenwich Village Follies* was preparing for its annual tour, Mary began to fret about leaving New York and her musical studies. Hearing Flo Ziegfeld was rehearsing for a new show, Mary admitted, "I decided to do a daring thing."[23]

The *Ziegfeld Follies* was the mecca for all vaudevillians. Every performer craved a chance at the *Follies*. It played to the best house, and through promoters and publicity, it became a high point in the performers' lives. In the 1920s the Ziegfeld girl replaced the Gibson girl as the epitome of American feminine beauty. Everyone adored the Ziegfeld girl. He glorified his female cast members, using silks, paints, powders, and lighting. He created the illusion of feminine beauty even when nature hadn't been so kind. No other producer equaled Ziegfeld.

Mary conceded that no *Greenwich Follies* girl would "consider herself faultless enough for Ziegfeld's national institution." In spite of her awe Mary knew "the road to a reputation for quality in musical comedy led through the New Amsterdam [Theater] and I wanted the theatrical security of being a former *Follies* girl." She continued, "After thought, I decided that the worst that could happen to my application was refusal; and there was always the possibility it might be considered."[24]

So Mary sat down and mapped out her campaign. While planning her strategy, she was invited to appear in a benefit concert during the time the troupe was on tour in Philadelphia, Pennsylvania. She had assembled a fifteen minute sketch choreographed for her own talents. Mary said, "[I] amazed the owners of the *Greenwich Village Follies* by going on 'cold' as appearing without a background of chorus girls for the first time is called, and getting as many recalls as the headliners on the program." This unexpected success gave her courage as well as a $50 increase in salary, now $125 a week, plus using her own sketch with special setting while the show was on tour.[25]

Mary made no commitment—still determined to remain in New York for continued study. Knowing rehearsals were underway for a new show, Mary took her first pilgrimage to the producer's office in the New Amsterdam Theater where the *Ziegfeld Follies* were staged. "The elevator man was dismally unimpressed upon my arrival—'just another new one,' was his attitude. The same perfection of indifference prevailed in Ziegfeld's outer offices. When I at last claimed the attention of a proud office boy long enough to murmur something about Mr. Ziegfeld I was told coldly that the boss was not in. 'And besides, look at the hundreds waiting to see him,' he added in discouragement."[26]

Mary regarded the two great offices in despair and judged his estimate was not exaggerated. She also "noted that 999 of the number were girls—painted girls in black satin dresses, befeathered hats, invisible stockings, highest of heels and millions of dollars' worth of rouge. My first aghast thought was 'Heavens, I'm not dressed up enough for this place.' My skirt and blouse with its round collar and tiny white cuffs were of blue serge—the stuff never wears out—and bought in California. My heels were flat, and make-up in the morning had not occurred to me. I had no inflated ideas about feathers, nor had I overcome my small-town training in the matter of the suitability and economy of a simple wardrobe." In awe of all the gorgeous trappings, Mary felt shabby in comparison. "Had I only known it, Ziegfeld hates girls who come to him all dressed up like a four-alarm fire."[27]

This was the first of many journeys from Philadelphia. Three times a week for the next four weeks, Mary was aboard the early morning express to the metropolis. This routine consisted of wiping off the last of the cold cream at midnight, followed by a short nap, and up at dawn for the two-hour train ride to New York. She sat among the many other anxious hopefuls for five or six hours in the Ziegfeld office. A hurried taxi ride took her back to Pennsylvania Station where she boarded the train for the two-hour return ride. Mary was in costume and make-up ready for appearance in the show at 8:30 p.m.[28]

Observation soon taught Mary that only one girl, the secretary right outside the office, could open the door. Seating herself next to the secretary, Mary soon "ceased to be just another face to her and became Mary Lewis of the *Greenwich Village Follies*." Just as she felt she could not endure one more excursion from Philadelphia to New York, she found herself invited into the hallowed chamber. "Chill with panic, hearing nothing but my clamoring heart," Mary was escorted into Ziegfeld's office. "Behind a huge desk a man sat and looked at me and never moved. Even his eyelids seemed unblinking. Presently he said in the famous high monotone: 'Hello, and who are you?'"[29]

Florenz Ziegfeld—there was no one that could compare to him. He combined showmanship, zest, courage, taste, and flamboyance into his productions and he was an acute judge of talent. Mary gulped, "I'm Mary Lewis." "What do you want?" Ziegfeld asked. "I want a job," replied Mary. Ziegfeld laughed and Mary began to breathe again and joined him in laughter. She said, "My laugh and my smile were always my open sesame. And frozen though I was I had probably smiled as I walked into the room." Motionless, the great producer asked, "Aren't you with the *Greenwich Village Follies*?" Mary answered, "Yes, they want me to go on tour, but I want to go into the *Ziegfeld Follies*." "What do you want to do?" Ziegfeld questioned. "I want to sing," Mary answered. "Sing something," he commanded.[30]

Mary walked over to the piano, sitting with her back to the image, she felt his silent presence. The phone rang constantly adding to her nervousness. After Mary had sung two jazz numbers, Ziegfeld walked around his desk, approached the piano, and looked at her showing no emotion. "And so you want to be a *Follies* girl?" Ziegfeld inquired. "I don't want to be a *Follies* girl. I want to sing. I want to be a principal." Mary aimed high.[31]

"All right. I'll give you $150 a week. Go get your contract," said Ziegfeld. No more was said. Dumbfounded, Mary obeyed and terminated her agreement with the *Greenwich Village Follies*.[32]

Endnotes Chapter 8 New York

1. Lewis, "From the Slums," *LHJ*, June 1927, p. 66.
2. Program Greenwich Village Theatre, *Greenwich Village Follies 1920.*
3. Lewis, "From the Slums," *LHJ*, June 1927, p. 66.
4. John Murray Anderson, (1886-1954), was educated in Edinburgh where he was introduced to the theater. During a 36-year period, Anderson created, in many cases wrote, and produced 34 major musical shows and revues (29 on Broadway and 5 in London); 7 circuses for Ringling Brothers-Barnum & Bailey; 4 aquacades for Billy Rose; 11 pageants; 61 film house presentations; and 24 fancy night club shows. He wrote or helped write the lyrics for 64 songs. Fifty-fourth *Variety* anniversary edition, Jan. 6, 1960, p. 263. "Robert Baral's Reprise: Pre-Beatnik Greenwich Village and Murray Anderson's 'Follies.'"
5. Lewis, "From the Slums," *LHJ*, June 1927, p. 66.
6. Ibid.
7. Ibid.
8. Charles Bancroft Dillingham, (1868-1934), was an American theatrical producer who presented over 200 plays on Broadway, most of these musicals. In 1910 he opened the Globe Theater in New York and, for more than 20 years, he managed the productions there. He also headed the Dillingham Theater Corporation. *The Encyclopedia Americana International Edition*, 1984, Vol. 9, p. 118.

9. Florenz Ziegfeld, (1869-1932), was born in Chicago, the son of the founder of the Chicago Musical College. The first of his revues, which were Ziegfeld's distinctive contribution to the American stage, was the *Follies of 1907.* This was followed by more than 20 consecutive annual editions of *The Ziegfeld Follies,* which was billed as an "American institution." They were spectacular displays, combining lavish, imaginative sets, and costumes with an abundance of attractive girls. Under the slogan, "Glorifying the American Girl," Ziegfeld created a model of feminine beauty that became the fashion, emphasizing slenderness and grace. He engaged the foremost composers, librettists, and lyricists to write his shows and top-notch comedians to supply humor. His work established a standard of taste and artistry that left its mark on stage entertainment. *The Encyclopedia Americana International Edition*, 1984, Vol. 29, p. 774.
10. Lewis, "From the Slums," *LHJ*, June 1927, p. 66.
11. Ibid., pp 66,68.
12. Ibid., p. 68.
13. Ibid.
14. Ibid.
15. Ibid.
16. Ibid.
17. Ibid.
18. *Variety*, 6 Jan. 1960, p. 263. New York Public Library Theater Collection. Program *Greenwich Village Follies 1920*, New York Public Library.
19. Ibid. Leo A. Marsh, New York *Telegraph*, 31 Aug. 1920, New York Public Library Theater Collection.
20. Geraldine Farrar, (1882-1967), an American soprano, enjoyed a brilliant career in opera and on the concert stage. Her striking dramatic and musical ability, coupled with her charm and personality, placed her among the outstanding American singers. She excelled in the role of Madama Butterfly. She sang with the Metropolitan Opera Co. from 1906 until she retired in 1922. She was born in Melrose, Massachusetts. *The World Book Encyclopedia*, 1961, Vol. 6, p 52.
21. Lewis, "From the Slums," *LHJ*, June 1927, p. 68.
22. Ibid., July 1927, p. 79.
23. Ibid., June 1927, p. 68.
24. Ibid., July 1927, p. 28.
25. Ibid.
26. Ibid.
27. Ibid.
28. Ibid., pp. 28, 79.
29. Ibid., p. 79.
30. Ibid.
31. Ibid.
32. Ibid.

Mary Lewis loved the gown she wore as the Pink Rose in the *Follies of 1921*. Victor Herbert complimented Mary when she sang the number composed by Herbert. *LHJ* May 1927, page 3.

Ziegfeld considered Mary Lewis the most beautiful prima donna he ever hired. The lavishness Florenz Ziegfeld flung into his *Follies* stunned Mary Lewis. Photo by Ira D. Schwarz.

PROGRAM CONTINUED

SCENE 3—
Musical Number—"RADIO" (Scene painted by H. Robt. Law Studios)
By Gene Buck and Dave Stamper)
Dialogue by Ralph Spence
Sung by Alexander Gray and Mary Lewis
And Messrs. Whitcomb, Shannon, Truscott and Lambert

SCENE 4—
"LACE-LAND"
Song—"Weaving"..............................Sung by Mary Lewis
(Lyrics by Gene Buck; Music by Victor Herbert
(Scene by Joseph Urban)
(Lace Ballet devised and staged by Ned Wayburn)
Characters:
The Lace Maker..................................Mary Lewis
The Dutch Visions—Irene Marcellus, Beulah McFarland, Gertrude Selden and Polly Nally.
The Trousseau:
Lace Stockings............Clara Beresbach
The Parasol..............Frances Reveaux
The Handkerchief.........Helen Worthing
The Fan.................Beulah McFarland
The Bridal Gown............Sonia Ivanoff
The Veil......................Jessie Reed
Butterfly ....Marie Shelton
Pages.........................Madge Merritt, Addie Rolf
Ballet of Motives—Misses Stoneburn, Rich, Rees, Dana, Conroy, Manning, Earle, McLaughlin, Vernon, Vreeland, Valentine and Pearl Eaton.
The Inspiration..................................Mary Eaton

SCENE 5—"SONGS I CAN'T FORGET" (By Gene Buck and Louis Hirsch)
Sung by Thomas Spencer, Mary Lewis and "The Follies Four"
Some New Talent in the Following Order:
"Glow Worm"......................................Mary Dahm
"Bedalia" ....Anastasia Reilly
"La Poloma"......................................Hilda Moreno
"French" ....Leonora Baron
"Alexander's Ragtime Band"........................Pearl Eaton
"Annie Rooney"...................................Hallie Manning
"Robt. E. Lee" ....Hazel Webb
"Hiawatha" ....Marion Rich
"Sweet Adeline"....................................Mary Lewis

SCENE 6—"THE FILMLESS MOVIES"
(By Franklin P. Adams, Nate Salsbury and Emil Breitenfeld)
Andrew Tombes

PROGRAM CONTINUED ON SECOND PAGE FOLLOWING

16th annual production of Ziegfeld Follies, New Amsterdam Theatre, program page 39, week beginning May 21, 1923.

8

The Follies

The Ziegfeld *Follies* are considered to have reached their zenith in the 1921 and 1922 editions. The *Follies of 1921* featured Mary Lewis, Fanny Brice, W.C. Fields, Raymond Hitchcock, Ray Dooley, Van and Schenck, dancer Mary Eaton, and John Clarke. The script was written by Willard Mack, Channing Pollock, and others. Music was composed by Jerome Kern, Victor Herbert, Rudolph Friml, and B.G. DeSylva. Costumes were by James Reynolds, the young Irishman who had also designed for the *Greenwich Village Follies*.[1] Sets were by Joseph Urban, a vibrant designer from Austria who was left stranded in the United States at the outbreak of World War I.[2] John Steele rejoined the show later. Other principal singers were Mary Milburn, a protégée of Mr. Herbert; Vera Michalena; and Florence Denishawn.[3]

It was Ray Hitchcock who had given Mary the advice the preceding year to try her luck on Broadway. Hitchcock was a droll comedian who wove impossible tales into joyous comical situations. Comedienne Ray Dooley was cast in various roles. W.C. Fields, with his big nose, top hat, and rasping nasal voice, was a combination of strange characteristics. Fields remembered the 1921 *Follies* as an historic show. His main comedy scene took place in the subway with a family starting out on a vacation. Other supporting players were Dooley, Hitchcock, and Fanny Brice. The racket of the approaching train heralded the burlesque as the family tried in vain to enter the car. Years later Fields told a friend: "the 1921 *Follies* was my happiest year with Ziegfeld and the best revue I ever saw in my life."[4]

Although it was Mary who opened the *Follies of 1921*, all eyes (and ears) were on the "funny girl," singing comedienne Fanny Brice. Fanny made the headlines. She was the laugh of the season with a burlesque of actress Ethel Barrymore playing Camille supported by Hitchcock as

Armand. Fanny introduced the French song, "Mon Homme," or "My Man." The press and the public were on her heels or at her feet.[5]

Fanny had received her first contract with Ziegfeld as comedienne in 1910. On her way to the top she attracted the attentions of Nick Arnstein and Fanny fell madly, head-over-heels in love. Although at the time Arnstein was married, the couple began living together and later married. Nick never settled for anything but the very best. To Fanny, not known for her beauty, poise or grace, Nick stood for manners, education, and good breeding. He also possessed, unfortunately, a capacity for dreaming and scheming.[6]

As a result of his schemes, warrants went out for his arrest in February, 1920, for masterminding bond thefts amounting to five million dollars. Nick went into hiding, but was able to keep in contact with Fanny using W.C. Fields as a messenger boy. Although still protesting his innocence, Arnstein sent word he was ready to give himself up.[7]

After Fanny and her driver had made rendezvous with the fugitive, in a daring move, the car swung into a New York City police parade. As the route swung past the reviewing stand on Fifth Avenue, Nick saluted the city's high ranking police officials who glared at the hunted fugitive as he rolled past. After dropping Nick at the Criminal Court Building, Fanny appeared for her *Follies* performance. The couple's second child, a son, was born and three weeks later, Fanny was in rehearsal for the new *Follies*. Nick, after trial and sentencing, was deposited at Fort Leavenworth prison in Kansas.[8]

Fanny immortalized "Second Hand Rose" and "My Man." No one was dry-eyed as Fanny, dressed as a French peasant girl in a torn skirt and mussed hair, shared a part of her personal heartache. She closed her eyes, caressed herself, and sang the plaintive lament. Everyone knew she was baring her soul as she yearningly mourned for Nick. The song might have been written for Fanny. It was one of the few times she sang straight without the comedy routine.[9]

To forget her sorrows, Fanny's home became the scene of nightly parties following the *Follies* performances. She was the favorite of the social set and loved to cook as she entertained the elite of New York's upper crust. Although the *Follies* cast rallied around to protect her, Fanny brazenly faced the press. She answered their most impertinent, intimate questions with wisecracks. They followed her everywhere. The couple divorced, but Nick remained Fanny's "man" for the rest of her life.[10]

Mary found a difference between the *Greenwich Village Follies* and the *Ziegfeld Follies* in the discipline and routine. There was a schedule with an hour space and a name designated for that time slot. The girl was called to rehearse and she did, barring illness or death. Never with Ziegfeld was Mary subjected to the continuous, exhausting practice sessions around-the-clock as she had been with Anderson.[11]

Before the show opened, the last few days of practice lasted until midnight for the cast. Ziegfeld, though, was at work eighteen hours a day. No one but the master knew what the show would be like. He shaped, slashed, and honed the production into a flawless opening performance.[12]

The lavishness Ziegfeld flung into his *Follies* made Mary breathless.[13] The sets by Joseph Urban were skilled perfection with paints applied to the background canvas by use of pointillism, small dots of color, a technique of the Impressionist school. Only Urban achieved the magical effects with lighting and the subdued art work.[14]

The cost of the wispy costumes appalled the thrifty country girl. In the 1921 review Ziegfeld showed a little more of the American girl (and Mary) than the public was accustomed to seeing at that time. "Perhaps the loveliest I ever wore was the one I used in the 'Rose' number. Its bodice was a pointed diamond basque with no straps. Its hoop skirt was a heap of rose petals, each edged with diamonds. This was worn in the act I shared with Michalena, the blue rose, Denishawn, the yellow rose, and Milburn, the red." Mary was the pink rose.[15]

"After I had sung my song in this number," Mary said, "Victor Herbert walked over and said, 'What a nice voice you have.'" Mary was surprised and touched to be recognized by the great composer and accepted the compliment graciously."Everything was so beautiful, so dainty, so fragile. Workmanship, materials, money, nothing was stinted. One lovely white brocade I wore came from the most important shop in New York," said Mary. "A great Paris dressmaker made some of my things. Even Ziegfeld must have paid hundreds for them."[16]

"But the scantiest costume was the one I used as the lady animal trainer in the Hitchcock skit. It had been designed originally for another member of the company—a woman with a beautiful figure, thinner and more compact than mine. The bodice of this costume was made of four diamond handkerchiefs, quite small, caught together at the corners, two in front and two in back," she described. "The trousers were two strips of black *passementerie* [beaded braid strips] held together with diamond strips, one on each side of the leg. With it I wore diamond crystal shoes." When telling her own story in 1927 she conceded "such attire would be thought modest and adequate, but then, when nudity was not so usual, I thought I could never go through with it. When I was told I had to wear the thing I tried to make it decent with tights," she explained, "but when Ziegfeld saw me he said, 'Go take those tights off. They're terrible.'"[17]

"I took them off, but when it was time for me to go on before the mob, I couldn't." Mary was hysterical. As she tried to protest, the manager shoved her out into the revealing lights on stage with, "Aw, go on, Mary, be a sport." Mary was crying so hard she couldn't sing. Van and Schenck, also in the skit, tried to sing it for her, but forgot the words in the hullabaloo.[18]

By the time the *Follies* had played thirteen weeks in New York, it was ready to take on tour. Michalena left the company and Mary was awarded her songs and skits making seven numbers in which she appeared. Mary introduced the song, "Kiss in the Dark," music by Herbert.[19] When the show went on the road, the girls traveled in a private train with a special compartment for each girl. They stayed in the finest hotels and opening nights were crowded with the society's elite.

Away from home, parties filled the recesses from rehearsals and performances. There Mary was initiated into the cynicism associated with being a *Follies* girl. She found the prejudices against the girls and the legends of their ruthlessness and gold-digging completely wrecking her trust in humanity."Parties were the only respite on tour," Mary said, "Cynicism is the chief reward of such fêtes. A small-town girl of seventeen to twenty, admitted to the *Follies* because of her beauty, her voice or her nimble feet, as green as they make 'em, believing in the trueness of lovers, the fidelity of husbands, the integrity of fathers and Santa Claus, soon abandons illusions. The tales she regarded as "incredible and simply silly in nine cases out of ten, unfortunately the tenth is always widely advertised. Most girls regarded the Ziegfeld show just as I did—as a necessary stepping stone to musical comedy and the movies" rather than for romantic involvement. "They work like horses, with their five or six singing and dancing lessons a week. They are young and they are human, but mostly as straight as they make 'em. They haven't time to be otherwise," she later said.[20]

Mary soon found the parties boring and was irritated at the time slipping away. She was accustomed to a routine of dedicated study and practice. Feeling herself drifting, she began to scheme to return to New York. Underground information had revealed Ziegfeld's plans to reopen the New Amsterdam Roof, a room at the top of the New Amsterdam Theater, the setting for the *Midnight Frolic*.[21] Designer Urban had fashioned the roof into a glittering night club with a moveable stage, glass balconies, and stunning rainbow lighting. There was dancing and inter-table telephones, the forerunner of the night club floor show. The innovation struggled amid the prohibition regimentation.[22]

Mary called Ziegfeld from Boston and told him of her desire to return to New York. "If you get in Sunday night, do you think you can have three songs learned by Monday night?" "Yes," Mary answered quickly." All right, you can leave Sunday," was the response.[23]

Mary was elated. This was just before Christmas in 1921. After the roof show closed, a new *Follies* would be prepared allowing her one unbroken year in New York for study. Mary arrived in Manhattan Sunday morning as instructed and met with song writer Dave Stamper. They rehearsed the new songs and Mary opened as prima donna the following night. Not sure of the words, she scribbled them on a little scrap of paper which she held in her palm.[24] Her salary now enabled Mary to fulfill her dream. At last, five years after determining to be the pupil of this man, Mary contacted William Thorner. Knowing he judged a voice quickly and didn't bother with trivial talent, Mary was nervous. She sang one little song for him the first audition and was told to return the following day. The third day he asked abruptly, "What is the thing you want to do? Have you ever thought of opera?" Mary confessed it had been a dream—a hopeless dream. "If you want to work," Thorner told her, "I think you've got the voice to make the Metropolitan."[25]

That year, in 1922, Mary began earnestly to study and practice. At this point, her natural mother reentered her life. Mary never explained how the reunion came about. Mary's only mention of her mother is: "I rented a little flat and mother came on to take care of it for me. We prepared our own meals and I rarely went out."[26] Mary continued to support her mother the rest of her mother's life.[27] Mary kept up the image of the *Follies* girl by wearing a handsome coat to and from the theater, while underneath she wore an inexpensive cotton dress.[28]

Mary studied twice a week with Thorner. She engaged a coach and began working on Puccini's *La Bohème* three or four days a week besides studying Italian and French. The schedule was possible only because the roof "Frolic" didn't open until 11 p.m. and was out at 1:30 a.m. Mary went straight home for sleep and was able to have an hour's nap after dinner before the evening performance. She admitted she could never have coped with such a strict routine had she been starring in the regular 8:30 p.m. *Follies*.[29]

The rooftop show ran three months, closing before rehearsals began for the 1922 *Follies*. Mary had then progressed with her lessons in foreign language and her vocal efforts. Ziegfeld was so impressed that he crowned her the only prima donna that year.[30] He considered her the most beautiful lead singer he ever hired.[31]

The *Follies of 1922* opened June 5 featuring Mary, Will Rogers, Gilda Gray, Evelyn Law, Mary Eaton, Gallagher and Shean, and the Tiller Girls from London. Mary remembered Martha Lorber joined the cast. The script was by Ring Lardner, Ralph Spence, and Gene Buck. Costumes were by James Reynolds, Tappé, and Charles Le Maire. Urban again was master of set design.[32]

This *Follies* was pronounced the most expensive. It was climaxed by Charles Le Maire's costumed spectacle, "Lace Land," which achieved theatrical glorification. Lyrics were by Gene Buck, music by Victor Herbert. The most costly costume of all was worn by Mary. It was the famous "radium" costume of peasant design, made of alternate ruffles of lace and organdy. The lace was treated with radium about once a week by the wardrobe mistress.[33]

The rare and precious element had only been identified by Pierre and Marie Curié only twenty years before. Its novel, glowing quality was popular providing the luminous light in watch dials. Each tiny particle of the radioactive material gave off the eerie glow. At that time, its dangerous radioactive effects were unknown. It was obtained from uranium and was very expensive. Ziegfeld had a reputation as a reckless spender and the backers loved to let him spend. Mary was flattered to be chosen for this headlining apparition. When the lights were turned out, the ghost of the dress and Mary's face, luminous in the glow from the peasant cap of lace, were all that could be seen on stage while she sang "Weaving."[34]

After her unwitting radiation treatments each night, Mary's health broke down in July. She blamed herself with her reckless enthusiasm of study and performance for the onslaught of what she called, "Neuritis." For three months she languished in the hospital. Her arms refused to lift without great effort and her energy was sapped. For Mary it was as bad as the time she had lost her voice in California, although with this, the financial effects were disastrous. Symptoms of radiation sickness can be signs of infection, such as chills and fever, muscle aches, headache and dizziness.[35]

"But all things must end," Mary cheerfully said, "and in November I was able to rejoin the *Follies* and resume my work with Thorner." Mary stayed with the show until the following June in 1923.[36] The *Follies of 1922* was the longest run of any review of the series produced in Ziegfeld's lifetime. It played 67 weeks in New York and 40 weeks on the road.[37] Besides the "Lace-Land" extravaganza, Mary's name was listed first on the program as "Miss Take," a character in Act I, Scene 1 of "Blunderland." Other appearances were with Alexander Gray in Scene 3 musical number, "Radio." "Lace-Land" was Scene 4. Mary sang "Sweet Adeline" in Scene 5, her part in "Songs I Can't Forget," by Gene Buck and Louis Hirsch.[38]

Mary remembered the time between rehearsals on the New Amsterdam Roof. The cast sat in groups, talked, or sprawled in a corner watching humorist Will Rogers chew his gum and twirl his lariat. Mary must have been a favorite with Will, another Midwesterner who was born in Oklahoma Territory. His mother's name was Mary. His wife, Betty, was from Arkansas. Will studied the newspapers daily so every routine was fresh. He made shrewd, witty cracks at politicians and got away with it.

Will was a sort of father-confessor to the show girls.[39] Asked about the girls, he replied, "They've made me love 'em. Most of them are working for their living and working darned hard, too. You ought to see 'em at rehearsals. They know how to work and there's no nonsense about it either. There's not half of this stage-door johnny evil you hear about."[40]

The end of the season brought an unexpected turn of events for Mary.

Endnotes Chapter 8 The Follies

1. Randolph Carter, *The World of Flo Ziegfeld*. (New York: Praeger Publishers, 1974), p. 172.
2. Baral, Robert. *Revue - The Great Broadway Period*. (New York and London: Fleet Press Corporation, 1962), pp. 56-57.
3. Carter, *The World of Flo Ziegfeld*, p. 172.
4. Robert Lewis Taylor, *W.C. Fields—His Follies and Fortunes*. (New York: The New American Library, 1967), p. 146.
5. *New York Times*, 21 June 1921, *Times* Theatric Reviews, New York Public Library.
6. Carter, *World of Ziegfeld*, p. 127.
7. Norman Katkov, *The Fabulous Fanny, the Story of Fanny Brice*. (New York: Alfred A. Knopf, 1953), pp. 112- 114.
8. Ibid., pp. 128-129, 136.
9. *New York Times*, 21 June 1921, *Times* Theatric Reviews, New York Public Library.
10. Julien Phillips, *Stars of the Ziegfeld Follies*. (Minneapolis, Minnesota: Lerner Publications Co., 1972), pp. 47-49.
11. Lewis, "From the Slums," *LHJ*, July 1927, p. 79.
12. Carter, *World of Ziegfeld*, p. 91.
13. Lewis, "From the Slums," *LHJ*, July 1927, p. 79.
14. Carter, *World of Ziegfeld*, pp. 44-45.
15. Lewis, "From the Slums," *LHJ*, July 1927, p. 79.
16. Ibid.
17. Ibid.
18. Ibid.
19. Ibid. Oral interview, 1988, with Doris Vinton, the Ziegfeld Club. The charitable organization provides aid for women of the theater in need.
20. Lewis, "From the Slums," *LHJ*, July 1927, p. 79.
21. Ibid.
22. Carter, *World of Ziegfeld*, pp. 46-47.
23. Ibid.
24. Ibid.
25. Ibid., p. 80.
26. Ibid.
27. Dougan, "Enigma," p. 265.
28. Little Rock *Arkansas Democrat*, 22 July 1923, Lewis file, Little Rock Public Library.

29. Lewis, "From the Slums," *LHJ*, July 1927, p. 79.
30. Ibid.
31. Letter to Dougan, June 1975, from Doris Vinton, Ziegfeld Club, New York.
32. Carter, *World of Ziegfeld*, p. 172.
33. *New York Times*, 21 July 1921, *Times* Theatric Reviews, New York Public Library.
34. Lewis, "From the Slums," *LHJ*, July 1927, p. 79. "Weaving" was written by Victor Herbert, lyrics by Gene Buck. Program *Ziegfeld Follies*, 16th annual production.
35. Ibid., p. 80. With radiation accidents not severe enough to cause immediate death, side effects may not appear for years, Guthrie, The Health Resource. In the early 1900s radium-based paint was used to paint the faces of watches, clocks, and other items to make them glow in the dark. Dial painters dipped bushes in the radium paint and pointed them with their lips in order to paint the tiny numbers. Their lips were usually coated with the paint and patches of their skin and clothing glowed in the dark. The women thought it so safe they sometimes painted their teeth and faces and then turned off the lights to provide their own and co-workers amusement. They did not know the substance was killing them. Plants where radium was used to paint watch faces, etc., were in Ottawa, Illinois; Orange, New Jersey; Waterbury, Connecticut; and on Long Island, New York. With the welfare of workers at the heart of its mission, in the 1920s the National Consumers League began to investigate the toxic effects of hazardous materials used in factories—in particular, radium. In 1924 the deaths of four young dial painters and illnesses among many other young women doing this work convinced the League and its counterpart in New Jersey, that a new, unknown industrial poison was the culprit. The NCL and the New Jersey Consumers League led a successful lobbying effort to add radium mesothorium necrosis to the list of compensable diseases under New Jersey's Workman's Compensation law. Some lawsuits filed ended in settlement; but most of the women who got sick never sued. Their deaths were often attributed to other causes—anemia being one of the most common. Experts, including scientists at Argonne National Laboratory (located 25 miles south of Chicago), now affirm that radium did kill some of the women. The number of women who died of radiation poisoning is not known but some experts believe radium caused hundreds to die or live in bad health for years. National Consumers League, *Radium Workers Protected Due to Early League Efforts*, http://www.natl-consumersleague.org/radium.htm and Chicago Tribune, 30 Sept. 1998, Section 13, pp.1, 6, 8, *Half life*, by Martha Irvine, Associated Press.
36. Lewis, "From the Slums," *LHJ*, July 1927, p. 80. No further mention is made of the "Lace Land" spectacle.
37. Green, Stanley. *Broadway Musicals Show by Show* (Milwaukee, Wisconsin: Hal Leonard, 1985) p. 123.
38. Program *Ziegfeld Follies*, 16th annual production.
39. P.J. O'Brien, *Will Rogers--Ambassador of Good Will, Prince of Wit and Wisdom* (n.p., 1935), p. 61.
40. Donald Day, *Will Rogers--a Biography* (New York: David McKay Co., 1962), p. 123.

The lace on the cap Mary Lewis wore in the *Follies of 1922* was dipped in radium. The costume was sensational when the lights were dimmed framing Mary Lewis's face in a ghostly glow. It also caused a serious and lingering illness for the prima donna that season. Nickolas Muray. *LHJ* May 1927, page 5.

9

A New Career

Invited as a last minute guest to a party, Mary joined others in a *bon voyage* affair for a couple leaving for Europe. Another guest at the gala was Otto Hermann Kahn, an American banker and opera patron.[1]

Born in Germany, the son of a banker, Kahn entered the finance business first in Germany and then worked in London before coming to the United States in 1893. He was a partner in the financial firm of Kahn, Loeb & Company. He reorganized the Metropolitan Opera Company in 1907-1908. Deeply interested in music, the patron induced Giulio Gatti-Casazza to become general manager of the Metropolitan.[2]

Mary said, "My host, knowing something about me and how hard I had been working, and with a kindly idea of helping me to opportunity, made a point of insisting that I sing. And I sang to my own accompaniment some snatches from *Bohème* rather nervously. Mr. Kahn was very kind and asked if he might not hear me to better advantage, perhaps in the studio of my teacher. The next day, Thorner, hearing of Mr. Kahn's request, arranged to have him come to one of my lessons."[3]

"After this informal hearing," Mary continued, "Mr. Kahn decided to see to it that I was given an audition at the Metropolitan. This was not because I was thought ready for opera by anyone," she explained, "least of all by myself, but because I was most anxious to have Gatti-Casazza tell me whether my voice warranted my abandoning the *Follies* and security for the hazards of opera and study abroad. Fearing to be misunderstood or thought swollen with conceit, I carefully stressed my reason for desiring an audition."[4]

"How well I remember it!" Mary later said, "Tight with nerves, I ran errands all morning, ate a heavy luncheon and did all the things I shouldn't have done. Then at the appointed hour I was led into that dingy stage door of the Metropolitan on Thirty-ninth Street and was plunged at once into Italy. Here and there was a French or American tourist, but Mussolini's people predominated. They stood in groups and argued with passion, or telephoned with operatic gestures."[5]

"The stage of the Metropolitan is vast and incredible," Mary described. "I groped through dimness to the piano. Looking out into the great vault of the auditorium, I could not see the roof. Up and up climbed balconies and melted into shadows. Half a dozen eyes gleamed at me uncannily from the orchestra chairs and routed my shivering courage. I sang an aria from *Bohème* and some French songs and was told to leave my name and address so that judgment might be duly forwarded. The reward of the ordeal was Mr. Gatti's verdict that I had the voice and needed perhaps two years aboard to learn operatic routine, and languages and to acquire repertoire. This was all I needed. The fair awards of musical comedy were just ahead of me and my salary was climbing, but I relinquished them without fear or regret to pursue my operatic chimera."[6]

Mary further explained that after the first audition, there was talk of supplying funds from the company, if she was unable to fund her own venture. When Mary heard of the plan from Thorner, she said, "I declared that I would not accept such a thing under any circumstances. If I went to Europe, I would manage it myself and be under obligation to no one."[7] Reports indicate Gatti-Casazza was ready to sign her immediately, which would have put her under sponsorship of the Met.[8]

"On this bold note," Mary said, "I abandoned musical company, got rid of my apartment, settled my affairs, took what money I had and embarked for Europe on the great adventure." She had signed a three-year contract with Ziegfeld. The final year was allowed to be a sabbatical while she pursued study.[9]

Tired from the grueling routine of performing and studying, Mary hoped for rest when she sailed. "I had planned to bask in the Riviera sun to swim and laze and forget driving ambition. And then," she continued, "when the weariness of the three hard, vacationless years past had left me, I had intended to go to Italy and gain routine in some of her many minor opera houses."[10]

"En route I paused in Paris to hear Marie Kousnezova[11] in Puccini's *Tosca*, and after the second act I hastened to her room to proffer excited praise. The overly efficient woman unexpectedly repaid my tribute by taking me under her wing, crystallizing my plans, introducing me to her manager, Alexander Kahn, and finally arranging an audition for me with Raoul Gunsbourg." Kousnezova had also studied under Thorner.[12]

The results of the July 13 audition were cabled to the world from Paris! Albert Wolff, director of the Opera-Comique in Paris asserted that opera singers should not sing jazz as it "disharmonized the vocal chords beside vulgarizing the soul." Wolff further declared: "no American girl could think of singing in grand opera without at least five years study in France and Italy."[13] The "old world" felt it had a monopoly on operatic talent. The cable service reported: "To prove the contrary, Mary Lewis, who abandoned the revue stage to storm the opera, sang before Gunsbourg and Arturo Serrano, director of the Royal Opera in Madrid, and Alexander Kahn, the well known impresario." Mary sang "Caro Nome" ("Dearest Name") from Verdi's *Rigoletto* and the Juliette's Waltz ("Ah! Je veux vivre" or "Oh! I want to live") from Charles Gounod's *Roméo et Juliette*.[14]

At the end of the test, Serrano shed tears as he said, "At last we have a potential successor to Mary Garden." He added, "The fruits of her savings have taken her to her goal, and have placed her on the way to realize the supreme ambition which has fired the breast of countless American girls who have lacked all too often, the willingness to sacrifice to the end—to earn greatness." Gunsbourg's opinion was "Mary Maynard Lewis has found that a start in 'jazz' has been no serious handicap to success in grand opera."[15]

As a result of the test, Mary received contracts for several operatic and concert appearances for the future. Plans of a vacation were ruined with this stroke of fortune except for ten days snatched in Italy. During this time, instead of vacationing, Mary sang for agents and was offered some small engagements and arranged for a bit of Italian study.[16]

Hurrying back to Paris, Mary secured a French coach and an Italian maestro to accompany her and began work with Jean Périer, choir director, of the Opéra-Comique on several roles. This busy routine was interrupted one day by manager Alexander Kahn, who called to ask, "By the way, do you happen to know the role of Marguerite in *Faust*?" Mary replied she did not. "Can you learn it in three weeks?" he wanted to know. "If you can, I think I can arrange for a debut in Vienna," he told the startled Mary. Overcome by the speed her career seemed to be taking, she determined, "I'll get the score and have my accompanist play it over and see whether it will be too much for me to conquer in such a short time or not." After three weeks had passed, Mary declared herself ready to "have sung the opera backward, had anything so outlandish been called for, sketched the correct costumes and sets and conducted the orchestra." Her own memorization was reinforced by attending the Paris Opera twice to watch others perform the part.[17]

Kahn had taken Mary at her original word and had arranged for the Vienna debut. Mary declared herself "calm and ready." Her poise was shattered when she arrived in Vienna and found herself billed as the "Great French Opera Singer from the Paris Opera." Mary said, "Gazing at the blatant placards paralyzed me. It is bad enough to have to make a debut at all, but to be compelled to appear for the first time at the great Volksoper in Vienna, with Felix Weingartner at the baton, announced as a finished artist, was an operatic nightmare indeed."[18] After orchestral rehearsal, Mary felt more secure. The *mise-en-scene*, or staging, was one pitfall she dreaded. "But," she said, "fortunately the rehearsal went off well and no one suspected that I had never before set foot on any stage in the role."[19]

On the evening of the debut, October 19, 1923, Mary said she was "calm, unafraid and determined. Too well trained in the theater to be conquered by stage fright, I allowed confusion to seize neither faculties or courage." Tingling with excitement, Mary made her first operatic appearance looking out into the vast grandness of the cavernous theater. Up, up, and up the plush balconies tiered, filled with patrons used to the very best of operatic talent.[20]

Mary was surrounded by some of Vienna's best artists. Trajan Gosavescu, perhaps best remembered for being murdered by his irate wife, sang the title role. Emmanuel List, a noted bass, was Méphistophélès. The Martha, Viorica Ursuleac, was most noted for her roles in Richard Strauss' operas, as well as being the wife of conductor Clemens Kraus.

Gounod's *Faust* is a tragic French grand opera, adapted from Johann Wolfgang Von Goethe's account of man's tragic journey through life to hell and heaven, with the devil as companion and God as the final goal. It is considered the greatest German literary creation. Too vast for treatment in a single opera, Gounod's *Faust* is limited to a single episode of Faust and of Gretchen (Marguerite in the opera). It was given in German countries under the name of the heroine, so as not to offend the ghost of Goethe. The rest of the cast sang in German, while Mary, presumably, used the original French.

Faust is an old man, weary of books, learning, and life, who succumbs to the temptation of the devil, Méphistophélès. When shown a vision of the beautiful soprano, Marguerite, played by Mary, the old man is given regeneration for the pleasures of youth and love. When Marguerite dies in prison, the devil returns to carry Faust to the regions below. The production includes exquisite scoring with Marguerite's "Spinning Wheel Song," "Once There Lived a King in Thule" ("Il était un roi de Thulé"), that leads into the "Jewel Song" ("Ah! Je ris de me voir" or "I see the beauty that is smiling back at me") as some of the favorites.[21] The role of Marguerite also includes the powerful church scene with Méphistophélès, and the opera ends with the well-known trio, begun by the soprano.

Mary found the applause reassuring and modestly related, "The next morning the press was generous, more than kind, and I glowed at warm, unexpected praise."[22] The audience had watched critically as she began the famous "Jewel Song," and when it was over, the applause reverberated to the highest gallery. "Bravo, bravo! Greater than Jeritza," they proclaimed.[23] Operatic performances are gauged by standards of greater than, not as good as, more powerful than, and so forth. To be proclaimed greater than the beloved Maria Jeritza, the Czechoslovakian dramatic soprano, was indeed the highest praise. After conquering the European audiences, Jeritza had begun singing at the Metropolitan in 1921.

The news of Mary's successful debut was cabled around the world. "Greater than Jeritza" they echoed. So runs Mary's story and the clippings that appeared in the American press. Vienna critics reported she had a tendency to sing a semitone sharp, but compared her favorably with Mary Garden.[24] The performance received little attention in the Viennese press.[25]

Soon after the debut in Vienna, Mary met and had opportunity to sing for Franz Lehár, the Hungarian operetta composer. His famous work was the operetta, *The Merry Widow*, which by that time, had been produced world-wide. "When I told him of my operatic aspirations, he frowned and launched upon a tirade," Mary related. Lehár insisted, "I must give up opera and go in for operetta. There was more money in it and a readier fame." Lehár offered to write an operetta especially for Mary that would have its premiere in Paris, besides prophesying a great and financially rewarding future if Mary heeded his advice.[26]

"When he paused for breath," Mary continued, "I told him gently that I had worked hard, as hard as anyone I had ever known, to get as far as I had and that I had given up everything that other girls of my age enjoyed. I had known only concentrated work instead of any fun or social pleasures and that my heart was set on opera as my reward for all this sacrifice. But I assured him if I should find that I did not have the qualities that go to make a great opera singer, he might be certain that I would return to musical comedy." The case was closed, as far as Mary was concerned.[27]

Recognition from the Vienna debut brought a month's engagement at the Staadtheatre in Bratislava, Czechoslovakia. In the middle of December she was given the roles of Marguerite in *Faust*, Gilda in *Rigoletto*, and Micaela in Georges Bizet's *Carmen*. She then debuted at the Monte Carlo Opera in January 1924, in the role of Musetta in *La Bohème*.[28] Monte Carlo in Monaco is one of the most fashionable seaside resorts on the French Riviera on the Mediterranean Sea. In the course of her career, Mary played both soprano roles, Mimi and Musetta, in Puccini's ever popular score. Both parts gave Mary crowd pleasing opportunities. Mimi had the first act aria "Mi chiamano Mimi" while Musetta's Waltz, "Quando me'n vo soletta," invariably stops the show in the second act.

The heroine is Mimi, a beautiful young woman with tuberculosis, who lives in a garret and supports herself doing needlework. On Christmas Eve she knocks on a nearby attic apartment to seek a light for her candle. The apartment is the living quarters of Rodolfo, a writer; and his friends, Marcel, a painter; Colline, a philosopher; and Schaunard, a musician. Rodolfo is alone when Mimi needs help and the pair fall immediately in love; but are soon separated and reunited, just as consumptive Mimi coughs away her life. Part of the liveliness of the opera is the boisterous fun of the four friends in the Paris Latin Quarter. Marcel and Musetta continue a quarrelsome love affair.[29]

Mary continued with the Monte Carlo company the rest of the 1924 operatic year. On April 6, 1924, she was recitalist at Casa Del Mare at Roquebrune-Cap Martin, near Monte Carlo. Her appearance was at the invitation of Osbourne O'Hagan. Guests included members of royalty and some military generals and their wives. According to the review Mary was a hit. She was described as "divinely tall and most divinely fair in a plain gown of blue which, in the darks of it was like the depths of the sea, and in the lights, suggested heaven. A vision of azurine radiance, and rich Old Masters' shadow, and of living loveliness, with that irresistible dimple, and glints of gold in the coiled crown of her hair...." After more words of glowing praise the article found, "In short, the Recital of Mary Lewis must be writ large in Red Letters in the Chronicle of the music at Casa Del Mare. Mary was invited back for recitals at Casa Del Mare by the host, O'Hagan, whom she later referred to as her "adopted father" and Agnése Greenwood, as her "adopted sister."[30]

During the period while performing at Monte Carlo, Mary traveled to London, England, where an audition with the British National Opera Company brought an engagement for three performances, Musetta in *La Bohème*, and two in Jacques Offenbach's *The Tales of Hoffman (Les Contes d'Hoffmann*) for the coming London season. Performances were all given in English. Maggie Teyte, star of the company and a well-loved soprano, was slated to sing the role of Antonia. Mary had never performed or seen *The Tales of Hoffman* and began diligently rehearsing.[31]

Tales is a French opera in which the poet Hoffmann is drinking with a crowd of students in a tavern at Nurenberg. He offers to tell the story of his three experiences with love. Olympia is the heroine of the first act, a mechanical doll whom Hoffmann loves as he looks through magic glasses. The second, Giulietta, lures him with her charms and then deserts him. The third, Antonia, is a virtuous woman who loves music but is unable to sing because she is afflicted with consumption of the lungs. Antonia is urged to sing, then dies from exertion. Hoffmann then declares that for himself there nothing left but to drown his sorrows in drink. Hoffmann is visited by the Muse while alone in his room and reminded that he still has his art. Sometimes the same soprano fills all three roles, but the British producers used three different singers.[32]

The season opened in June with Mary scheduled to appear in July in *La Bohème*. On the morning of the opening of *Tales*, Mary received a phone call telling her to hurry to the theater to perform that evening in the role of Antonia. Miss Teyte had lost her voice! Mary had been studying opera long enough and hard enough to be comfortable with the arias, but she hurried to rehearse the staging techniques. In telling her own story, she said, "It never occurred to me there was anything heroic or remarkable in my singing the role on such short notice and I went on that night quite as a matter of course."[33]

She unpretentiously admits, "The next morning the newspapers headlined me, marveled at my rising so expertly to emergency, ran my picture and made much of the fact that I was a former chorus girl who had reached the heights of opera. And in their department," she continued, "the critics said only the kindest things about my singing."[34]

Mary neglected to state that, as the singers took their bows, the usually reserved English audience called her back with thunderous applause for fifteen curtain calls! Such a demonstration had never occurred before and never happened again in His Majesty's Theater. The management was forced to turn out the house lights to quiet the delighted Londoners so the show could continue.[35]

The directors of the company immediately responded with contract revision awarding Mary thirteen appearances instead of her previously scheduled three. The London *Times* reported: "as Musetta probably Mary Lewis sang and acted precisely as Puccini intended."[36] Mary appeared as Mary in a new English opera, *Hugh the Drover*.[37] The tale of rural life in England a hundred years before was written by Ralph Vaughan Williams. Tudor Davies, noted Welsh tenor, was cast as Hugh.

The opera is set in a Cotswold town in about 1812 during the Napoleonic wars. The heroine Mary, daughter of the town's Constable, is to marry John the Butcher, whom she dislikes. The marriage was arranged by her father. But at the village fair on the eve of May Day, Mary falls in love with a stranger, a drover named Hugh. He overhears Mary's confession of distaste for John and her Aunt Jane's philosophical attempt to console her. Hugh's lyrical account of his life arouses Mary's love. Their impassioned duet is interrupted by the Showman's announcement of a prize fight. Hugh, seeing his chance, fights John for Mary's hand and wins; but John persuades the populace that Hugh is a Bonaparte spy and has him put in the stocks to await the arrival of the army. That night Mary steals the keys and sets Hugh free, but their escape is foiled by the return of the celebrating villagers. The Constable disowns Mary. The soldiers arrive and recognize Hugh as a friend and patriot and John is recruited instead. The opera ends with Hugh and Mary taking to the open road and a vagabond life.[38]

The rural scenes give composer Vaughan Williams an opportunity to introduce several folk-songs in addition to original melodies which might be mistaken for old folk-songs. Williams conceived the plot for the opera in the early 1900s and was ready to introduce it in 1914. A collector of folk-songs, Williams said, "...I see hardly any chance of an opera by an English composer ever being produced, at all events in our lifetime..." but did not let that discourage him from devising an opera with English words, English music, and an English subject. The outbreak of World War I ended any prospect of a production. In 1924, both the Royal College of Music and the British National Opera Company vied for the first performance. It was in rehearsal by the Royal College of Music when the newly formed B.N.O.C. hurriedly had five private dress rehearsals between July 4 and 11.[39]

The B.N.O.C. won the race when the under-rehearsed production premiered on July 14, 1924. Mary's appearance brought praise not only in music reviews, but the news columns as well. The reporters commented on Mary's noticeable southern American accent, pronouncing it quite "quaint." Mary decided it was time to learn to speak the King's English correctly, especially since the British National Opera Company presented all of their operas in English. She engaged a coach, but found erasing the drawl was a more difficult task than learning Italian and French, languages that required only learning, not unlearning.[40] Ironically, around this time, Will Rogers was springing from the *Follies* into becoming an international philosopher, capitalizing on his drawl as an asset.

Hugh the Drover was presented a number of times in London before the company toured the provinces and the season ended with a special performance at Number 10 Downing Street for the Prime Minister.[41]

Following the success of the *Hugh the Drover* performances, His Master's Voice (HMV) assembled most of the members of the original cast and recorded extended excerpts in September. Mary appeared in eight of the ten sides and was particularly effective in the love duet with Tudor Davies.[42]

A month later the recording company called Mary back. During the next year eleven different arias were recorded, of which only four were ever published. Part of the problem was that the new electrical recording process was replacing the old acoustic horn. All four of her published HMV sides were acoustically recorded and an additional three were assigned catalog numbers although never issued.[43]

Lost, at the time, were the two arias from *Faust*, "Il etait un roi de Thulé" and "Ah! Je ris de me voir" ("Jewel Song)" Although two of her *Manon* arias were published, "Je suis encore tout étourdie" ("I am still completely dazed") and "Allons! Il le faut!...Adieu, notre petite table" ("Farewell, Little Table"), an additional two were not. "Suis-je gentille...Obéissons quand leur voix appelle" ("List to the Voice of Youth") was one of the sides scheduled for publication, but "Je marche sur tous les chemins" ("I walk on all the roads") even after seven attempts did not pass. Also lost was one of the three arias from Jules Massenet's *Thaïs*. Both "Dis-moi que suis belle" ("Mirror Song") and "Te souvient-il du lumineux voyage" ("Does he remember you from the beautiful voyage"), the latter perhaps her signature aria, passed and were published, but "L'amour est une vertu rare" ("Love is a rare virtue") although recorded in the new electrical system, remained along with her six attempts at "Depuis le jour" ("Since the day") from *Louise* (Gustave Charpentier) both unpublished and lost.[44]

After the season was completed, Mary returned to the continent for a ten day vacation in Milan and Venice, Italy. She then filled her engagements at Monte Carlo to sing Micaela in *Carmen* along with three appearances in Nice, one in *Carmen* and two in *La Bohème*, and three song recitals at Casa Del Mare.[45]

She spent three weeks at Casa Del Mare where her friends there and at Monte Carlo were startled with her pet rattlesnake, which has been presented to her in June when she was singing with the National Opera Company in London. A big box had been delivered at the stage door of His Majesty's Theatre with sounds of something moving inside. There, half-concealed in a bed of grass and dried Texas bluebonnets, was a baby Texas rattlesnake. With the fangs removed, it had been the pet of Tex Morgan, one of the cowboys. The note was signed: "Luck and love to our singing Texas sister." The snake was christened "Tex" and traveled with Mary to the Riviera.[46]

Mary then returned to Paris where she again encountered Lehár, who informed her she was to play the lead in one of his operettas. With a mind of her own, Mary declared she had no intentions of complying. She left for a tour in the south of France, where she received a wire from the director of the Casino de Paris. Mary did not know the director and declined his offer to sing in a Lehár operetta, even though the enticement guaranteed "price no object." Mary wired back appreciation of his interest and offer, but she was much too busy at the present time to accept.[47]

Again in Monte Carlo a short time later, Mary was stopped in the lobby of her hotel by the director of the Nice and Marseille Opera Company who told her the director of the Casino de Paris had scheduled a revival of *The Merry Widow* with the opening date arranged when Lehár declared, unless Mary Lewis was engaged for the lead role, the operetta would not go on. The director threw himself on the mercy of Mary, who realized his predicament, but again told him of her ambition to sing opera. Mary said, "The director made a guarantee of a six-month's engagement with his company after completion of *The Merry Widow*." With this, Mary relented and signed a contract for 150,000 francs for ten weeks, one of the largest salaries paid for musical comedy in Paris. Mary admitted two factors in relenting—the money was tempting, and she was fatigued from her year of concentrated study and appearances in prestige performances.[48] She also said, "I have never learned the art of fasting."[49]

Lehár had made a fortune from his most successful operetta, *Die lustige Witwe* or *The Merry Widow*, but the fortune disappeared in investments with Vienna stockbrokers. His determination to secure Mary Lewis as the leading lady for the Paris revival was one of his better decisions. The setting of the original production in German was in the state of Pontevidrinia. The revival in which Mary Lewis starred was translated into French as *La Veuve Joyeuse*. Pontevidrinia became the state of Marsovy. Cast names were changed from the German version to the French: Hanna Glawari, the merry widow, to Missia Palmieri, a young American lady; Danilo Daniowitsch, the suitor, to Danilo; Baron Zeta, the state's ambassador, to Baron Popoff; Camille de Coutancon, the French officer, remained the same. The intrigue in the plot remained basically the same.[50]

As Missia Palmieri, "the merry widow" of the State of Marsovy, Mary fell into the intrigue of the light-hearted plot. Baron Popoff, the state's ambassador, tries to induce its wealthiest subject into keeping the funds at home. He worried that, because Missia was so rich and beautiful, she might be snapped up by a foreigner, so Popoff tries to play "matchmaker" dragging the Count Danilo into the act. Danilo was Missia's suitor before she married the rich old banker who left her a widow. Unwilling to be tagged as one of those after her fortune, Danilo has found other interests among the girls at Maxim's in Paris, where he serves as an attaché in the Embassy. Intrigue complicates the plot as Baron Popoff's wife is about to embark upon an affair with a French officer and her love letter to Camille de Coutancon, written on a fan, comes into Missia's possession. Thinking it is from Danilo, Missia (Mary) sings the famous "Vilia, O Vilia." Danilo's pride keeps him away, not wanting to be thought of as a fortune hunter. Missia gives out information that, under the banker's will, she will lose her inheritance if she remarries. Danilo proposed and is accepted. All ends happily as Missia discloses the money she loses is assigned to the second husband. Great fun is had by all as the principals whirl and swoop and sing Lehár's "Merry Widow Waltz."[51]

Mary Lewis sang *The Merry Widow* in French at the rebuilt Apollo Theatre. Critics reported the production to be very expensive. While Mary's lack of volume and variable French were cited, the influential André Message observed: "The long run which *The Merry Widow* will surely have, will give Miss Lewis time to correct these few small faults we are able to find with her."[52] The production also played in Deauville, Ostend, and other resorts.[53]

As a reward following completion of the contract, Mary said, "I awarded myself the most glorious vacation I had ever had in my life—a month in Venice, untroubled by money worries or work." There on the sands of the Lido, she met Morris Gest, producer, and accompanied him to Salzburg to see *The Miracle* and to meet director Max Reinhardt.[54] During this time Mary sang at a Red Cross Gala at the Hotel Excelsior on the Italian Lido. This was sponsored by the Principessa di San Faustino for the benefit of the Italian Red Cross.[55]

Mary was given an audition by Mr. and Mrs. Herbert Johnson representing the Chicago Opera Company. Even though Mary told them she was contemplating another year of study and experience in Europe before making a commitment, the Johnsons offered a negotiable agreement. Mary was given approval to appear in Chicago either in that season, 1925-26, or the next, as she wished. The offer was for a 12 week season at $500 a performance.[56]

Several months after this conversation with the Johnsons, Mary felt it was time to return to America, where she hoped to become established with the Metropolitan or the Chicago Opera Company. When Mary informed her manager of her intention, Kahn contacted the American companies. While his client was waiting for a reply, a cable from the Schuberts was delivered with the message: "Can you sail immediately, playing title role in *Princess Flavia*, music by Romberg, salary one thousand weekly, answer Schubert."[57] The brothers were engaged in forming an American theater dynasty.

Yielding to temptation, Mary was on board an ocean liner four days later. Arriving in New York October 2, 1925, Mary said, "Fortunately Jeritza, Ina Claire and Fanny Ward were on the same boat and I escaped the cameramen and reporters without effort." Arriving at her hotel, she phoned Jack [John T.] Adams of the Wolfsohn Musical Bureau and was told immediately: "It's too bad you didn't see your way clear to grab the opportunity of adding to all the publicity that followed your appearances in Vienna, Monte Carlo, Paris and London." He also dissuaded her of any ideas of taking part in any musical comedy, at least for a six-month period.[58]

Ziegfeld sent a letter to Otto Kahn, chairman of the Metropolitan Opera Company, October 3, 1925:

> As you will remember, you wrote me a letter on April 24, 1923, in which you stated that Mr. Gatti-Cazzaza and the directors of the Metropolitan Opera company had heard Mary Lewis at an audition in the Metropolitan Opera House and they were unanimously of the opinion that she possessed an unusually good voice and promising qualifications for an operatic career.
>
> You asked me at that time to release her from her contract with the Follies in order that she might devote herself exclusively to

studying for a year or so. This I did, after you had told me in Palm Beach that it was your intention, when she had completed her studies, to put her in the Metropolitan Opera House. Although at that time I explained to you how valuable Miss Lewis was to me, I did not want to stand in the way of anyone with prospects such as you outlined for her, and I allowed her to leave the Follies.

She went to Europe where she did study and she made her appearances in opera over there which, if the newspapers are to be believed, were a great success.

She came in to see me on Saturday and I had been told that the Shuberts were negotiating with her, which she confirmed, for her appearance at the Century Theater in a musical show. Now I feel that if you are not prepared to carry out your idea of placing her with the Metropolitan Opera House, surely, in view of my contract with her at the time from which I released her on the condition that she would be able to play there, that she should not be allowed to play with anyone but myself if she is to go back into musical shows.

I believe she has the intention of seeing you and I hope that her qualifications now are such that you feel she is capable of fulfilling all that you anticipated she would be able to do when I allowed her to leave the Follies.

With kindest regards, Sincerely yours, F. Ziegfeld.[59]

The Metropolitan Opera Company had just signed soprano Marion Talley and was contemplating waiting until the next year before signing Mary Lewis, until they heard the Chicago Opera Company was negotiating with her. Mary signed a contract with the Metropolitan Opera Company on November 5, 1925.

Adams arranged for an appearance for Mary to sing with the State Symphony October 26 in concert conducted by Ernst Von Dohnanyi. It was reported by critics after this appearance: "the soprano had shown a good flexible voice with an unusual wide range." She was accompanied by Ellmer Zoller, who remained her faithful musical companion throughout her career. Her program included a variety of selections including "Depuis le jour" from *Louise*, "Rain," "The Answer," "My Lovely Celia," and "The Holy Child."[60]

She also was engaged to sing with the Harlem Philharmonic and on the radio, WEAF, November 1. The one hour program was linked to twelve other stations.[61] A telegram, rush message, was received from her mother in care of Radio Station WEAF network at 9 p.m. saying: "Sorry can't cut through Chicago station too strong am well love mother." Wolfsohn Musical Bureau received a telegram sent November 23 at 1:23 a.m. from the Philharmonic Society of New Orleans, Louisiana: "Heard Mary Lewis radio is she available. The same day Wolfsohn Bureau replied: "Mary Lewis available March third fee one thousand dollars."[62]

In preparation for her second audition at the Met, Mary remembered her former blunders and used common sense taking care of herself on the days when she was to sing. She practiced, ate luncheon, took a nap, and at 5 p.m., casually walked into the dingy stage entrance on Thirty-ninth Street. Mary said, "Not being excited over the outcome or elated at opportunity or anxious to please, I sang perhaps better than usual." Her self-confidence was bolstered with her other financially rewarding prospects, if this venture should fail.[63]

"After my first song Gatti-Casazza came and patted my shoulder and said, 'Bravo!' and smiled at my dumbfounded stare," Mary said. While the conductors added their approval, Mary told herself she was dreaming as she listened to instructions to return soon to sign a contract with the Metropolitan Opera Company.[64]

The contract with the Met was signed by Mary Lewis on November 5, 1925, and by general manager, Giulio Gatti-Casazza. The agreement for the 1926-1927 season was for a minimum period of twelve weeks and up to a maximum period of twenty-eight weeks between the beginning of November and about the middle of May. The exact length and dates of the engagement were to be decided by the Company and indicated to the Artist in writing not later than May 31, 1926.[65]

The standard contract provided that Mary's salary was to be $150 per week during the period of her engagement. The Metropolitan Opera would furnish her with train transportation while she was under contract, but disclaimed responsibility for any loss of luggage. Mary was to receive $15 as day for hotel expenses during her travel, but this rate did not apply to tours undertaken by the entire company outside of New York.[66]

The agreement called for the Artist to sing and perform whenever required by the Company not more than three times per week, not more than twice in succession, and never twice on the same day. In event that at one performance two or more operas were to be given, all the operas constitute one performance. The costumes for roles or parts were to be furnished by the Company except for gloves, feathers, stage jewelry, wigs, tights, boots, shoes, and other similar articles to be furnished by the Artist.[67]

> Mary agreed to sing and perform in the following roles or parts:
>
> In Italian: Mimi and Musetta in Puccini's *La Bohème*, Gilda in Verdi's *Rigoletto*, Manon in Puccini's *Manon Lescaut*, Nedda in Ruggiero Leoncavallo's *I Pagliacci*, Lauretta in Puccini's *Gianni Schicchi*, Susanna and Princess [sic - Countessa] in Wolfgang Amadeus Mozart's *Le Nozze di Figaro*, and Tosca in Puccini's *La Tosca*.
>
> In French: Princess in Rimski-Korsakow's *Le Coq d'Or*, Thaïs in Massenet's *Thaïs*, Juliette in Gounod's *Roméo et Juliette*, Manon in Massenet's *Manon*, Louise in Charpentier's *Louise*, Giulietta, Antonia, and Olimpia [sic] in *The Tales of Hoffman*, Marguerite in *Faust*, Rozenn in Edmond Clémont's *Le Roi d'Ys*, and Micaela in Bizet's *Carmen*.[68]

Mary Lewis received a letter from Ziegfeld with congratulations and he expressed his delight Kahn kept his word. He also said, "I think if you have any more interviews you should state the fact that I canceled a two years contract so as to enable you to go to Europe after you sang for Gatti-Cazzaza at the request of Mr. Kahn and that he had given you great encouragement." He also added, "You certainly have a good press agent. Who is he? I want to engage him. The papers in Baltimore, Washington and Philadelphia all have front page stories just the same as had New York. Now would be the time to get a good musical show and clean up." He also invited Mary to please stop in to see him if she would be downtown the coming week.[69]

She sang again over WEAF November 22 as guest soloist with the State Symphony Orchestra in an Atwater Kent Radio Hour broadcast from the Astor Gallery in the Waldorf-Astoria. With Ernst von Dohnanyi conducting, Mary Lewis sang two songs at 9:15 p.m. for her second contact with the microphone.[70] One of the earliest radio programs broadcasting good music was the Atwater Kent Hour. The Sunday evening program of the world's finest music featured stars of opera and concert hall.

As her final appearance January 7, 1926, before the New York opera debut, she sang six arias for the State Charities Aid Association at the Fifth Avenue mansion of Mr. and Mrs. Vincent Astor at No. 840 on the Avenue. The *Musical Courier* reported Mary Lewis wore a dress of pale green and "her lovely, easy floating tone completed the aesthetic enjoyment of the afternoon." *New York Variety* reported she "looked charming in a simple graceful afternoon frock of blue." Proceeds of $4,000 were donated to the mental hygiene committee of the Association. Ellmer Zoller was Mary's accompanist. Reports of the event were also carried in New York's *Tribune*, *Town Topics*, *Times*, *Evening Post*, and Chicago's *Musical Leader*.[71]

Endnotes Chapter 9 A New Career

1. Lewis, "From the Slums," *LHJ*, July 1927, p. 80.
2. Encyclopedia Americana, 1968 ed., s.v. "Otto Hermann Kahn."
3. Lewis, "From the Slums," *LHJ*, July 1927, p. 80.
4. Ibid.
5. Ibid.
6. Ibid.
7. Ibid.
8. Little Rock *Arkansas Gazette*, 14 Sept. 1924.
9. Lewis, "From the Slums," *LHJ*, July 1927, p. 80. *Arkansas Democrat*, 22 July 1923, Lewis file, Little Rock Public Library.
10. Ibid.
11. Maria Kousnetzoff, (born 1880 in Russia, died 1966 in Paris), a ballet dancer followed by her debut as an opera singer (1905) in St. Petersburg. She made successful guest appearances in France and England. In the United States she sang with the Manhattan Opera (1909) and the Chicago Opera (1916-17). She was also active as a dancer. She returned to Russia during World War I and later came to Paris in 1920, where she first appeared as a film actress. In 1927 she founded the Opéra Russe in Paris. *A Concise Biographical Dictionary of Singers - From the Beginning of Recorded Sound to the Present*, K.J. Kutsch and Leo Riemens translated from German by Harry Earl Jones. Chilton Book Company, Philadelphia, New York, London, 1969, p. 227.
12. Ibid., Dougan, "Enigma," p. 266.
13. Little Rock *Arkansas Democrat*, 22 July 1923.

14. Ibid. Also, Lewis, "From the Slums," *LHJ*, July 1927, p. 80.
15. *Arkansas Democrat*, 22 July 1923.
16. Lewis, "From the Slums," *LHJ*, July 1927, p. 83.
17. Ibid.
18. Ibid.
19. Ibid.
20. Ibid.
21. *The World Book Encyclopedia*, 1961 ed., s.v. "Opera," by Konrad Neuger.
22. Lewis, "From the Slums," *LHJ*, July 1927, p. 83.
23. Orr, *Judsonia*, p. 292.
24. *New York Times*, 14 June 1924.
25. Dougan, "The comparison to Maria Jeritza is particularly suspect. Jeritza was a dramatic soprano, which Mary was not; her roles and Mary's never overlapped. The comparison with Mary Garden was far more accurate, for had tragedy not intervened, Mary Lewis could have become a singing actress taking up Garden's roles." Notes to author, Sept. 1998.
26. Lewis, "From the Slums," *LHJ*, July 1927, p. 83.
27. Ibid.
28. Ibid.
29. *The World Book Encyclopedia*, 1961 ed., s.v. "Opera," by Neuger.
30. Mary Lewis's scrapbooks #1, courtesy of Holdridge. Menton, France, Monte Carlo News, *The Continental Weekly*, 12 April 1924. Research did not uncover background information concerning Osbourne O'Hagan or Agnése Greenwood.
31. Lewis, "From the Slums," *LHJ*, July 1927, p. 83.
32. Ibid.
33. Ibid.
34. Ibid.
35. Clipping, n.p., n.d., Lewis file, Little Rock Public Library.
36. Mary Lewis's scrapbooks #1, courtesy of Holdridge. "The Homecoming of Mary Lewis," n.d., n.p.
37. Lewis, "From the Slums," *LHJ*, July 1927, p. 83. A drover is one who drives a collection of livestock to market.
38. Michael Kennedy, cover 1975 reproduction of original recording, Pearl label, Pavilion Records Limited, 48 High Street, Pembury, Kent, England.
39. Ibid.
40. Lewis, "From the Slums," *LHJ*, July 1927, p. 83.
41. Frank Howes, *The Music of Ralph Vaughan Williams* (London, 1964), p. 497, cited by Dougan, "Enigma," p. 268. W.R. Moran, "The Recordings of Mary Lewis," *The Record Collector* 23, Ipswich, England, Dec. 1976, p. 184.
42. Dougan, notes to author, Sept. 1998.
43. Ibid.
44. Ibid.
45. Lewis, "From the Slums," *LHJ*, July 1927, p. 83.
46. Mary Lewis's scrapbooks #1, courtesy Holdridge, n.d., n.p.

47. Lewis, "From the Slums," *LHJ*, July 1927, p. 83.

48. Ibid.

49. Mary Lewis's scrapbooks #1, courtesy Holdridge, Paris, 13 April 1925.

50. John Drinkow, *The Operetta Book* (New York: Drake Publishers, 1973), p. 45-46. Program booklet, *La Veuve Joyeuse, saison* 1924-25. Mary Lewis's scrapbooks #1, courtesy Holdridge.

51. Program booklet, *La Veuve Joyeuse*, Mary Lewis's scrapbooks #1, courtesy Holdridge.

52. *New York Times*, 5 Nov. 1925, p.1.

53. Mary Lewis's scrapbooks #1, courtesy Holdridge, n.d., n.p..

54. Lewis, "From the Slums," *LHJ*, July 1927, p. 83.

55. Mary Lewis's scrapbooks #1, courtesy Holdridge. Paris (France) *Times*, 25 Aug. 1925.

56. Lewis, "From the Slums," *LHJ*, July 1927, p. 83.

57. Ibid.

58. Ibid.

59. Mary Lewis's scrapbooks #2, courtesy Holdridge.

60. *New York Times*, 1 Nov. 1925, sec. IX, p. 19; 8 Jan. 1926, p. 15.

61. *New York Times*, 1 Nov. 1925, sec. IX, p. 19.

62. Ibid. Mary Lewis's scrapbooks #1, courtesy Holdridge.

63. Lewis, "From the Slums," *LHJ*, July 1927, p. 83.

64. Ibid. Mary concluded her own story written in a series of three for the 1927 *Ladies' Home Journal*. Her narrative style and descriptive vocabulary give credit to Anna's rigid expectations from her pupil.

65. Contract agreement Metropolitan Opera Company, New York, and Mary Lewis, 5 Nov.,1925.

66. Ibid.

67. Ibid.

68. Ibid.

69. Mary Lewis's scrapbooks #2, courtesy Holdridge.

70. *New York Times*, 23 Nov. 1925, p. 3.

71. Mary Lewis's scrapbooks #2, courtesy Holdridge.

Tudor Davies and Mary Lewis starred in the original production of *Hugh the Drover* by Vaughan Williams. It was staged by the British National Opera Company in 1924. Pearl Pavilion Records LTD, 1975. Photograph courtesy of Pavilion Records, repertoire available on GEMM CD 9468.

10

At The Met

Hundreds stood in line for hours to purchase tickets on January 28, 1926. The occasion was Mary's debut at the Metropolitan Opera Company cast as Mimi in *La Bohème*.[1]

The following day, critic Samuel Chotzinoff reported for the New York newspaper, *The World*: "At the end of the third act a crowded house wouldn't stop applauding until the veteran Antonio Scotti (who had witnessed many memorable debuts...)[2] and other principals [Edward Johnson, Canadian tenor; Léon Rothier, German bass; and Elizabeth Kandt] who were taking curtain calls with Miss Lewis sneaked into the wings, leaving the erstwhile chorus girl, cabaret singer and Ziegfeld star alone on the stage." He continued: "Then there was more applause, and people near enough to the stage threw violets at Miss Lewis—there must have been at least two dozen bunches that she gathered into her little black apron—and Mr. Scotti and the principals laughingly sneaked back on the stage and all joined hands and bowed. A new debut was successfully accomplished."[3]

An unidentified clipping reads:

> The Broadway that heard and saw Mary Lewis seven years ago when she came to New York as a chorus girl in the *Follies* fresh from her triumphs as a California bathing beauty, heard her again yesterday afternoon when she made her debut at the Metropolitan Opera House....For Miss Lewis her debut was the end of seven years of unremitting toil and the beginning of years of even greater effort, but for the crowd that packed the Metropolitan it was at the climax of a romantic career seldom paralleled in American musical history.[4]

The company was making an effort to recognize American performers rather than depending upon the established European artists, although the productions were sung in the original languages, requiring mastery of multi-lingual skills as well as musical ability. The unidentified critic continued:

> Miss Lewis, admitted even by the music critics to be in fine voice, received an ovation unequaled in the Metropolitan since the days of Geraldine Farrar and her battalions of worshiping 'Gerry Flappers.' And the applause...was spontaneous and tremendous and the shouts of approval and encouragement were followed by an avalanche of flowers that well-nigh buried the stage in a bewildering profusion of fragrance and beauty. Five times after the fall of the first-act curtain Miss Lewis was called before the footlights to receive the homage of the huge audience. The demonstration was against the rules of the Metropolitan, but no one made a protest and the house officials made no move to stop the shower of violets and other blossoms.[5]

Mary had a charisma, the vibrancy reached out to enchant the crowd. The applause rang out from patrons filling the five balconies and the tiers of boxes, besides those seated on the main floor. "It was apparent very early that this was an occasion, for the audience was not the usual Metropolitan assemblage; rather it was composed of persons who not only love music for music's sake, but who had been stirred by the story of the rise of this determined Arkansas girl who would not be held down by the chorus....Very likely Miss Lewis would have been cheered regardless of the quality of her voice, because of the romance of her career, but her hearers became even more fervent and tempestuous when they found that not only did she have stage experience and an ability to act that is not precisely common in grand opera, but that she also had a voice of unusual quality. Her appearance did not mark the discovery of a great voice, but it did mark the appearance in opera of a new American soprano with great gifts, who probably will be a prima donna of the first magnitude."[6]

Both reviews contained references to Mary's Cinderella story, and her escape via the traveling troupe and subsequent adventures. Chotzinoff of the *World* pointed out the shortcomings in Mary's efforts as well as others of the cast, as critics are paid to do. He noted: "She sang with better artistry [than her appearance with the State Symphony] but whether it was due to nervousness or an unfamiliarity with the size and acoustics of the opera house Miss Lewis sang everything either soft or loud." He also contended, she had a tendency to sing sharp instead of most singers' propensity to sing flat. He did admit: "Miss Lewis' singing of Mimi had many notable features. The quality of the voice is lovely. The tones are firm and rounded, with no trace of a tremolo. The lower register is a little weak and the middle not very much stronger, but the upper register is brilliant, and, when Miss Lewis chooses to make it so, it is sensuous. What is more important still, Miss Lewis seems to possess a deal of musical intelligence and good taste, and it was pleasant to watch her avoid obvious effects and opportunities for meretricious display. The one serious fault in her singing is a tendency to sacrifice vocal beauty for dramatic effect [a result of her theatrical training!]. Many of Puccini's loveliest moments Miss Lewis whispered brokenly in a laudable effort to convey the depth of her feeling and the progress of her operatic illness. On the histrionic side her impersonation was modest, tender and touchingly sincere, and in spite of her cheerful plumpness and guileless countenance the audience was visibly touched."[7] Mary, the little waif who almost starved to death in the gutters of the south, was battling against the opposite effects of starvation. Chotzinoff was less kind with the other principals in the cast.

Several other critics were less impressed. Olin Downes of *The New York Times* found her voice light and unequal in its registers. Downes found "the upper tones the freest and most effective."[8] W.J. Henderson, venerable critic of the *Sun* was not impressed—saying, that her "creditable" performance gave little indication of a major talent, while Elizabeth Kandt as a new Musetta sang "in such a way as to make Miss Lewis seem better than she was."[9]

A photograph of Lewis taken in her dressing room with conductor Gennaro Papi shows the pair buried under an avalanche of floral tributes in honor of Mary's debut. She was described as being one of the youngest stars to sing at the Met,[10] although she probably would have lost the distinction had her true age been posted. She was one of the first singers to come from the musical-comedy stage.[11]

"Yesterday afternoon she reached the end of the long trail and arrived at her goal," concluded one of the reviewers.[12] Although many of her friends were unable to attend, Mary Lewis received cards, letters, and telegrams of congratulations from Europe as well as the United States.[14]

The Victor Talking Machine Company, soon to become RCA Victor, as radio was growing in popularity, had never issued Mary's English recordings. Instead, starting in December 1925, and continuing until 1928, Mary worked intermittently in Victor's studios. Sixteen different arias and songs were recorded, from which eight were published. The new electrical system made Mary's voice sound somewhat harder than the old acoustic process, but all the published records were artistic and to some extent financial successes.[15]

The longest entry in the catalogues was her signature aria, "Te souvient-il du lumineux voyage" from Massenet's *Thaïs.* Best known in instrumental versions as the "Meditation from *Thaïs*," it is really a duet, but no baritone appears in either of Mary's recorded versions. The two-sided disc also contains Nedda's aria from *I Pagliacci*, "Qual fiamma avea nel guardo!...Che volo d'augeli." Victor took eleven takes of the Jewel Song, "Ah! Je ris de voir," from *Faust,* but never issued it.[16]

The remainder were songs. Three test recordings, two accompanied by Elmer Zoller, never prompted further exploration, and "Love's Old Sweet Song" (G. Clifton Bingham-J. L. Molloy) went to six tries without a success. Equally unsuccessful was "Blue Danube Waltz" (properly "On the Beautiful Blue Danube") by Johann Strauss. Nine takes failed to produce a satisfactory recording.[17]

On the other hand, the delightful "La Danza" ("The Dance") (Pepoli-Rossini) passed on the first take, as did "Les Filles de Cadix" (A. De Musset-L. Delibes). "Dixie" (Dan E. Emmett) took only two and "The Old Folks at Home" (Stephen C. Foster) required but three. Most surprising was that "Little Grey Home in the West" (D. Eardley Wilmot-Hermann Löhr), the song Mary had used unceasingly in early Broadway days, needed ten takes.[18]

Meanwhile Mary's operatic career continued in New York. On February 19, 1926, she appeared as Nedda in *I Pagliacci* with Vittorio Fullin, Scotti, Giordano Paltrinieri, and Lawrence Tibbett. Conductor was Papi.[19] She had earned the title of "Mary Lewis of the Metropolitan Opera." When her success was attributed to "luck," Mary Lewis retorted: "Lucky means lots of hard work and being ready when the opportunity comes to jump in and grab it."[19]

Endnotes Chapter 10 At The Met

1. Mary Lewis file, New York Public Library, n.p., 1926.
2. Antonio Scotti was an Italian baritone, a member of the Metropolitan Opera Company from 1899 to 1933.
3. Samuel Chotzinoff, *The World*, New York City, 29 Jan. 1926, p. 13.
4. Lewis file, New York Public Library, n.p., 1926.
5. Ibid.
6. Ibid.
7. Chotzinoff, *World*, New York, 29 Jan. 1926, p. 13.
8. *New York Times*, 29 Jan. 1926, p. 18.
9. Irving Kolodin, *The Story of the Metropolitan Opera 1883-1966*. (New York, Alfred A. Knopf, 1967), p. 328.
10. New York *Telegraph*, 10 Sept. 1926, Lewis File, New York Public Library. Also, Wentworth, "Ugly Duckling," *Screenland*, July 1930.
11. Kolodin, *Story of the Metropolitan Opera 1883-1966*, p. 327.
12. Lewis file, New York Public Library, n.p., 1926.
13. Mary Lewis's scrapbooks #1, courtesy of Holdridge.
14. Dougan, notes to author, Sept. 1998.
15. Ibid.
16. Ibid.
17. Ibid.
18. William H. Seltsam. *Metropolitan Opera Annals*. (New York: The H. W. Wilson Company in Association with The Metropolitan Opera Guild, Inc.), 1947. p. 444.
19. Dayton *Herald*, 18 Oct. 1926. Mary Lewis's scrapbooks #2, courtesy of Holdridge.

Mary Lewis played the role of Musetta in Puccini's opera *La Bohème*. *Opera and the Ballet*, July 1924, London, England. Mary Lewis's scrapbooks #1, courtesy of Holdridge.

Hundreds stood in line for hours to purchase tickets to see Mary Lewis, former *Follies* star, cast as Mimi at the performance of *La Bohème*. Photo by Mishkin, n.d., n.p. Mary Lewis's scrapbooks #2, courtesy of Holdridge.

Mary Lewis sang the role of Nedda in *I Pagliacci*. One of the songs Mary Lewis recorded was "Che volo d'augeli" ("Ye Birds without Number") for Victor. Strauss-Peyton. *LHJ* June 1927, page 26.

11

Welcome Home

The Little Rock *Arkansas Democrat* headlined: "Mary Lewis Given Greatest Welcome State Ever Knew," on March 26, 1926. The only other gathering of such a multitude several years previous was to hear opera singer Amelita Galli-Curci. But Mary was accorded the "greatest demonstration of welcome ever accorded any individual of that state."[1]

Arriving at Little Rock from Hot Springs, Mary was welcomed by Governor Thomas Terral at the State Capitol, where a golden "Key of the City" was presented by Mayor Charles E. Meyer. The head of the Little Rock Chamber of Commerce extended his greeting. This was followed by a procession which filed through the governor's reception hall for an hour.[2]

Mrs. Alice Henniger, former teacher and friend, had accompanied Mary from Hot Springs, where Mary had given an operatic concert at the Auditorium. Following the official welcoming, Mary was the guest of honor at a luncheon given by school friends from the Henniger School of Music. That evening in her hotel room, Mary read hundreds of messages containing good wishes from those who were unable to be present.[3]

The next morning, Mary and manager, Jack Adams, slipped away for a brief visit with James K. Lewis, her former father-in-law. The elder Lewis had followed her career with interest and saw her perform with the Rockettes in New York's Radio City Music Hall. Although young Keene Lewis had remarried in 1923, he also had seen her perform. Keene was perfecting his talents as an amateur painter. He was owner of Hollis Mill Company of Little Rock.[4] Keene Lewis can be recognized, disguised as the young beau, in Mary's three-part story written in 1927 for the *Ladies' Home Journal*.[5] Not mentioning the marriage, Mary asserted that she next saw the young man opening night of the *Greenwich Village Follies*. "He had become a painter," she noted.[6]

During her stay in Little Rock, Mary, Governor and Mrs. Terral, and Mrs. Henniger toured points of interest in the city. A special visit was made to see her foster mother, Anna Fitch, in the Hillcrest addition where Mary darted around to see the familiar and the unfamiliar. She admired the new backyard fence and checked the sturdy growth of what the reporter called, "a rare plant," her holly bush.[7]

A photographer was on hand for a picture-taking session. Anna was pleased enough, in her tight-lipped, unsmiling way, to send a copy to be published in her Ohio Wesleyan Alumni news. Approaching the eighty-year mark, Anna did not attend the evening concert.[8]

By 8 o'clock that evening, motor cars filled the streets around the old high school auditorium filled with an overflow crowd seated even upon the stage. The guests were welcomed by Mrs. Henniger, who was president of the Little Rock Musical Coterie, sponsors of the civic concert series.[9] How proud she was to introduce a former pupil who had achieved international fame and opera status!

In acknowledgment of the wave of applause, Mary bowed, said a breathless word or two, and then SANG. The account declared that if there were any skeptics of her musical powers, they soon ceased to exist. "The entire range of the vocal scale she took with equal facility and ease. Liquid pure as a flute were her tones as they poured forth in all their legato loveliness in a program of numbers heavier than any previous artist has given here.... Whether in French, German, English or Italian, the tonal purity and enunciation was marvelous, unexcelled."[10]

Then the floral tributes began to appear, large and small, and in every shape the florist could devise. The parade of young and old, male and female admirers seemed never to end until Mary was overwhelmed. In gratitude she tried, but failed, to sing, "Home, Sweet Home," and while wiping the tears away, she finished by playing the tune softly. It mattered not, as no other eye in the crowded house was dry either.[11]

Judge George B. Rose was called upon for help to ease the tension, and the emotion of the moment was smoothed by his patter until Mary could proceed with the concert program. "And in a few moments everybody forgot all about everything except the liquid golden notes of her voice; feasting their eager eyes on every line of her gracious loveliness,—so stately, remote, and other-worldly; and yet as intimately dear as anybody's little daughter, just home for the Easter vacation and unexpectedly lovelier than even the fondest imagination had dreamed. So that was Mary Lewis' concert!"[12]

At a reception at the Lafayette Hotel, along with the Governor and Mrs. Terral and Mrs. Henniger, Mary greeted the throngs that streamed past. It was after midnight when dinner was finally served. At the head table with Mary and the dignitaries was her mother, Mrs. Maynard, who came down for the concert from her son's home in Chicago.[13]

Among the music and laughter, Mary responded to one dance invitation. It was an exhilarating evening. It was so exciting that Mary almost missed her train! The baskets, wreaths, and bouquets of floral tribute were to be distributed to the hospitals and churches in the city. Mary took only one tiny bunch with her— "some old fashioned posies from a little hill garden out on the Heights—a bit of home"[14]—from Anna's flower garden. At 2:30 a.m. Mary hugged her last hug, said the last good-bye, and waved as the train pulled away from the station at Little Rock. How different, she remembered, from when she left in 1918 and there was no one at all to say farewell![15]

Governor Terral immediately sent a letter to Otto H. Kahn, chairman of the Metropolitan Opera Company, telling of the overwhelming reception Mary Lewis's home state had given and claimed her as their own. He continued with "She fought her own way without assistance from any one. She deserves all the credit and we are indeed proud of her and of her accomplishments.... We have had the pleasure of seeing and listening to many great artists, but none in voice will surpass the voice of Mary Lewis.... Her voice sounded as though it gently drifted from the misty, milky heavenly pathway onto earth's rugged surface. God has been good to her in that she has been blessed with a voice that seemed was handed to her by an angel of God. No greater gift could come to any one." He concluded with a request that she come back to Arkansas soon.[16]

Kahn responded that he was pleased the Governor and fellow citizens had found it in their hearts to give so enthusiastic a reception and recognition to Mary Lewis. "She is thoroughly worthy of it. She has fully earned it. She is endowed, not only with a lovely voice which she uses with admirable taste and skill, but also with a very good brain, a manner and disposition which gain friends for her everywhere, and a sterling character.... I know how much of courage, of hard work, of self-denial and of determined striving has gone into the making of the success of that fine 'Arkansas product.'" He continued: "It is a heartening thing to all who have faith in young American talent, who want it to have its due share of opportunity, encouragement and recognition, and who are seeking, as best they can, to serve the cause of art in America."[17]

A rumor was printed in the middle of March 1926, concerning Mary's engagement to Count Bondy von Bethlen, son of the Premier of Hungary. She received a cablegram from Paris dated March 16, 1926, reading: "Congratulations for engagement with Bethlen's son send truth anyhow for papers." The cablegram was signed, "Jean."[18] Mary was reported to be under written pledge by her managing agency not to marry for five years. The contract was said to have dated from 1923. A year later, Mary said the report of the marriage clause, as well as the report of her engagement to the Count, were "sheer nonsense."[19]

Mary appeared in several commercials for Lucky Strike cigarettes and for Chickering pianos, saying: "My first music lessons at the age of eight were taken on the Chickering and it is an inspiration that I am again to be associated with it in my career."[20]

For the rest of the 1926 Metropolitan Opera season, Mary sang five times in three roles: as Giulietta, the courtesan in *The Tales of Hoffman (Les Contes d'Hoffmann)*; Mimi in *La Bohème*; and Nedda in Leoncavallo's *I Pagliacci* both in house and on tour in Atlanta in April.[21]

Marion Talley, who had generated even more excitement than Mary, appeared nine times in four roles. Talley's debut was three weeks after that of Mary Lewis. In support of the coloratura soprano from Kansas City, Missouri, a large delegation from her home state was present. W.J. Henderson's review was not particularly favorable.[22]

When the two sopranos sang together in *The Tales of Hoffman*, with Talley as Olympia the mechanical doll and Mary as Giulietta, comparisons were in order. Talley's stage presence was compared unfavorably to that of Mary Lewis, while Mary's "vocal difficulties were largely forgotten."[23]

The plum role, Antonia, went to Lucrezia Bori. Other colleagues during Mary's first year at the Met were Giuseppe DeLuca and Giuseppe Danise, Italian baritones; Adamo Didur, bass from Galatia (central Turkey); Rothier; Giacomo Lauri-Volpi, Italian tenor; Scotti; Fullin; and Lawrence Tibbett, an American baritone.[24]

When not scheduled for performances at the Met, Mary was booked for tours and concerts. She sang at a morning musicale at the Hotel Biltmore. At Carnegie Hall in recital she included Handel and Mozart arias, French songs by Claude Debussy, Maurice Ravel and Gabriel Fauré, and ended with "The Holy Child." The concert was sponsored by the National Association of Women Painters and Sculptors.[25] In May of 1926 she sang Marguerite in *Faust* in Massachusetts at the Springfield Bay Music Festival. Rothier sang Méphistophélès. The recital by Mary Lewis, and by Marion Talley on the following night, would be their first appearances at the Springfield Bay Music Festival. Record ticket sales were posted.[26]

Summer found Mary again in Europe, where she helped celebrate Independence Week in Paris and performed the role of Mimi at the Opéra Comique on July 1.[27] Mostly she devoted herself almost exclusively to study and hard work. On her debut in *La Bohème* in Paris she received flowers with gift cards enclosed from Osbourne O'Hagan and "sis" as well as from others including Morris Gest and Henri Defreyn, her co-star in *The Merry Widow*.[28] From Salzburg came word "that Max Reinhardt, no less, became interested in her career during the Summer and that he, aided and abetted by the inevitable Morris Gest, has offered her the leading role in a new opera which he is to stage in America this Winter for Mr. Gest."[29]

A cable report from Paris dispatched word that Mary Lewis sailed on the *Aquitania* and would arrive in New York the following Friday. The *Aquitania* of the Cunard Line was considered one of the most beautifully decorated liners ever to go to sea. She was over four city blocks long. For the enjoyment of the passengers the ship included: the Caroline smoking room, Palladian lounge, Louis XVI restaurant, the Adam drawing room, the Jacobean grill room, and an indoor pool decorated with replicas of Egyptian ornaments in the British Museum.[30]

This time Mary took her manager's advice and found herself making headlines accompanied by several photos concerning her return. The welcome back in New York gave time only for an appearance at the Radio Industries banquet at the Hotel Astor on September 15.[31]

The New York *Telegraph* on September 11, 1926, reported: "She is back as she left—dimple in the right cheek as saucy as ever, hair the same natural Scandinavian luster, eyes the same captivating blue and freckles showing here and there. She grew almost indignant when one brazen reporter dared suggest that she was taking on weight. She lives in constant fear of expansion, but so far she has been able to preserve that alluring figure which none but her enemies, if she has any, can call other than buxom. To prove to her own satisfaction that her lines remain in status quo, she purchased while abroad a dress made of material colored with wide horizontal lines. Now the fashion experts insist that such a dress cannot be worn by a heavy woman. The pattern of the cloth emphasizes every bulge, hill and dale. If that be true, then Mary Lewis' lines, even exaggerated by the dress goods, is just about right."[32]

According to another description: "In her hair is the light of the sun's glow, wavy, abundant and becomingly dressed. Her eyes twinkle more beautifully than any stars above, and to the rosebud mouth are added teeth which look as though she held a string of pearls between ruby lips."[33]

Paul Norwood wrote: "The pretty miss came back before she wanted to only that the voice which charmed the New Amsterdam audiences and now thrills those at the Met could be heard over 35 radio stations September 15. On that day the Radio Industries will hold a banquet at the Astor and Mary's will be the only musical one thrown into the microphone. If the audiences listen in she will be heard by more people than have ever caught a single voice over the air."[34] It was estimated that 15 million people would hear her sing. Mary Lewis's appearance was through the courtesy of A. Atwater Kent, who manufactured one of the most popular and best-selling radio sets. This was the first of a series of musical concerts to be broadcast to promote the sale of the radios.[35] Many, unfamiliar with the mysteries of radio, actually believed they had to buy an Atwater Kent set to tune into these hours; naturally the sponsor did nothing to discourage them.

Mary then embarked on an extensive tour sponsored by Wolfsohn Musical Bureau, taking her from Hartford, Connecticut, to New Orleans, and to the Pacific Coast, where in San Francisco Mary was back at the scene of the beginning of her career.[36] There were 4,000 in attendance at her recital at the Exposition in San Francisco. She represented Atwater Kent in presenting radio set number 1,000,000 to San Francisco Mayor James Rolph, Jr. He, in turn, presented Mary Lewis with a Key to the City.[37]

Along with all this traveling and publicity events, Mary did not neglect the serious side of her art. She performed a Carnegie Hall recital December 13, 1926. One critic noted that her high notes were neither freely produced nor always on pitch and found her French and English songs the best. In the English, it was reported: "Every word could be heard, and the voice gave the effect of being used in its natural setting."[38] Mary Lewis remembered Anna's earlier training in elocution.

Christmas 1926, brought a simple Christmas greeting to Anna from New York.[39] Mary returned to the Metropolitan in February, 1927, where she sang only five times that season. She appeared as Nedda in *I Pagliacci* opposite Johnson and DeLuca. In *Tales* Mary was Giulietta; Talley again was Olympia; Bori, Antonia; Mario Chamlee the poet; while Didur, DeLuca and Rothier divided the villians. The main attraction was the great Feodor Chaliapin in *Faust* and Mary was Marguerite.[40] The Russian Chaliapin was an eccentric non-conformist. March 15, 1927 Mary sang one performance as Giulietta in *Les Contes d'Hoffmann* in Brooklyn, and on May 10, the same role in Rochester, New York.[41]

On tour, Mary made her first appearance in Chicago as a recitalist.[42] One unidentified review noted: "It is difficult to tell from the reviews whether she delighted the music critics, to whom she was new, more in the ear or in the eye." They wrote commentaries alternating phrases having to do with the picture and the sounds she made. "And altogether she made a happy success."[43]

On April 3, 1927, Mary Lewis came to the rescue of Atwater Kent's radio program. The scheduled artist, Beniamino Gigli, was ill and could not perform. Mary and Allen McQuhae sang.

Mary ended the 1926-27 season in April embroiled in a suit with Warner Brothers' Vitaphone pictures.[44] She had been one of the first prima donnas to be signed by Vitaphone for one of the first talkies. History would have been made had the project been completed. Earlier sound tracks were recorded on special phono discs that played the length of the reel, not always in synchronization. In about 1925 a practical method of producing movies with sound was developed. Vitaphone was called the "marvel of the century." This revolutionized the motion picture industry and ended the silent film era.[45]

An abridged version of *Tales*, starring Mary Lewis, was being filmed in the old Manhattan Opera House. The heat failed and Mary sat around all day, thinly clad, warming herself, reportedly, with a teacup of Scotch. According to Vitaphone, she was drunk and the performance was unusable. Mary indignantly denied the allegations. She admitted to having a small amount of brandy for medicinal purposes, and presented depositions by her agent and other artists stating that she was not drunk. Mary complained of having pernicious anemia all her life.[46] Although Mary had been raised in a strict anti-alcohol environment, she had long ago started to drink. However, this Vitaphone episode was the first indication that drinking had begun to interfere with her life. In time, it would become one of her personal demons.

Al Jolson, with his soulful rendition of "Mammy," received the notoriety for starring in the first part-talkie feature, *The Jazz Singer*, which was filmed in the Manhattan Opera House and presented to the public October 6, 1927. Suddenly a whole new medium for opera singers was opening up.

Vitaphone filmed and marketed during the year of 1928, "The Story of Mary Lewis," which was shown in theaters equipped to play the new film product. The story of her rise to the Met was described as one of the most dramatic in the history of the stage. One clipping reported: "Miss Lewis will display her charming personality and rare voice in a Vitaphone presentation." These features included stars of the musical and theatrical world: Mary Lewis, Ted Lewis and his famous New York night club orchestra, comedian George Jessel, Al Jolson, Van and Schenck, John Barrymore, and Fred Waring and his Pennsylvanians orchestra.[47] Among those listed to be the first to bring the sound pictures to the public included opera stars: Mary Lewis, Marion Talley, Beniamino Gigli, Guieseppe DeLuca, John Charles Thomas, Reinald Werrenrath, and Giovanni Martinelli.[48] Mary Lewis was mentioned in listings of both classical and secular artists.

The surprise ending of the season came when Mary and Michael Bohnen, bass-baritone of the Met, decided to get married.[49]

Endnotes Chapter 11 Welcome Home

1. Kay Tallquist, *Arkansas Democrat*, 28 March 1926.
2. Ibid.
3. Ibid.
4. Obituary, Keene Lewis, n.d., n.p. Courtesy Mary Woodward Lewis.
5. Letters to author from Mary Woodward Lewis.
6. Lewis, "From the Slums," *LHJ*, May 1927, p. 50.
7. Tallquist, *Arkansas Democrat*, 28 March 1926.
8. Fitch scrapbooks.
9. Tallquist, *Arkansas Democrat*, 28 March 1926.
10. Ibid.
11. Ibid.
12. Ibid.
13. Ibid.
14. Ibid.
15. Ibid.
16. Mary Lewis's scrapbooks # 2, courtesy of Holdridge.
17. Ibid.
18. Mary Lewis's scrapbooks #1, courtesy of Holdridge.
19. *New York Times*, 14 Mar. 1926, p. 3. Clipping, n.p., n.d., Lewis file, New York Public Library.
20. Fitch scrapbooks. Mary Lewis's scrapbooks #2, courtesy of Holdridge.
21. Dougan, notes to author, Sept. 1998; Seltsam, *Metropolitan Annals*, pp. 446, 448-449. Quaintance Eaton, *Opera Caravan* 1883-1956. (New York: Metropolitan Opera Guild, 1957), p.299.
22. Seltsam, *Metropolitan Opera Annals*, 450-451.
23. *New York Times*, 13 Mar. 1926, p 21.
24. Seltsam, *Metropolitan Opera Annals*, 444, 446, 449.
25. *New York Times*, 30 Jan. 1926, p. 13.
26. Springfield (Massachusetts) *Union*, 14 May 1926. Mary Lewis's scrapbooks #2, courtesy of Holdridge.
27. *New York Times*, 30 June 1926, p. 25.
28. Mary Lewis's scrapbooks #2, courtesy of Holdridge.
29. *New York Telegraph*, 6 Sept. 1926.
30. William H. Miller, Jr. *The First Great Ocean Liners in Photographs 1897-1927.* (New York: Dover Publications, Inc. 1984), pp. 68, 94. Courtesy of Charles F. Martin.

31. *New York Telegraph*, 6 Sept. 1926.

32. Paul Norwood, *New York Telegraph*, 11 Sept. 1926.

33. Dougan, "An American Tragedy," *Opera News*, July 1984, p. 33. According to Mildred Fitch, oral interview 1983, when Mary began her professional career, she had her teeth capped to remedy an unsightly gap between her two front teeth.

34. Norwood, *New York Telegraph*, 11 Sept. 1926.

35. Mary Lewis's scrapbooks #2, courtesy of Holdridge.

36. An undated typed itinerary of her 1926 tour in the Lewis family papers, cited by Dougan, "Enigma," p. 272. See also appearances.

37. Mary Lewis's scrapbooks #2, courtesy of Holdridge. San Francisco *Chronicle*, n.d.

38. *New York Times*, 13 Dec. 1926, p. 26. Mary earlier credited Anna with the elocution lessons which served her well throughout her career. Even now opera singers do not use amplification because they have worked long and hard on developing their breath control and on aligning their vocal registers—head, chest and middle—to form a unified column of sound with firm diaphragm support. Singing with good technique means singing that projects words clearly at every volume level as far back as the last row of an opera theater or concert hall. Today pop singers' voices are amplified and their recordings are doctored in the studio to produce a sound that usually has little to do with the actual size and quality of their voices. Opera singing is the most natural kind of singing that the audience will hear. Chicago *Tribune*, 25 Oct. 1998, p. 4, section 7.

39. Fitch scrapbooks.

40. Seltsam, *Metropolitan Annals*, 461, 463, 464, 466.

41. Metropolitan Opera Company, Mary Lewis file; Eaton, *Opera Caravan*, pp. 302, 304.

42. *New York Telegraph*, 7 Feb. 1927.

43. Lewis file, New York Public Library, n.p., n.d.

44. Jack Warner, studio chief, and his brothers, Sam, Harry, and Albert.

45. *New York Times*, 16 Aug., 1927, p. 29; Ibid., 12 Oct., 1927, p. 29.

46. Ibid. According to Janice Guthrie, The Health Resource, anemia can be a symptom of malnutrition (childhood or dietary) and of radiation sickness, a result of the fabulous radium-treated dress Mary wore in the Follies.

47. Mary Lewis's scrapbooks #2, courtesy of Holdridge. Utica, New York *Press*, 13 April 1928; Augusta, Georgia, 21 June 1928; 9 Sept. 1928, n.p.; New York *Morning Telegraph*, 18 Nov. 1928.

48. Mary Lewis's scrapbooks #2, courtesy of Holdridge. New York *Morning Telegraph*, 18 Nov., 1928.

49. *New York Times*, 1 Mar. 1927.

After achieving fame on the stages of Europe and New York, Mary Lewis was given “the greatest welcome the state ever knew” when she returned to Arkansas in March of 1926. Governor Thomas Terral and Mrs. Terral accompanied Mary Lewis on a visit to her foster mother, Anna Fitch. Photo by Forbes, Fitch album.

One of Mary Lewis's favorite roles was that of Giulietta in *The Tales of Hoffman*. Mishkin. Author's file.

12

Bohnen

Ten years Mary's senior (more by her press age), Michael Bohnen made his operatic debut in Germany at the age of twenty-three. He was the leading bass-baritone at the Metropolitan Opera from 1923 to 1932. Bohnen was known for many things, and was called the "strong man of the opera," "the last of opera's giants," "tirelessly re-creative," "known for his lively spontaneous personality," and "a God."[1]

His voice was exciting. According to biographer Hans Borgelt: "The voice was seductive, disquieting, appealing to the entire nervous system; it did not merely report a fact, it expressed editorial comment. He was a master of gesture, movement and mimicry, singer and actor fused into a masterful personality which held his audience in a spell of fascination." Bohnen described himself merely as a "singing actor."[2]

Born in Cologne, Germany, the son of an engineer, Bohnen was named *Kammersänger*, Court Singer, by Kaiser Wilhelm II soon after his operatic debut. The title was earned after Bohnen performed as Gurnemanz in *Parsifal* in Berlin without rehearsal. He performed in both bass and baritone roles in Wagnerian operas. His technique was further developed at Bayreuth, singing there in 1912 at the invitation of Cosima and Siegfried Wagner.[3] Cosima, Wagner's wife, was the daughter of Hungarian composer, Franz Liszt. Siegfried was one of Wagner's sons. The Bayreuth theater had been maintained by Wagner's family as a training ground for study of the master's works.

Bohnen began in 1919 to produce and act in films. Of the thirty undertaken, the eight-part *Herrin der Welt* was considered a milestone in film history.[4] Bohnen made the transition from silent films to even greater triumphs in talking films.[5]

Bohnen sang, by request, in London, and at the Vienna Staatsoper under the direction of his good friend, Richard Strauss. Bohnen also was famous for operetta performances, and he recorded on several labels,[6] both German and U.S.A.[7]

Although Germany was suffering financially following the first World War, Bohnen said, "I won't have anybody put limits on my earnings."[8] He was referring to the "Gagenconvention," which meant opera managements had bound themselves not to pay the opera stars higher fees than stipulated in the convention. Bohnen considered himself an exception.[9]

Bohnen was beckoned to the Metropolitan by Gatti-Casazza in 1923 after he had appeared at Wiesbaden, Berlin, and Bayreuth in Germany, Vienna, London, and Stockholm. Physically a giant, six-foot-three inches in height and weighing three hundred pounds, he was a superb athlete. He professionally boxed and wrestled; was a champion competitor in swimming and billiards; an artist in oils, watercolors and sculpture; and he collected trophies racing automobiles.[10]

Not all accounts agree on Bohnen's physical appearance. A review in an early Viennese Press stated: "When he stands on the stage one is captivated before he has sung a note—and although the singer is only medium sized—how one was surprised when Bohnen appeared in the concert hall, a middle sized, bit fat, comfortable German town dweller with round glasses on his nose–yet on stage he appears to be a giant. It is not physique that makes Bohnen appear large, but the spirit, great talent, weight of personality."[11]

"He was one of the truly great operatic artists of the twenties," wrote Irving Kolodin. "When you went to a Bohnen performance in which he was at his best you could not separate the vocal experience from the dramatic, for they were both completely interrelated."[12]

He was not always at his best. The multi-talented Bohnen was also temperamentally explosive, capricious, and egotistical. He was impatient and didn't care who he lambasted. He was compulsively creative and unconfined by tradition. Besides the greatest of praise, his reviewers resorted to terms which included: "eccentric," "bumptious," "erratic," and they criticized him for "buffooneries."[13]

While singing "Schweig! Schweig!" the aria in the finale of the first act of Carl von Weber's *Der Freischütz* (The Freeshooter), he lifted a heavy oak table above his head with one hand.[14] The opera was based on an old tradition among the German huntsmen. Bohnen was cast as the villainous Kaspar, who tempts the hero into a compact with the devil. Whoever sold his soul to Zamiel, the Demon Hunter, would receive seven magic bullets, which would always hit the mark—but at the firing of the seventh, the hunter must yield his soul to Zamiel, if he had not found another victim for the demon. For every convert, the hunter received seven more bullets. In the ensuing struggle between the forces of good and evil, good is eventually triumphant.[15]

Opera singers were given the freedom to design their costumes to suit their own interpretation of the roles. Bohnen chose to wear armor as Wotan in Wagner's *Die Walküere*. "It made me feel more like a God,"[16] he said as he performed the Wagnerian epics based on Germanic and Viking folklore. By using built up boots, he appeared as a seven-foot-tall Méphistophélès in *Faust*. He also chose, instead of a traditional red devil, to be garbed in gloomy ash-gray, which he said represented the "earthbound" qualities of Satan.[17]

Bohnen appeared in twenty-one roles at the Met and a total of 174 performances. Besides *Der Freischütz* and *Faust*, his talents were displayed in *Mona Lisa*, *Der Rosenkavalier*, *Die Verkaufte Braut* (*The Bartered Bride*), *Tannhäuser*, *Lohengrin*, *Die Meistersinger*, *Tristan und Isolde*, *Parsifal*, and all of *The Ring* operas. He varied his costumes and interpretations at whim. Management, colleagues and critics were confounded.[18] Once upon his arrival from Europe, Bohnen picked up a telephone booth containing opera star Lawrence Tibbett, and carried it across the room.[19]

He swept Mary off her feet!

Endnotes Chapter 12 Bohnen

1. David E. Prosser, "Unruly Giant," *Opera News*, 31 Jan. 1970, p. 24.
2. Ibid.
3. Ibid., p. 25.
4. Ibid.
5. J.F.E. Dennis, "Michael Bohnen," *The Record Collector* 27, Jan. 1983, p. 202.
6. Prosser, "Giant," p. 25.
7. Dennis, "Bohnen," *The Record Collector* 27, Jan. 1983, pp. 230-239.
8. New York *Herald Tribune*, 27 April 1965, Bohnen file, New York Public Library.
9. Dennis, "Bohnen, *The Record Collector* 27, Jan. 1983, p. 203.
10. Prosser, "Giant," p. 25.
11. Dennis, "Bohnen," *The Record Collector* 27, Jan. 1983, p 207.

12. Prosser, "Giant," p. 24.
13. Ibid.
14. Ibid.
15. Charles O'Connell, *Victor Book of the Opera*, RCA Co., 1936, p. 162.
16. Prosser, "Giant," p. 24.
17. Prosser, n.p., n.d., Bohnen obituary.
18. Lawrence Gilman, New York *Herald Tribune* 29 May 1932, Bohnen file, New York Public Library.
19. Prosser, "Giant," p. 25.

Michael Bohnen chose a gloomy ash-gray instead of the traditional red devil for his appearance as Méphistophélès in *Faust*. Author's file.

13

Mrs. Michael Bohnen

Headlines on April 15, 1927, informed the public: "Mary Lewis, soprano, of the Metropolitan Opera Company, became the bride last evening of Michael Bohnen, bass-baritone of the same company, in a ceremony which was a surprise to every one, even to some extent to Miss Lewis and Mr. Bohnen themselves."[1]

Bohnen and Lewis had known each other since her debut in Vienna in 1925, but since he didn't speak English and she didn't speak German, friendship was slow in blossoming. The season at the Met continued along this same line. The courtship developed six weeks before the ceremony, although others backstage had no idea romance was blooming, and Bohnen and Lewis never appeared on stage together. As the season neared an end, the pair impulsively came to a decision for an immediate marriage.[2]

The first announcement of their intention came to William Guard, press agent of the Met, when they told him they wanted to be married that afternoon and asked Guard to get in touch with New York's mayor, Jimmy Walker. As the marriage license bureau was closed, Guard reached James Gannon, chief clerk, who returned to City Hall to issue the parchment. Meanwhile, Guard went to City Hall along with Dr. Karl Riedel, assistant conductor, and opera star, Lawrence Tibbett, and several others. The reserves held the reporters and photographers at bay.[3]

The wedding was set for 4 p.m., and at that time Guard said, "It is an ideal day for a wedding," to which the sprightly Mayor Walker replied, "It is indeed." The little group waited for the principals to appear and exchanged stories, mostly about Bohnen's super-powers, for amusement.[4]

Two hours later, after 6 p.m., Mary and Bohnen arrived breathlessly. They had taken the wrong subway! As they tried to avoid the rush of street traffic, they boarded at 59th street, but took an uptown train. When the trolley crossed the Ship Canal, the nuptial pair realized they were in error, changed trains to return, and were trapped in the rush-hour jam![5]

The group was ushered into the private office of Mayor Jimmy Walker who performed the ring ceremony. After he pronounced them man and wife, someone suggested he might kiss the bride. Looking up and down the powerfully built bridegroom, Mayor Walker declined. "Consider it done," he said evasively.[6]

Bohnen gave his age as thirty-nine. He had been married previously and divorced the year before, leaving two sons in Germany. Mary's age was listed as twenty-seven. Her divorce from J. Keene Lewis was cited, one of the few times it appeared in print. The usual Cinderella tale followed.[7]

To the accompaniment of photographers' flashbulbs, the couple left City Hall for an unknown destination. Mrs. Bohnen intimated they would have "a quiet little supper" at her house at 128 West 59th Street. A very short honeymoon was planned, as Bohnen was shipping out on Monday for a series of engagements in Berlin on May 1. Mary had musical commitments in New York and would join him in June.[8]

The following day, Bohnen sang the role of Gurnemanz in a matinee of *Parsifal* with Mary in the audience at the matinee. As he was in his dressing room at the Met putting on his make-up for his part, Bohnen, not realizing anyone was present, burst into song. He adjusted his artificial, long, white whiskers, and said in broken English, "I am so very happy ."[9]

Of their courtship, Mary explained, "You see he couldn't speak English and I couldn't speak German, but I admired him a great deal and liked him and we were good friends—as good friends as two people can be who can scarcely exchange a complete sentence between them." Mary went on. "We began being really good friends when the Metropolitan company went to Atlanta just about this time last year. But we couldn't talk. So I decided to study my German and he decided to study English, and now we can talk to each other in both languages," she finished with triumph.[10]

Mary confided her plans to reporter Dorothy Dayton and included the wonderful qualities she found in her new bridegroom. "She married him because he is the first man whose career she has been more interested in than her own. He is the first man for whom she has felt that she is 'willing for him to be the big one'... She married him because he combines both fatherly and motherly instincts and 'wants to look after you and protect you. And so you can't help but love him,' Mary dimpled with her blue eyes shining."[11]

Dayton quoted Mary: "You see he has a wonderful sense of humor, and he is such a jolly person and so good natured. So big hearted. And he is so interested in my career. I don't think a woman can love a man unless he has a more forceful personality than her own, and unless she can respect and admire him for his talent. She must feel that his ability, his judgment, are greater than her own. I have always been a very dominant person and interested in my own career," Mary admitted, "but I am perfectly willing for him to be the big one. He is the first man I have ever felt that way about."[12] In other interviews Mary declared they had agreed both would pursue their careers.[13]

Mary accompanied Bohnen to the Hamburg-America liner *Reliance* for a final farewell Monday evening—and decided to go along, concerts or no concerts without consulting anyone. With only an hour left before departure, the bride and groom rushed off the ship and jumped into a taxi. Arriving at the bride's apartment, they threw Mary's wardrobe into trunks and bags, and dug up an old passport. The Bohnen called for three more taxies, loaded them with Mary's luggage, and sped back to the pier.[14]

As this was taking place, one of their friends purchased Mary a ticket and, on their arrival, the bridal pair were ensconced in Bohnen's stateroom. They could not occupy the liner's honeymoon suite, as it was taken by another couple. That new bride had been seven years as secretary to one of the officials of the steamship company and was given use of the suite for that voyage.[15]

"What about your concert engagements?" asked the reporters.

"My engagements will have to cancel themselves," said the bride breathlessly clutching Bohnen's arm. "I didn't have time to cancel them. We're too much in love to be separated yet. I couldn't bear to be separated now."[16]

"All ashore that's going ashore!" the stewards shouted, and the singers' friends were hustled off ship. They stood at the end of the pier as the happy newlyweds stood at the rail waving, shedding tears, and shouting good-byes.[17]

Four days before the wedding Mary Lewis signed her second contract with the Metropolitan Opera Company for the 1927-28 season. She agreed to place at the Company's disposal the same operatic roles as in the previous year's contract. She also agreed not to sing or render any services for the purpose of reproducing or transmitting the voice by wireless apparatus and/or any other device or process between then and the middle of May, 1928, without the Company's written consent. Salary was again $150 per week with options for the 1929-30 season at a salary of $200 per week and for the 1930-31 season at $250 per week.[18]

Mary had a contract to appear in Rochester, New York, for the Metropolitan Opera Company May 10, 1927. She was to sing Giulietta in *Les Contes d'Hoffmann.* The role was sung by Bori.[19]

On her arrival in Hamburg on May 1, 1927, Mary announced she had no intention of sacrificing her career. Acknowledging she had turned her back on the Met and her contracts, Mary defended herself saying, "However, I could not bear to part with him. I packed three suitcases and came. That's that." She had received some threatening cables from her managers, who were dealing with irate producers. Mary was disconcerted, but replied, "I fully intend to return to America for my Chicago engagement August 1." She parried questions as to whether Bohnen would return with her.[20]

The Berlin reporter found Mary's troubles had faded with the thrill of riding beside Bohnen at seventy-five miles an hour on the Hamburg-Berlin road. Bohnen was scheduled to drive a car in the Wiesbaden races in June. With his new bride's encouragement, he reported with assurance, more racing medals would be added to his collection.[21]

Mary was seated in the front row for Bohnen's performance May 2. She sat beside American Ambassador and Mrs. Schurman, along with other embassy staff members.[22] Mary asked a *New York Times* foreign correspondent "to tell her friends that she was blissfully happy and certain she had found her soulmate. If it was understood how much she was in love, no one would censure her for forgetting her contracts to be with her husband."[23] The pair were involved in a romantic episode worthy of an opera score.

On May 11, Mary visited her adopted home, Casa Del Mare, in Monaco, as the guest of Osbourne O'Hagan. On the day following her arrival she sang as "only divas sing at home," and it was spontaneously decided to arrange a recital. With only four days to issue invitations Mary Lewis said, "I will sing my best even if only 20 people turn up, just as I would if there were 2,000—for I shall be singing for my father." Her accompanist was Seneca Pierce. As the climax of an aria from *Manon* was reached, "Miss Greenwood, who was referred to as Mary Lewis' adopted sister, suddenly appeared in the upper gallery and wafted over her all-surprised sister a thousand rose petals she had secretly gathered from the garden." The recital, which was reported in glowing prose, was billed as "The Home Coming of Mary Lewis." Mary's visit ended on May 16, when she left to rejoin Bohnen in Berlin. It was reported that if his engagements permitted the newly married couple would visit the Casa for an extended visit, but if that was not feasible, Mr. O'Hagan and Miss Greenwood would join them in Lucerne, Switzerland. While at Casa Del Mare, several luncheon parties were given in Mary's honor which included many "distinguished persons." Mary planned to study with Pierce in Berlin.[24]

A tour of recitals in the European capitals was arranged for Mary while Bohnen was performing around the Berlin area. They sang together for the first time that summer in Berlin. A notice read: "It was a great artistic pleasure that was prepared for us in yesterday's performance of Gounod's opera *Faust*. The leading roles were brilliantly filled in a manner seldom encountered and besides this, one learnt [sic] an interesting artistic personality in Mary Lewis, the wife of Michael Bohnen, in the role of Marguerite. She is of uncommon sympathetic appearance and has a full extended soprano voice which brought her triumphs at the New York Metropolitan Opera. Bohnen himself as Méphistophélès was once again vocally and artistically unbeatable.... Richard Tauber and Heinrich Schlusnus who were also in the cast."[25]

Tauber, a tenor from Austria, gained world-wide popularity through his appearances in operas, operettas, and recordings. Schlusnus, a German baritone, was distinguished by the entirely personal and warm sound of his voice. He was known as the most famous singer of German Lieder.[26]

Lewis and Bohnen possessed the entire vocal range. Bohnen, with four octaves, earned the unique double-billing as bass-baritone. Mary took up where he left off soaring to the highest soprano notes.

As Mary boarded ship in the fall to return to the United States, Bohnen returned the compliment and refused to part. He joined her for the voyage with no baggage except for two shirts and an extra collar.[27] In early August, they were captured by a photographer as they arrived in Chicago for Mary's operatic debut in that city. Strongman Bohnen is shown hoisting a rather plump Mary down from the steps of the *Century* train.[28]

On Wednesday, August 10, 1927, Mary Lewis was cast as Giulietta in *The Tales of Hoffman* at Ravinia, a distinctive, open-air acoustically-kind, rustic pavilion where the Chicago Symphony Orchestra played its summer season. The *Aurora Beacon News* critic found, "... all who love Ravinia and the most beautiful music in the world in a setting such as heaven itself cannot surpass, should make the trip out...during the present weather and a full moon." The 1,500 seats had been snapped up, porches were jammed with listeners, and hundreds more were seated outside on chairs, or on the grass in the beautiful park. The evening weather was so ideal that many of the beautifully gowned women and their well-dressed masculine escorts sat in the cool air, eating their picnic suppers with superb manners.[29] Among those who attended were Rev. Frank Fitch and his wife, Mildred, of Earlville, Illinois; and his son, Finley, and his wife, Blanche, of Yorkville, Illinois. Mary and her foster brother met there for the first and only time. Frank was old enough to be her father![30]

Critic Edward Moore headlined his review: "Miss Lewis At Least Rates As Operatic Beauty." He wrote, "Mary Lewis is a beautiful woman who knows how to walk across the stage." He deferred comment on her operatic abilities until he heard her sing in another opera. In a bizarre review, he panned the score more than the performers. He thought the "Barcarolle," which Mary sang with Ina Bourskaya on pitch, was to their credit since it seemed not to be written for human voices. He concluded: "What was needed was a new score."[31] Mary also appeared Sunday as Mimi in *La Bohème*.[32]

On October 31, 1927, Mary returned again to Little Rock, this time to initiate the new high school auditorium at her alma mater. She sang in the first public function to be given in the building. Tickets were $2.50, $2.00, and $1.50. The manager of the Civic Music Course, under the auspices of the Musical Coterie, was Mrs. Frank Vaughan.[33] This school, then Little Rock High School, would later be renamed Central High School and was the scene of the famous civil rights crisis in 1957.

A reception, touted as one of the most beautiful affairs of the autumn season, was sponsored by Judge and Mrs. George B. Rose. Invitations to 700 had been sent to pay honor to Miss Mary Lewis, Metropolitan Opera Star and a former Little Rock girl.[34]

The spacious rooms in the lovely Rose home were decorated with beautiful paintings and treasures from the Old World which added elegance to the ambience. A silver basket filled with pink roses and snapdragons centered the dining room table, flanked by tall, pink tapers in silver holders. The hosts, Miss Lewis, Senator and Mrs. Joseph T. Robinson, Mr. and Mrs. Clarence Rose, Governor and Mrs. John E. Martineau, and Dr. and Mrs. Charles H. Brough received the guests in the parlor, while other dignitaries presided in the reception hall and the dining room. Frozen ices were served in the morning room.[35] Guests at the reception included no less than one current and two past governors.

It was the sort of event the Victor Talking Machine Company loved. One advertisement read: "The story of Mary Lewis—the American girl who climbed to the heights of grand opera from musical comedy—has been told so many times that to repeat is becomes banal. However, in the two years since her debut at the Metropolitan Opera Company, that mecca of all aspiring singers, and the four since she first determined to scale those dazzling heights, Mary Lewis has made a distinct and lasting impression, quickly and firmly establishing herself in the front ranks of contemporary artists."[36]

"Each concert she gives," Victor continued, "enhances her artistic stature, and her operatic appearances have received the acclaim of her hearers. Possessing youth, beauty, a personality that is dazzling in its radiance, in addition to a voice of unusual loveliness and brilliance, Mary Lewis is a splendid example of what pluck and determination can accomplish. Each time she is heard she sings her way into the hearts of her hearers, and according to one critic, 'a spellbound audience realized it was in the presence of a superb artist.'"[37]

Victor also wanted the reader to purchase Mary Lewis's records. Mary had recorded in 1926 "Little Grey Home in the West," the song she used to audition her way into a Dillingham contract. On the reverse side was, "From the Land of the Sky-Blue Water,"[38] based on an actual Indian melody and legend, written and published in 1908 by Charles Wakefield Cadman. He was interested in recognizing and preserving authentic Indian music. Cadman was a pioneer in realizing that the native heritage of America was being lost. Victor had also released a recording of "Dixie" by Mary Lewis.[39]

On November 21, Mary was billed to broadcast on radio at the Capitol Theater in New York. As Mary was to take her turn at the microphone, Major Edward Bowes announced because of contract restrictions Mary was singing at the Capitol, but not over the radio.[40]

After having been members of the same operatic company for two seasons, Lewis and Bohnen were finally cast to perform together in *I Pagliacci* in a matinee performance February 13, 1928, on the Metropolitan stage. Bohnen brought down the house and upstaged Mary and the other performers. As the clown, Tonio, Bohnen made his entrance walking on his hands![41]

The opera is a play within a play. Canio, the leader of a troupe of players in rural Italy, suspects his wife, Nedda, of being unfaithful. In her aria, the one Lewis recorded, she wishes that she was as free as a bird. Tonio, the clown is a gross character in love with Nedda. When she rejects his advances, he reports his suspicious to Canio. As the players are acting out their drama for the rural audience, Canio casts aside his acting, confronts Nedda, and stabs her lover dead. "The comedy is ended," Canio then proclaims to the audience.[42]

A crisis occurred in the performance when Mary, as Nedda, was to whip Tonio. The whip caught in Mary's shawl, and Bohnen escaped his lashing. Giovanni Martinelli, one of the Met's leading tenors, was the Canio. That evening Jeritza was cheered by a holiday crowd as Carmen with a new Toreador, Ezio Pinza, Italian bass, later of South Pacific fame.[43]

When soprano Grace Moore made her debut at the Met as Mimi on February 7, 1928, a delegation from her home state of Tennessee, including two United States Senators, pelted the stage with a barrage of violets which recalled the debut of Mary Lewis.[44] Moore also came up through the ranks of musical comedy and revues and studied in Europe.

Mary sang only four times that season with the Metropolitan Company. She sang Nedda again opposite Edward Johnson and Mario Basiola. In *Tales* she joined Nina Morgana, Queena Mario, Armando Tokatyan, DeLuca, Rothier, and Didur. Her other performances were in *Faust* were Chaliapin, Chamlee, and DeLuca.[45]

Wolfsohn tours scheduled Mary Lewis for a recital at Miami Beach, Florida, and a concert at the Civic Auditorium in San Francisco, California, in February, and in March she appeared in recitals in Pennsylvania, New Jersey, Connecticut, Louisiana, North Carolina, and Toronto, Canada.[46]

In a March 11, 1928, Carnegie Hall recital her program included Italian songs by Lotti, Paisello, and Faccio; Lieder by Strauss, Brahms, and Marx; French songs by Hahn, Debussy, Satie, and Delibes; and some unusual English numbers—"Symphony in Yellow," by Griffes, "The House that Jack Built," by Sidney Homer; and one of Mary's favorites, "The Nightingales of Lincoln's Inn." Rossini's "Tarantella Napoletani" ended the program. Her Italian, French, and English numbers were well received. As a southern girl, she included "Carry Me Back to Old Virginny" as one of her encores. Other numbers for encores were "The Song of India," and Rossini's "La Danza."[47]

A visit to Hot Springs, Arkansas, was made to visit old friends and family in April. A newspaper photo dated April 13, 1928, was captioned, "Songbird Goes Back To Her Nest."[48]

Accompanying her husband, Mary again headed for Europe that month, canceling her performances at the Newark, New Jersey, festival. Life with Mary was never dull! A tour of concert recitals in Europe was arranged for Mary.[49]

Meanwhile, there was consternation among the executive committee of the Newark Music Festival Association, where Mary Lewis was scheduled to sing on May 14. "Search in vain for Mary Lewis" was a headline in the Newark *Star-Eagle*. They reported the singer mysteriously disappeared from her New York home, and the committee feared Miss Lewis would not keep her engagement.[50] A servant said Miss Lewis had gone and had left no address.[51]

Jack Adams, of the Wolfsohn Musical Bureau wrote a letter to the committee enclosing a doctor's certificate which stated that "she needed a rest" and would be unable to sing at the Newark Festival. The letter frankly said Adams suspected Miss Lewis and her husband, Michael Bohnen, had sailed for Europe on the *Aquitania*, but a wireless to the ship had been returned to the Wolfsohn Bureau. Calvin M. Franklin, a partner in the bureau and personal manager for Miss Lewis, arrived at Newark to consult with the committee and said he "had washed his hands of her for all time."[52]

Franklin recalled that about a month before Mary Lewis, while on a concert tour in the Midwest, wrote asking that three concerts be canceled: Bangor, Maine, on May 2; Lynchburg, Virginia; and the Newark Festival concert. She wanted to go abroad with her husband. When Wiske, head of the Newark Festival event, was informed of her request he told the Wolfsohn Bureau the festival association would sue the singer and also seek an injunction to prevent her from leaving the country. Mary Lewis then is said to have responded, "Very well, I will sing." This was how the matter was left until the medical certificate, without comment from Mary Lewis, reached the Bureau.[53]

Knowing Bohnen was to sail on the *Aquitania*, Franklin sent his attorney to the ship. The attorney reported he could not find Miss Lewis, but had been able to locate her trunks on board. A cablegram addressed to Mary Lewis, *Aquitania*, was sent after the ship sailed, but it was returned. A subsequent cablegram sent to Mrs. Michael Bohnen was not returned.[54] Mary was finding, like others in the performing arts, that while her managers were promoting her career, they were also controlling her life. Mary rebelled.

In Germany Mary sang in concert with Bohnen in Berlin on June 5. Following her October 11 recital, German and English newspapers reported: "Mary Lewis Wins Berlin." Other concerts were given in Budapest, Prague, and Vienna. She went "home" to Casa Del Mare to sing in a recital for O'Hagan on December 2, 1928.[55]

While the Germans were watching the Bohnen romance, they also were watching the Fatherland's emergence from post-war restrictions, lifted in 1925. The German craftsmen and scientists were perfecting the inflatable blimp which had been used to rain down fire on the heads of the British during World War I and had been used for German intercity commuting.

The *Graf Zeppelin LZ 127*, named for the inventor, made its debut in 1928. The maiden oceanic voyage to Lakehurst, New Jersey, was met with cheers on both sides of the Atlantic in mid-October. On the return to Germany, a nineteen-year-old blond golf caddie slipped aboard as a stowaway. He was soon discovered and put to work sweeping the floor and washing the dishes. Chief Steward Heinrich Kubis did not appreciate his uninvited assistant, and Captain Hugo Eckener, at the helm, was not happy. "When the papers hear of this, they'll make him a hero. Then we'll have to fight off stowaways every trip we make."[56]

The captain was right. For a week the wire reports kept the lad on the front page, and he received offers from editors for his story. He was invited by many German families to be a houseguest; among the hosts were Mary and Michael Bohnen. The *Chicago Tribune* pulled out a file photo of the couple, captioning it "Fete Stowaway."[57] After a spectacular around-the-world trip in 1929, the *Graf* settled down to commuting between the German settlement in Rio de Janerio, Brazil, and Germany.[58]

In Europe at an audition for Erik Charell's production, *Casanova*, operetta, Bohnen had been standing in the wings watching the twenty-five- year-old Spanish dancer, La Jana, audition. As she left the stage, he congratulated her on her performance and received a kiss in reply. The kiss led to more.[59] In 1928 composer Ralph Benatzky and his librettists put together the operetta assembled from the works of Johann Strauss. Bohnen recorded excerpts.[60]

As the roving lover, Casanova, Bohnen was featured in a series of tableaux set in theaters in Italy, Spain, Austria, and in Bohemia. The show also featured intermission entertainment of well-known personalities, including La Jana in the cast. During 1928-1930 it ran for over 100 performances as well as the tours.[61]

A Christmas Eve wireless communication from on-board the British White Star liner, *Majestic*, reported the ship was carrying 11,000 bags of Christmas mail and 1,000 passengers, many of them Americans homeward bound. The ship had been delayed a day at Southhampton, England, by fog. Despite head winds and rough weather, the liner expected "to reach Quarantine before dawn and to send her passengers ashore for Christmas dinners at their own firesides." Mary Lewis was among the passengers who missed celebrating Christmas at sea. Her name was one of the eight celebrities on board listed in the newspaper release.[62]

In 1929 Mary played Marguerite three times, once opposite Bohnen with his seven-foot Méphistophélès, and she also appeared in a Metropolitan concert in the "Garden Scene" from *Faust*.[63]

A recipe was printed in the New York City *Life*, captioned "Kitchen Helps." The tested recipe read: "How to cook a 4-minute egg. Bring water to boil, place Mary Lewis "Meditation" from *Thaïs* on phonograph, drop in egg. At conclusion of the song, remove egg."[64]

Mary again appeared in concerts in Iowa, Nebraska, Maryland, New York, New Jersey, Missouri, and Pennsylvania. She sang on an Atwater Kent radio concert over WEAF which included some little known Spanish folk songs of California. The Symphonic Orchestra was directed by Josef Pasternack. A telegram was sent to the radio station, National Broadcasting Company, from her mother in Chicago, "Program coming in fine, give Mary Lewis my love from her mother." Other congratulatory telegrams were received from around the country.[65]

Bohnen received acclaim January 19, 1929, at the American premiere at the Met of the controversial German "jazz" opera, *Jonny Spielt Auf* by Ernst Křenek. In this burlesque on the post World War I decade, Bohnen played Jonny, a colored jazz band leader. Coach for the role was his friend Al Jolson, a master of the "blackface" minstrel.[66]

Jonny spielt auf or *Johnny strikes up* was introduced in the United States by Bohnen. The opera was the most famous work of Austrian composer Křenek. Introduced in Europe in February of 1927, it achieved short-lived international success. Of particular interest was the technique of combining jazz elements and fashions of the contemporary world into traditional opera framework. The opera was written in two parts with eleven scenes. Other roles were Max, a melancholy musician; Anita, a beautiful singer; Daniello, a charming violinist and owner of a valuable violin; and Yvonne, Jonny's sweetheart. Others in the cast included Florence Easton as Anita, Editha Fleischer as Yvonne, Friedrich Schorr as Daniello, and Walther Kirchhoff as Max.[67]

The plot finds Max and Anita falling in love until Anita must leave for Paris, where she is to sing. Daniello is a guest in the hotel where Anita lives. Jonny, the young black musician in the hotel band, attempts to seduce the singer and she is rescued by Daniello, who then tries to buy off Jonny with 1,000 francs. Out of spite, Jonny steals the violin and hides it in Anita's banjo case. Yvonne quarrels with the hotel manager over Jonny's strange behavior and is fired. She is hired by Anita, who by now is having an affair with Daniello, but she soon tires of him and leaves. When Daniello finds his violin is missing, he searches everywhere. Jonny, then, has to follow the women to keep track of the valuable violin.[68]

Act two finds Jonny telling Yvonne about the stolen violin. Daniello follows the group to the hotel where he hears his violin, which Jonny is playing. Daniello informs the police, who pursue Jonny to the railroad station where he hopes to make an escape to Amsterdam. Jonny meets Anita and Max there, as they are on their way to America. Jonny puts the violin among Max's suitcases and Max is arrested as the thief. Yvonne knows the truth, but Daniello tries to stop her from telling as she is jealous over Anita's affection for Max. Daniello falls to his death beneath a train. Jonny confesses he is the thief. Max joins Anita on the way to America, which is the symbol of his new found faith in life. Jonny, with the violin, climbs to the top of the station to perch on the station clock, which turns into a globe and Jonny fiddles on top of the world while the crowd below dances the Charleston to his tune.[69]

Special praise was accorded to Bohnen for the opera finale. He tap danced through an entire change of scenery, climaxed by a leap to the top of the piano for his finale. This success brought Bohnen a Warner Brothers contract to star in a film version of the opera.[70]

At the Metropolitan Mary appeared in *Faust* with all three as Marguerite, opposite Chaliapin twice and Bohnen once. Mary also appeared in a Metropolitan concert singing the Garden Scene from *Faust*.[71]

As he prepared to fulfill his Warner Brothers contract, Bohnen bought a house at 554 Moreno Avenue in Hollywood. As his wife, Mary moved in and had some of his furniture shipped from Berlin to make him feel more at home. Bohnen was reported to have been vexed Mary had not asked him first before preparing the domestic domain. There in Hollywood, the mecca of romance, the marriage terminated. "A clash of artistic temperaments" was said to be the cause.[72]

Bohnen left Hollywood with three documents. First, an agreement to pay Mary $35,000. Second, to sell the interest in the house and contents on the ground floor and car in the drive to a Carl Brehme[73] of Maple Drive for a price of $10. The low price was given because Bohnen wished to leave immediately. Brehme was to pay any bills due. Third, Bohnen had a release from the Warner Brothers contract, providing he did not take any film offer in the U.S.A. without its consent.[74]

Mary filed for separate maintenance on August 2, 1929. On August 30, Mary filed for divorce. On August, 1930, after the customary one year-long cooling-off period, Lewis received an uncontested divorce. Although she was granted alimony, Bohnen stopped payments.[75]

If the marriage between the two headstrong personalities was a mistake in the first place, Mary's second mistake, years before, was breaking her commitments for scheduled engagements and getting on the boat with Bohnen to cross the Atlantic for their honeymoon. In the divorce proceedings, Mary charged Bohnen had struck her in view of passengers on their honeymoon cruise. He abused her on their Paris honeymoon, and in Berlin, struck her with such force that a door panel was broken. Later in New York, she alleged Bohnen tried to force her to jump from a hotel window—fortunately she didn't.[76] After the divorce her career never again reached its pre-marriage heights.

Mary Lewis had chosen a man who could dominate her—and dominate he did! Mary consoled herself with food and drink. She never again seems to have publicly mentioned the disastrous marriage. In contrast, Bohnen exploded with a barrage of accusations in a series of articles published in the German tabloid, *Die Stern*, from November 1953 to January 1954 after Mary was deceased.[77]

In order to make his story more popular, Bohnen took liberties making what is written an unreliable source. James F.E. Dennis, editor of *The Record Collector*, referred to *Die Stern* as a "scandal sheet." In his biography of Bohnen, Dennis wrote: "According to Bohnen, Lewis had chased him for the two previous years," although during that time she was concentrating on her own career and had first performed at the Met only one year previous. Voted three consecutive years the most beautiful woman in America, and at the peak of her opera career, she could not have been the drunkard Bohnen accused her of being. Dennis found reports of Mary's drunkenness unfortunate,"...but it is my impression that Bohnen drove her to it."[78] Bohnen's story contradicts the press releases (and often contradicts itself), saying he was coerced into being a reluctant bridegroom.[79]

Bohnen's final performance at the Metropolitan was on April 13, 1932. He then returned to Germany. Bohnen and the dancer, La Jana, lived together in Berlin when not performing elsewhere. Born in Vienna in 1905, La Jana (Henriette Hiebel) grew up at Frankfurt am Main. Her dancing career began in a sleazy Paris cabaret, and she worked her way to fame.[80] There is no record of marriage, although a *New York Times* February 2, 1933, release captioned: "Former Husband of Mary Lewis Has Pneumonia in Vienna." The article states that Bohnen was seriously ill with double pneumonia and his wife, La Jana, well-known stage dancer, was summoned to Vienna.[81]

It seems unlikely they married. When Bohnen was fulfilling his contract at the Met in New York, La Jana found other escorts, including German Crown Prince Wilhelm and Paul Joseph Goebbels. After a tempestuous relationship, accompanied again by physical abuse, Bohnen bowed out in jealousy after the press reported her courtship by Prince Wilhelm. The Prince in turn bowed out to Third Reich Propaganda Minister, Paul Goebbels.[82]

Bohnen refused to support the Nazi party, which resulted in his relegation as a porter for the Siemens radio and electrical company.[83] During World War II, he spent some time in Buenos Aires, Argentina. At the end of the war, Bohnen returned to Germany and became head of the Berlin Municipal Opera for two years. He was decorated by both Berlin and West Germany in the 1950s. Malicious rumors of his affiliation with the Nazi regime were based on his association with the dancer, who had let herself be exploited by the party. The rest of his life was spent in retirement.[84]

Late in life Bohnen married Inge Behrend, apparently not a theatrical person. His last few months of near poverty were made easier due to an honorary pension from the Metropolitan Opera. He said he was happy to know his friends in America remembered him. He died shortly before his seventy-eighth birthday in 1965.[85]

Endnotes Chapter 13 Mrs. Michael Bohnen

1. *New York Times*, 15 April 1927.
2. Dorothy Dayton, n.p., n.d., Lewis file, New York Public Library.
3. *New York Times*, 15 April 1927.
4. Clipping, n.p., n.d., Bohnen file, New York Public Library.
5. Ibid.
6. *New York Times*, 15 April 1927.
7. Ibid.
8. Ibid.
9. Dayton, Lewis file, New York Public Library.
10. Ibid.
11. Ibid.
12. Ibid.
13. Mary Lewis's scrapbooks, courtesy of Holdridge.
14. *New York Sun*, 19 April 1927.
15. Ibid.
16. Ibid.
17. Ibid.
18. Contract agreement, Metropolitan Opera Company, New York, and Mary Lewis, 12 Nov. 1927.
19. Mary Lewis's file, Metropolitan Opera Company; Eaton, *Opera Caravan*, p. 304.
20. *New York Times*, 1927, wired from Berlin, May 1.
21. Ibid.
22. Ibid.
23. Ibid.
24. Mary Lewis's scrapbooks #1, courtesy Holdridge, n.d., n.p.
25. James F.E. Dennis, "Michael Bohnen," *The Record Collector*, Ipswich, England, 27 Jan. 1983, p. 226.
26. Jones, Harry Earl. *A Concise Biographical Dictionary of Singers - From the Beginning of Recorded Sound to the Present.* (Philadelphia, New York, London: Chilton Book Company), 1969, pp. 387, 431-432.
27. New York *Herald Tribune*, wired from West Berlin, 27 April 1965.
28. *Chicago Tribune*, n.d., Fitch scrapbooks.
29. *Aurora* (Illinois) *Beacon News* 11 Aug. 1927.
30. Oral interviews, Mildred Fitch, Finley and Blanche Fitch.
31. Edward Moore, n.p., n.d., Fitch scrapbooks.
32. Ravinia program, Fitch scrapbooks.
33. Program, Civic Music Course, Little Rock, Arkansas. Fitch scrapbooks.
34. Clipping, n.p., n.d., Fitch scrapbooks.
35. Ibid.
36. Ibid.
37. Ibid.

38. W.R. Moran, "The Recordings of Mary Lewis," *The Record Collector* 23 Dec. 1976, pp. 186-187.
39. Ibid.
40. *New York Times*, 21 Nov. 1927, p. 18.
41. Clipping, n.p., n.d., Bohnen file, New York Public Library.
42. O'Connell, *Book of the Opera*, pp. 316-317.
43. Clipping, n.p., n.d., Bohnen file, New York Public Library.
44. Seltsam, *Metropolitan Opera Annals*, p. 484.
45. Dougan, "Enigma," p. 273-274.
46. Mary Lewis's scrapbooks #2, courtesy of Holdridge.
47. *New York Times*, 11 Mar. 1928, sec. X, p. 10, Mar. 12, 1928, p 26.
48. Fitch scrapbooks. Chicago *Daily News*, 13 April 1928. Also numberous clippings in Mary Lewis's scrapbooks #2, courtesy of Holdridge. No further information is available concerning the friends and relatives Mary Lewis was reported to have visited. Research Garland County Library.
49. Dennis, "Bohnen," *The Record Collector*, Ipswich, England, 27 Jan. 1983, p. 226.
50. Newark (New Jersey) *Star-Eagle*, 23 April 1928, Metropolitan Opera Company files.
51. Newark *Ledger*, 24 April 1928, Metropolitan Opera Company files.
52. Ibid.
53. Newark *Evening News*, 23 April 1928.
54. Ibid.
55. Mary Lewis's scrapbooks #1 and 2, courtesy of Holdridge.
56. J. Gordon Vaeth, *Graf Zeppelin*, (New York: Harper & Bros., 1958), p. 63.
57. Fitch scrapbooks.
58. Ibid.
59. Dennis, "Bohnen," *The Record Collector*, Ipswich, England, 27 Jan. 1983, p. 227.
60. Ibid., p. 228.
61. Ibid.
62. Mary Lewis's scrapbooks #2, courtesy of Holdridge. New York City *Times*, 25 Dec. 1928. Although Bohnen was not mentioned, he was in the United States for appearances in January, 1929.
63. Seltsam, *Metropolitan Annals*., p. 448, 496-498
64. Mary Lewis's scrapbooks #2, courtesy of Holdridge. H.V.W., New York City *Life*, 2 Nov. 1928.
65. Ibid., #1 and #2.
66. Prosser, "Giant," p. 25.
67. Research Starved Rock Public Library System.
68. Ibid.
69. Ibid.
70. Prosser, "Giant," p. 25.
71. Seltsam, *Metropolitan Opera Annals*, p. 496-498.
72. Dougan, "Enigma," p. 275.
73. No further information is available concerning Carl Brehme.

74. Dennis, "Bohnen," p. 227.

75. Ibid.

76. Dougan, "Enigma," p. 275.

77. Dennis, "Bohnen," p. 225. Dennis refutes the credibility of *Die Stern* information. *The Star* could be more correctly translated *Der Stern* (masculine gender).

78. Ibid.

79. Ibid.

80. Ibid., p. 227.

81. *New York Times*, 2 Feb. 1933.

82. Dennis, "Bohnen," p. 227.

83. Prosser, "Giant," p.25.

84. Obituary, New York *Herald Tribune*, 27 Apr. 1965.

85. Obituary, n.p., n.d., Bohnen file, New York Public Library.

Mary Lewis and Michael Bohnen, both of the Metropolitan Opera, surprised everyone, even to some extent themselves, when they ended the 1927 season with a marriage ceremony performed by New York's Mayor Jimmy Walker. Photo by Freudy, unidentified source, Fitch album.

14

Hollywood

Not long after Mary's marriage ended, New York's Wall Street financial empire came tumbling down. The fall made a crumpled shambles of monetary affairs, not only of those in the United States, but across the Atlantic, too. Mary weathered the storm in California, sending her Christmas greetings to Anna in 1929 from Beverly Hills.[1]

Then Mary's career took a new direction. Hollywood announced that it "Snared a Song Bird With Sound." The talkies were emerging, and a novel way was found to make an agreement. Mary Lewis, soprano of the Metropolitan Opera Company, was captured on film making a verbal contract to appear in Pathé pictures. The agreement was recorded via camera and microphone on February 28, 1930.[2] The stunt indicated the extent to which talking motion pictures were branching from being a field of entertainment into a means of practical matters.

Sound revolutionized film. Although Enrico Caruso and Geraldine Farrar had appeared in movies, their voices had not been heard. Now, overnight, skilled veterans of silent stage whose voices were unfit for sound found themselves suddenly unemployed. At first, the studios rushed to turn out musicals in order to exploit the full potential of the medium. One unidentified photo captioned the event, the story of the unusual contract, adding: "and when the voice can be found with beauty, charm, and above all the ability to act, the singer is going to be caught if human wiles can do it, though she fly to farthest ends of the earth." And so Mary Lewis became ready to embark on a third career, her *Follies* and Opera careers being cited as openers.[3]

And again the press recounted her Cinderella tale: the abandoned child who later ran away to be free of unmerited and undue punishment. Sometimes the tale became a little jumbled, but always contained the same element of pathos. Finally, Mary was reduced to contagious laughter, as every interview contained the same repetitious biography.[4]

Mary found it quite easy to laugh, as she contracted for two films, agreeing to accept a salary of about $4,000 for each minute she appeared on screen.[5] The film was to be a story of her life, with Mary to be the first to star in her own film autobiography.[6] Mary's attributes, her beauty and her voice, were accorded the greatest of praise in the ballyhoo accompanying the venture.

Mary still had one major problem to overcome. She had to lose weight. Just how and when Lewis lost her extra weight cannot be satisfactorily explained. By one account in a July, 1930, *Screenland* the interviewer reported: "she had refused a film offer several months ago [probably about April] because she felt she was too stout to screen well." The interviewer says, "One can scarcely believe it now. She weighs only 120 pounds, which spells real slenderness for a girl five feet seven inches tall. Her face hasn't a surplus inch."[7]

The secret of how she lost twenty-three pounds is revealed: "She refuses to diet, feeling that this process is weakening and consequently fatal to a singer's vocal power. She has relied entirely on massage, going every day for six weeks to Sylvia Ulbeck, the *masseuse*, who has contributed to the health and beauty of so many screen stars. Sylvia suggested to Mary that two or three times a week would be enough if she found the daily beating and slappings, which made up reducing massage, too strenuous and painful. Mary decided in favor of the daily treatment. There is no procrastination or softness about her. If she is going anywhere, she takes the shortest and most direct route to her goal."[8]

An April 12 New York interview contended that Miss Lewis's proudest boast was not for her singing, or her acting, but her achievement of having lost nearly thirty-seven pounds in the past year. Her weight loss was attributed to daily morning check-ins with a doctor to be given her menu for the day. At that date, she is recorded to have weighed in at 135 pounds, five foot six inches tall.[9]

Also on that day she appeared at the Met singing Micaela in *Carmen* with a cast that included Pinza, Ina Bourskaya, and Antonin Trantoul. Unfortunately, one member of the audience later recalled she was "drunk as a lord, staggering all over the stage." Her last appearance at the Met was eight days later in a Sunday afternoon concert, singing the waltz from *Roméo et Juliette*.[10] It was announced she would return to Hollywood, and she confided her intentions to lose another ten pounds.

The plans for the autobiographical story were scrapped, with Mary citing, "They said there wasn't enough love interest." A story was begun for Mary to play a French peasant girl whose beauty and voice attract the attention of Marie Antoinette. She was to be a little peasant who is invited to live at a toy village built by the queen. Filming was begun in May, interrupted, and not resumed.[11]

By the summer of 1930 so many talking-singing-dancing pictures had been made in the rush to exploit the new media, that the market was saturated. The studios were looking for another format. And in 1930, the public was standing in line for bread, not for theater entertainment. Even the Met was having fiscal problems and a campaign was launched to "Save the Met" from ruin.

Mary sued Pathé for $22,500 for breaking the contract. Pathé, in turn, charged Mary Lewis "became intoxicated and involved in a scandal" and violated the "morals clause" of her contract. Pathé contended that she "became the subject of comment by publications reflecting upon her character and tending to lessen her drawing ability and popularity as an actress." No details were given.[12] The stars were expected to set good moral examples. Pathé declared it had loaned Miss Lewis "$2,500 to enable her to avoid being interviewed by newspaper reporters concerning the incident." They also added they had attempted to help her obtain sound and screen tests for employment at other studios.[13]

Given equal billing on the newspaper page was the headline "Hitler assails Hindenburg." In a verbal attack on the aging German president, Hitler spoke from a beer cellar celebrating the eleventh anniversary of the founding of the National Socialist Fascist movement. Adolph Hitler declared, "Nothing happens without my knowledge or approval, what's more, nothing is done unless I wish it. We'll use every means at our disposal to do away with the present regime."[14]

Mary suddenly announced she had "abandoned plans to make a talking motion picture for Pathé and that she was sailing for Cherbourg, France, May 7, on the *Aquitania*." According to the announcement, "Miss Lewis' collapse after singing two numbers over a nation-wide radio hook-up last Sunday evening, [May 4, 1930] had been caused by the shock she received when she learned that her father was critically ill." Miss Lewis stated she had arranged to fit into her broadcast program his favorite song, "Beautiful Blue Danube." One of Miss Lewis's friends said her father's name was Osbourne O'Hagan, he was seventy-eight years old, his permanent residence was London, and his summer home at Monte Carlo.[15] Mary was losing another important father figure in her search for a family of her own.

Other reports rumored Mary had been "hooked" off the stage for inebriation over a broadcast beamed live over all of the United States.[16] Disruption of the on-the-air performance threw the engineers, producers, and co-stars into pandemonium.

The movie contract was severed. Mary was fighting not only the battle of the bulge, but with the spirits in the bottles as well. Anna had warned her the Devil would get her if she didn't watch out.

All that remains of the talkie debut are some captivating photos and publicity releases of Mary sandwiched in between other Hollywood notables, Andy (of Amos and Andy), Joe E. Brown, Buster Keaton, Claudette Colbert, and a very young Loretta Young in a one-piece bathing suit.[17] Grace Moore made the transition after the 1932 season at the Met and went on to achieve a successful career in musical films.

During the summer of 1930, Mary gave a concert at the Hollywood Bowl. Reports said it was well-received. She was photographed touring the Christie Studios where she once appeared in the silents for $75 a week. As befitting a glamour queen, she was accompanied by her five dogs. She said she had left New York forever and it seems unclear if she sailed to Europe.[18]

She wrote to her mother, "My marriage to Bohnen did me so much harm, put me back so in my work, that it seems almost impossible to overcome the bad spell." She reported $180 and many debts and asked for her mother's prayers.[19] It was reported that her marriage with Bohnen cost her $40,000 in severed contracts.[20]

In an undated letter to her mother, probably from the early 1930s, Mary reported having had a tumor the size of a golf ball removed from her uterus.[21] It will always remain unknown if the tumor was caused by the earlier unwitting radiation she received wearing the dress and hat dipped in radium in the Ziegfeld *Follies of 1922*.

She appeared that fall, 1930, at the RKO-Keith Palace Theatre in New York during the week of November 22. It was billed as "Vaudeville

Debut of the Famous American Soprano, Late of the Metropolitan Opera Company." Although other acts were in the show, Mary's picture was on the cover of the program booklet. The biographical insert compared her life with her foster father with that of Charles Dicken's Mr. Murdstone. Anna's reputation as a foster mother had suffered earlier as being of the same pattern as the missionary's wife in "Rain." Following Mary's list of accomplishments in the Palace program, she is described as having "fifteen operas in her repertoire, speaks four languages and is justly considered to be one of the foremost sopranos of the day."[22]

Earlier one of Anna's neighbors, Mrs. Walter Terry, spoke out in defense of Rev. William and Anna Fitch. She wrote to the *Time Magazine*: "Under the heading Music in your issue of April 5, 1926, I read with eye-protruding astonishment the article 'In Little Rock' in which you grossly misstate the true manner of our Mary Lewis's departure from the City of Roses. Mary was no abused Annie washing pots and pans for the good parson and his wife—for she had been a matron of some odd years...Mrs. Fitch is a neighbor of mine and a wonderful character. Even Mary agrees with that... I wish the editors had time to investigate before they print these seemingly innocent articles, or that someone had got Mary's opinion and not written as if Mrs. Fitch were the cruel god mother...when she is the kind of grandmother one dreams about...tending her lilac bushes and baby chickens and her business. Please do not print any more articles making her a feminine Simon Legree [the harsh overseer in Uncle Tom's Cabin by Harriet Beecher Stowe]." The editor printed a rebuttal that "if unfair the wrong must be righted but Mary Lewis herself said she was spanked by Mr. Fitch if she did not practice her music enough to suit him and I would dance by myself in my room. My foster mother would punish me every time she caught me at it and I was continually at it."[23]

She appeared in a recital at Town Hall, 113 West 43rd Street in New York, January 29, 1931, accompanied by the faithful Ellmer Zoller at the piano. No further information is available.[24]

Mary retreated to her beloved Europe the following summer and wrote to her mother from Paris, "I have nearly worried to death since I came over here about work, the same as in America. It certainly has been one tough year and a half for me." She expressed her hope to get a role in an operetta, but said, "I feel never sure of anything now," echoing the other Depression-stricken unemployed.[25]

She did succeed in landing the title role in an operetta, *La Comtesse Maritza*, and was the only American in the cast of 125. The operetta was a French-language version of Emmerich Kálmán's *Die Grafin Maritza* (Countess Maritza). The operetta was arranged by Max Eddy and Jean Marietta. Her debut in the Viennese operetta in Paris at the Theater Ambassadeur was on May 9, 1931. A United Press release the following day reported that the first night audience was enthusiastic upon hearing the operetta sung entirely in French. The cast was accompanied by a Gypsy orchestra playing on stage while a select group of Paris musicians served in the pit.[26]

"I love being the Countess Maritza!" Mary Lewis told the press, "And something tells me that my reviving comic opera in Paris is going to be the best job I have ever done in my life." She said she was as excited as when she sang her first opera. Her French accent was pronounced perfect by the critics and her theatrics were considered unusual.[27]

Alexander Kahn, her former manager, said, "Miss Lewis is the most human actress on the stage today. Her stage and theatrical intelligence is remarkable and she is going to be the toast of Paris—mark my word."[28]

The operetta was set in Hungary in a contemporary period. Mary, cast as the beautiful, rich, and forceful Countess Maritza, is sought after by many suitors. To discourage them, she invents a ruse by throwing a gala affair to announce her engagement to a fictional Baron Koloman Zsupan. To her dismay, a man of that name turns up. To save face, Maritza has to acknowledge him as her fiancé. The plot thickens as Maritza falls in love with her bailiff, who, in reality is an impoverished, handsome count, Tassilo Endrödy-Wittemburg. He is a Viennese who has taken the job as bailiff in order to raise a dowry for his sister, Lisa.[29]

While Tassilo is trying to persuade the Countess Maritza to take an interest in the business affairs of her estate, she plays at flirting with him and he declares his love for her. Maritza finds a letter, written by Tassilo to a friend, telling of his intention of raising money. Thinking he is marrying her for her money, Maritza sends him away just as Tassilo's rich aunt arrives to offer him money. All ends well because Maritza had written a proposal of marriage in her "letter of reference" when she dismissed the servant. The cast, wearing traditional Balkan costume, cavort on stage to the Gypsy music played by the band on stage. "Come Gypsy, Play Gypsy" is an English language version of one of the favorites from the score.[30]

Probably while on tour with the production Mary sent Anna a postcard in June: "Just a line to say hello from Czechoslovakia! I hope you are in good health and spirts. Love, Mary Lewis.[31]

The next report of Mary was, as usual, the unusual. In the throes of a world-wide depression, she snagged herself a millionaire![32]

Endnotes Chapter 14 Hollywood

1. Fitch scrapbooks.
2. Frances Calhoun, "Snaring Song Bird," May 1930, p. 27. Also clipping, n.p., 28 Feb. 1930, Lewis file, New York Public Library.
3. Ibid.
4. Clipping, n.p., 12 April 1930, Lewis file, New York Public Library.
5. Gladys Hall, "She Obeyed That Impulse," *Motion Picture*, n.p., n.d., p. 111.
6. Calhoun, "Snaring Song Bird," p. 30.
7. Wentworth, "Ugly Duckling," *Screenland*, July 1930.
8. Ibid.
9. Clipping, n.p., 12 April 1930, Lewis file, New York Public Library.
10. John C. Sicignano, Nutley, New Jersey, 12 Feb. 1975, to Dougan, provided in notes from Dougan to author; *Metropolitan Opera Annals*, p. 516.
11. Ibid.
12. *New York Times*, 25 Feb. 1931, p 28.
13. Ibid.
14. Ibid.
15. Ibid., 7 May 1930, p 24.
16. Oral interview, Mildred Fitch, 1983.
17. Fitch scrapbooks.
18. Dougan, "Enigma," p. 276. *New York Times* 15 Feb. 1931, Lewis file, New York Public Library.
19. Ibid.
20. Clipping, n.p., 12 April 1930, Lewis file, New York Public Library.
21. Dougan, "Enigma," p. 278.
22. Fitch scrapbooks. RKO-Keith Palace program, p. 4.
23. Mary Lewis's scrapbooks #2, courtesy of Holdridge. *Time Magazine*, Cleveland, Ohio, 26 April, 1926.
24. Cover of program only, research New York Public Library.
25. Dougan, "Enigma," p. 276.

26. Mary Knight, United Press Correspondent, Paris, 8 May 1931, published 10 May 1931, Little Rock, unidentified, Fitch scrapbooks.
27. Ibid.
28. Ibid.
29. Drinkrow, *Operetta Book*, pp. 35-37.
30. Ibid.
31. Fitch scrapbooks.
32. *Chicago Tribune*, 18 Sept. 1931, Fitch scrapbooks.

Mary Lewis, Opera Star, at her home in Hollywood, where she is preparing for her debut in the talkies. Photo by Russell Ball, Fitch album.

The Victor Talking Machine Company advertised "Possessing youth, beauty, a personality that is dazzling in its radiance, in addition to a voice of unusual loveliness and brilliance, Mary Lewis is a splendid example of what pluck and determination can accomplish." Her profile appeared in the May 1930 issue of *Cinema*. Fitch album.

Mary Lewis's career took a new turn when she was signed by Pathé as the latest singing sensation of the silver screen. The caption says, "...we just want to tell you that Mary is not only a beauty and a singer—she's a real girl whose sense of humor and perspective have not been warped by success." Photo by Russell Ball, unidentified source, Fitch album.

15

Sailing

As Mary entered into a new chapter of her life, she also entered wholeheartedly in playing the celebrity game of "Hide-and-Go-Seek" with reporters. On September 18, 1931, a special release reported Mary Lewis had been the secret bride for several days of Robert L. Hague, a vice president of Standard Oil Company. Just when or where the marriage took place was a secret until the news was divulged unwittingly by Miss M. Gallagher, the singer's secretary and companion. Miss Gallagher became flustered when she realized she had made a slip. "Nobody is supposed to know it," she said, "It was to be a dark secret."[1]

Another dark secret was Hague's divorce from his third spouse, Edith Bobe, which had been made public only in March releasing information undisclosed for twenty-nine months.[2]

A September 19 Associated Press report disclosed Miss Lewis and Hague had left New York the previous night for marriage in Maine, accompanied by Hague's brother, Cuthbert. This report was correct—the marriage took place in Portland, Maine, on September 19.[3]

Just where, why, and when the romance commenced, culminating in marriage, remains a secret. It is certain they were acquainted for many years since Hague was well known in the world of the theater and was a friend of many actors and actresses; in fact, on holidays, he held an open house for unemployed thespians. He contributed to every charity connected with the stage.[4]

Hague definitely had been acquainted with Mary Lewis, whose star had shown so brightly on the New York stage. They shared a mutual background. Hague was the son of an Episcopal rector, Rev. Henry Hague, and his wife, Harriet. He was born in Lincoln, Rhode Island, March 2, 1880. As a young man, he enrolled at Worcester Polytechnic Institute, but he left without completing his term and ran away to sea where he shipped first as an apprentice on a fishing vessel sailing from Gloucester to the Grand Banks. After a rough experience on small boats, he signed on the four-masted bark, the *Susquehanna*, which sailed between Philadelphia and Japan.[5]

Realizing sails could not compete against steam, he left the sea, learning the machinist's trade in the Worcester plant of a subsidiary of American Steel and Wire Company. He tried his hand as a fireman on a railroad, graduating to a locomotive engineer with the New York, New Haven and Hartford line.[6]

In 1904 he again answered the call of the sea and signed on as an oiler on an American Hawaiian Company ship and he rapidly rose to an engineer and assistant superintendent in charge of construction for this line. In 1909 he was tapped to become assistant superintending engineer for the Standard Oil of California where he advanced to marine superintendent in charge of all operations designing construction.[7]

When the United States entered into World War I he was drafted by the United States Shipping Board as director of construction and repairs on the Pacific Coast. He was later summoned to Washington to take complete charge of repairs to Shipping Board vessels, and, along with the assignment, he directed the reconditioning of captured German ships to be used for the allied cause.[8]

Following the armistice, Hague joined the Standard Oil Company of New Jersey where he soon was named manager of the marine department. As the big company reorganized, Hague was made vice president in 1927 of the Standard Shipping Company. During his association with the New Jersey company, the number of tankers increased from eighty-one to 205 and tonnage from 897,000 to 2,150,000.[9]

He was well known on Broadway since his company's headquarters was located at 26 Broadway in 1927. His humor was appreciated by a list of celebrities including Jimmy Walker, Victor Moore, Oscar Shaw, William Gaxton, George Cohan, David Warfield, and virtually every other boulevardier in New York City.[10]

And it was well known he had a fondness of the opposite sex, especially the beautiful ones. He possessed millions and spent like a sailor on shore leave. He staked actors at liberty, backed shows for actresses, poured champagne at parties, and was the most jovial member of more than ten clubs.[11]

On Broadway it was known he was the man who saved "The Lambs," having reorganized the club and contributed generously to enable it to survive the Depression years.[12] "The Lambs," primarily a supper club, accepted for membership only men of the theater except for some outside members like Hague. For their own benefit, the "Lambs" staged an annual review called, "The Lambs Gambol." The club, formed in 1874, finally succumbed one hundred years after its founding.[13]

For all of his accomplishments he was best known as, "Hague, the husband of Edith Bobe, a modiste [a designer of women's fashions] who was a victim with her in a sensational jewel robbery in her apartment in 1924." Any reference to Hague includes this identifying tag, said, more or less, in one breath. The front pages of the press in 1924 heralded the story how Hague was escorting a very pretty modiste, Edith Bobe, to her home at 168 East 63rd Street. On the spring midnight eve, the pair was stopped in her vestibule by a masked gunman who demanded their valuables. Bobe stepped between the robber and Hague and exclaimed, "Take all I have but don't shoot him!" Hague was then struck senseless from the rear by an accomplice. The masked men took jewelry valued at $100,000 from Edith's fingers and throat and were never apprehended. Hague later made his third try at matrimony with Bobe.[14]

His first two wives were hidden in obscurity much like Mary's first marriage. One was Mrs. Alba Kneeland Hague of California and the other was Mrs. Stella Ritchie Hague, who received $500 a month in alimony.[15]

A dapper Hague and a svelte Mary are captured on Associated Press film as they reached Los Angeles on "their operatic honeymoon." Their marriage was announced to friends and family on oversized nautical Christmas cards. They wished "A Boat-load of Christmas Cheer for you and a Happy Cruise in '32." Hague is cartooned rowing a boat equipped with a barrel of oil and a tiny Christmas tree. The pirate's parrot quips, "A sailor's wife a sailor's 'star' should be! Yo Ho, Oh Oh," while the gulls echo, "He's moored at last and furled his sails," and "No danger now from wreck or whale." Mary is a musical anchor while the gull overhead calls out, "Shiver me timber, the skipper's got a singin' anchor!"[16]

As the wife of the shipping millionaire, Mary Lewis withdrew from the stage and sang only occasionally for friends. Listed in the *Who's*

Who in America in 1932-33, Mary Lewis gives recognition only to her last two marriages and is said to have been the daughter of Joseph Lewis and Hattie (Lewis) Kidd. By adopting her brother's name with Lewis, Mary conveniently satisfies her lineage, protective of the privacy of her early years. Her education is simply listed as "private [Anna's and William's] and public schools, Little Rock, including three years of high school."[17] Mary went sailing off to see the world.

Endnotes Chapter 15 Sailing

1. *Chicago Tribune*, n.d., wire from New York, 18 Sept. 1931, Fitch scrapbooks.
2. Ibid.
3. Clipping, n.p., n.d., Fitch scrapbooks.
4. *New York Times*, 9 Sept. 1939, Lewis file, New York Public Library.
5. Ibid.
6. Ibid.
7. Ibid.
8. Ibid.
9. Ibid.
10. Rob Roberts, n.p., n.d., Fitch scrapbooks.
11. Ibid.
12. *New York Times*, 9 Sept. 1939.
13. "The Lambs," *Notable Names in the American Theatre*, (James T. White & Co., 1976). Research by New York Public Library.
14. Roberts, Fitch scrapbooks.
15. Ibid.
16. Fitch scrapbooks.
17. *Who's Who in America in 1932-33*, p. 1413.

Mary Lewis and Robert L. Hague, a vice president of Standard Oil, captured the attention of a world torn by economic depression when the pair slipped away for a secret marriage and honeymoon in 1931. Associated Press, unidentified clipping, Fitch album

The surprise marriage announcement to friends and family was an oversized nautical Christmas card. Fitch album.

16

The Rich and The Poor

Anna received acclaim as "Mary Lewis' Foster Mother" as she celebrated her eighty-fifth birthday. "Friends from all parts of the city came to see her, bringing gifts and offering their congratulations" reported the Sunday, November 22, 1931, Little Rock papers. "'Cards [were received] wishing a happy birthday and many of them came from friends far and near. I don't know how so many people knew it was my birthday,' Anna smiled. There were baskets of flowers in all the rooms of the little bungalow and other presents—books, candy and fruit, and a great birthday cake, with icing shaped in the figure '85.'"[1]

After mentioning some facts about the late Reverend Fitch, the story gave a sketchy background of the Fitches' travels and told how they had taken into their home the little girl, Mary, whom Anna personally taught. Anna seems to have been rather stern with the *Arkansas Democrat* reporter: "Mrs. Fitch said she hoped the reporter would get everything right in the story, because, she said, someone writing about Miss Lewis some time back gave the impression that Miss Lewis' home life with the Fitches had not been happy." Then Anna showed the reporter where her "budding diva grew to young womanhood" under Anna's watchful eye.[2]

The reporter continued: "All the time that Mary lived at their home, the young girl was kept constantly at her music and elocution lessons. Mrs. Fitch attended to the academic education until it was time for Mary to enter high school. She and the little girl had been affectionate companions as a mother and daughter," the report continued. "As proof of their friendly relations, which still exist, she proudly displayed letters and postcards from the noted soprano."[3] One was the card Miss Lewis sent from Czechoslovakia. At the conclusion of the interview, Anna had her picture taken standing in front of the holly tree which Mary had found in Judsonia and brought with her to their new home on the bluff in Little Rock. There were three separate stories concerning Anna's birthday.[4]

Mary and her new husband seem to have left no trail during the year of 1932. The country was being buffeted by the financial storm which threatened to capsize its economic structure. One out of four workers was unemployed. The banks were closing, gulping down the savings of depositors, and the United States treasury was bankrupt. A tidal wave of terror was flooding over the country. Everyone was suffering—farms were being foreclosed, workers had no work, and there were few to support the businesses. The pensioned, like Anna, watched their savings disappear. On March 4, 1933, Franklin Delano Roosevelt was inaugurated as president and asked for executive power to fight the foe. While the republic rallied behind his leadership, Anna watched and wrote her cynical comments on current events.

Mary returned to radio broadcast over WMCA in New York on June 7, 1933. The seasoned performer completed her broadcast, although in great pain, and, as soon as it was over, was rushed from the studio to the hospital for an emergency appendectomy.[5]

One headline in August 1933 read: "Mary Lewis' New Hat Aids Trade Recovery." Interviewed by Amy Porter, Mary is said not to know much about economics, but is right when she says her new pink chiffon garden party hat with blue roses is going to aid in the recovery of this country." While this may sound like a great many garden party hats, Mary made it seem reasonable when she explained, "This hat was designed by an American designer and made right here in New York. So the money I paid for it stays in this country and will help pay wages of salesgirls, sewing girls and pay the textile manufacturer whose work produced the hat. Surely that is good for American business. Besides it's a prettier hat than I could get in France."[6]

Mary went on to say she considered it "the patriotic duty of all American women, especially those with money to spend, to buy their clothes in this country instead of in Paris or London or any foreign place." The article continued: "She does not buy even a pair of silk stockings abroad, unless, of course, all the old ones break into runs and she is stranded stockingless in Paris and cannot wait for a boat to arrive with the American product. Well, anyway, she buys nothing or nearly so in Paris although she is in and out of the pleasant city at least twice a year. In fact, she just returned from there with her husband."[7]

When asked what new Fall creations she brought back from Paris, Mary answered, "My Fall creations will be created right here, just as my Summer things were. And let me tell you there are more reasons than one for my preference for American clothes." The reasons were: "Because American clothes are cheaper than French, with the dollar pumping around and other financial bewilderments; American stores are more efficient and speedy in serving their customers; American clothes suit the American woman better than French clothes."[8]

Mary claimed, "It is a wonderful experience after you have been foolish enough to buy clothes in Europe, to walk into New York store and walk out with a new dress on, because if you are a very special customer in France and lucky, you may get a dress made to fit you in ten days." Mary expressed hope American women appreciate their own stores. "If we American women are the best dressed in the world, as we claim, we have only our own fine stores to thank, and so when we get a little money to spend on clothes, we should not chase ungratefully across the water to spend it." And Mary made a very pretty picture model for her American wardrobe.[9]

It was said Mary had half-a-million dollars in diamonds.[10]

Before the Christmas holidays, Mary appeared in a fund-raising concert for St. Benedict the Moor, a mission church, on December 17, 1933. Hague was known for having many years undertaken the presentation of a revue in Hoboken at the Majestic Theater turning over the gross proceeds to a mission Catholic church in one of the poorer sections of the city. It was the first church north of the Mason and Dixie line for black Catholics. Irish colleen Mary appeared with John McCormack, the popular Irish tenor, who was virtually a cultural institution during the preceding two decades. McCormack had a superbly flexible voice, amazing breath control, and beautiful enunciation.[11] The concert raised $10,000.[12]

A re-debut was announced upon Mary's recital at Town Hall on May 18, 1934, during which she combined selections in French and German Lieder. She also sang "The Sleep That Flits on Baby's Eyes" by John Alden Carpenter, Frédéric Chopin's "Lithuanian Song," and "Romance" from von Weber's *Preciosa*.[13] Included were two works new to New York, "Wiegenlied" from Franz Schreker's *Der Schalzgraber* and "Kirchenscene" (Church Scene) from Goethe's *Faust* by Jerome D. Bohm, who arranged the piece. He also was the accompanist. Bohm was of the New York *Herald Tribune* music criticism staff.[14]

According to reviewer F.D.P. [Perkins of the *Herald Tribune*]: "The occasion might have been regarded as a virtual re-debut, Miss Lewis having made few public appearances here since her departure from the Metropolitan Opera Company. Nor had she ever given in New York a performance of the vocal quality and interpretive capacity shown yesterday afternoon. The program was not of the type chosen by an opera singer making a temporary excursion into the concert field, but one calling for interpretative skill of a non-operatic type, an ability to sing concert music of many styles, periods and moods.... The concert suggested that Miss Lewis' vocal career has entered auspiciously a new phase which could lead to artistic attainments beyond those of her Metropolitan days." He continued, "As she gained in confidence she showed increasing ability to set forth a long, unbroken vocal line and project highnotes marked by clarity and smoothness."[15]

F.D.P. summarized among the best were songs such as Wolf's whimsical "Storchenbotshaft" and the Chopin work calling for lightness of touch and delicacy of coloring.[16]

D.H.H. of the *New York Times* stated: "The voice was still basically the same. The top notes were still shrill, the upper register brilliant, and her mezza-voce singing, displayed the slightly eerie and almost unearthly timbre that one associates with that of a fine boy soprano." The audience showered Mary Lewis with floral offerings and warm applause and she was called back for several encores.[17]

Mary then dropped almost out of sight for a year. A brief glimpse is caught by a Little Rock reporter on September 17, 1935: "Succeeding in her efforts to dodge publicity Mrs. Robert Hague, the former Mary Lewis, former opera singer, boarded an eastbound American Airlines plane here this morning en route to New York. Accompanying the former opera singer was Jack Kidd, her 17 year old nephew of Chicago and a man giving his name as Elmo [Ellmer, the Faithful] Zoller." Joe Kidd had departed from Little Rock for Chicago the previous day.[18]

Mary had arrived by plane Saturday from New York, having just returned from her second trip to Europe since Christmas and had flown down for a visit with her mother, Hattie Maynard of Little Rock, who was taking a course of baths at Hot Springs. A reporter concluded: "Since her marriage several years ago to Robert Hague of New York and retirement from opera, the former opera singer has shown a violent dislike to the publicity spotlight that played upon her so successfully during her career."[19]

Although not performing professionally, Mary Lewis was still kept busy performing in and supporting benefit events. On October 16, 1935, Mary and Hague were hosts for dinner for the artists cooperating in the interest to help save the Brooklyn Academy of Music. The event was held in their home at the Ritz Tower, 465 Park Avenue. Among the fifty-two guests were Zoller, Mr. and Mrs. Jack Adams [her former manager], and more than twenty famous stars of the Metropolitan Opera Company along with noted figures of the concert, stage, and lecture platform. The planning meeting was followed by a dance.[20]

For the benefit held at the Opera House of Brooklyn Academy of Music, October 22, Mary Lewis sang "Sortita d'Ofelia" from *Amleto* (*Hamlet*) by Franco Faccio[21], a little known 19th century opera, and in a quartet singing from *Rigoletto*, the only known time in concert, Mary sang in the famous quartet. Attendance figures were 1,827. The artists were entertained following the program at the Hotel Granada, which was described as "long" by an unidentified clipping. The report continued: "How could the dear public wait? (Who wouldn't wait to hear the glorious voice of a Mary Lewis—the voice that has a way of crystalizing dreams and by its lovely human quality almost brings tears to the eyes?)" Photos of Mary Lewis were featured in many of the newspaper accounts.[22]

On November 10, 1935, came this announcement: "Rumor Mary Lewis has husband's permission to resume her career and is interested in radio."[23] At a concert that day featuring Rafaelo Diaz at the Waldorf-Astoria, Mary responded to requests to sing and it was reported she "warbled like an angel and loud and long were the cheers" for the singer formerly of the Met and now wife of a millionaire.[24] Diaz, a light tenor, sang with the Metropolitan Opera from 1917-25 and 1926-30.

Mary Lewis sang over radio WYNC in a November 11, 1935, program honoring Joyce Kilmer, the poet and newspaper reporter who was killed in France in 1918. Mary recited: "I think that I shall never see, a poem as lovely as a tree." Then she sang, "Trees," the musical adaptation of the well-known poem written by Kilmer. Mary Lewis sang another selection (not identified) to close the broadcast.[25]

On November 17 Mary Lewis sang on a radio broadcast WMCA for the 11th annual dinner and ball for the Brooklyn Federation of Jewish Charities at Hotel St. George with over 2,000 attending. Among her numbers were "Eli, Eli." She was helped to learn the Hebrew number by a cantor, who was a Presbyterian. Prior to the broadcast a dress rehearsal of the musicians was held at the Hague home in the Ritz Towers, admission by invitation only.[26]

Also during November Mary sang at a Musicale at the Hotel Plaza and Mary and Hague were hosts for a dinner in honor of the 85th birthday of Mother Hague. On November 17 Mary sang on a radio broadcast WMCA for the 11th annual dinner and ball for the Brooklyn Federation of Jewish Charities at Hotel St. George. Two thousand persons attended. Milton Berle was also on the billing.[27]

The Hagues were guests at a reception and dance on the Starlight Roof of the Waldorf-Astoria, sponsored by the American Merchant Marine Conference Committee. Mary Lewis was vice-chairman of a Benefit Bridge Supper and Dance at the Plaza for the benefit of the Catholic Actors Guild. Mary was guest at a reception and ball by the Board of Directors of Radio Personalities. On November 24, Thanksgiving Eve, she sang at Fabian's Fox Theater for the benefit of the American Christmas Fund and Relief. As Mrs. Hague she received a thank you for sponsoring a boy into the Gramercy Boys' Club. She also received a number of requests for benefit performances.[28]

On December 9 Mary and husband Hague enjoyed an evening on opening night at the Metropolitan Opera, sharing their box with former Mayor Jimmy Walker and his wife and Zoe Atkins, the playwright and poet. On January 8, 1936, the Hagues were hosts for a reception at their home in the Ritz Towers for Atkins, whose new play, "O Evening Star," had premiered at the Empire Theater. Guests included the "handsome" Grand Duchess Marie, Ina Clair (of the Met), Elsa Maxwell, and Dorothy Parker, "gossip" columnists.[29]

At the end of the year Mary received a cable from London from Hague wishing her "Happy Birthday" although he was not sure of the correct date. She also received a card from Mother Hague, also not sure of the date.

On January 22, 1936, Mary Lewis accompanied herself on a hurdy-gurdy organ at the Virginia Day Nursery on 5th Street. The itinerant street musicians had been banned from the streets by New York Mayor Fiorello La Guardia.[30] Mary petitioned the Mayor to reconsider his decision. She sang simple Italian folk songs to the delight of the children. Mary said she wanted the children "to hear the instrument that brought music and joy into my life when I was a child. I learned to sing and to dance to it. Now children may grow up and never hear one." She said it was the tunes of the hurdy-gurdy that inspired her to a musical career. There were requests for songs from the children except for one little girl who was coaxed to speak up and say what she wanted. Loudly she said, "Please, Miss, I'd like the pearls on your dress."[31]

Also on January 29 Mary Lewis was interviewed during a radio broadcast on WABC. According to the script Mary was asked, "How did you happen to take up the side of the hurdy-gurdy against Mayor La Guardia's campaign to banish them?" She replied, "I think the hurdy-gurdy belongs to the sidewalks of New York or any big city." She explained that in seeing the delight of the children in the Day Nursery on the lower East Side reminded her of her own "woe-begone childhood."

The interviewer said, "It's difficult to imagine you—with your life of glamor—wealth—and success—ever having a childhood of stress." Mary replied "Oh, but I did! And until I was taken—a bedraggled and undernourished little waif—and adopted by a minister and his wife—the only highlights of childish fun I remember were dancing and singing in the streets to the tune of the hurdy-gurdy."

> Interviewer: 'The story of your phenomenal career certainly rivals the most glamourous Cinderella tale. I remember the sensation when you stepped from the *Follies* to the Metropolitan Opera—how long did it take you to achieve that?'
>
> Mary: 'It took me two and a half years to make that trip from 42nd Street to 40th Street! But, you know I had been singing in public from the age of eight—and had always continued my studies in piano, violin, and the pipe organ.'
>
> Interviewer: 'Did you study for opera over here?'

> Mary: 'Oh yes, I took a singing lesson every day while I was in the *Ziegfeld Follies*—besides studying operatic scores—Italian and French—then I made the big decision to give up my good job as a Ziegfeld prima donna—to go to Italy and starve while I studied music.'
>
> Interviewer: 'And what did Mr. Ziegfeld say about that?'
>
> Mary: 'At first he didn't think I was serious. But when I convinced him—he wished me good luck—So I dashed for Europe—studied and—starved—and sang in every place in Europe I had a chance to—Vienna, Paris, London, Monte Carlo. I came back determined to get an audition with Gatti-Cazazza at the Metropolitan.'
>
> Interviewer: 'The rest is history—I remember your debut at the Met—the front page stories—the accounts of your brilliant success! And now—that you have completed the dream of every Cinderella—by marrying a millionaire husband—how to you enjoy life without the excitement of the public?'

Mary explained while she had been enjoying housewifely duties she remained convinced that her path lay in her music and she expected to be back in public life through the radio.[32]

The following day, January 30, 1936, Mary was one of more than 5,000,000 men and women, from coast to coast, who would attend some 6,000 celebrations in honor of President Franklin Roosevelt's 54th birthday. These benefits were a nationwide marathon effort to raise funds to help with the treatment of those afflicted with the same contagious disease which had partially paralyzed young Roosevelt before his election as president. Mary assisted with planning the party presented by Rafaelo Diaz at the Central Park Casino. Diaz was Master of Ceremonies. Mary opened the program singing "My Man's Gone Now" from the American opera *Porgy and Bess* with the composer, George Gershwin, at the piano. Gershwin wrote many great musical works based on the rhythms, melodies, and moods of American popular music. *Porgy and Bess* (1935), his largest work, was the first truly American opera based on the tragedies and the great musical contributions of the America's blacks depicted in a setting near Charleston, South Carolina.[33]

Also singing at the President's Birthday Ball benefit was Joseph Lapima, a young baritone, who also suffered from the effects of polio. He was a protégée of Mary Lewis.[34]

Mary again sang the Gershwin number with the Vincent Lopez orchestra on February 4 for the benefit for United Order of True Sisters at the Hotel Biltmore. The busy social schedule continued with an invitation as guest at the Launching Stand for the tanker, "T.C. McCobb," at the Federal Shipbuilding and Dry Dock Co. at Kearny, New Jersey. She sang on February 10 for the benefit for the Catholic Actors Guild.[35]

The following day she entered half a dozen Dachshunds at the Westminster Kennel Club Show at Madison Square Garden. "All German dogs," she said, "with Irish names, Paddy and his sister Biddy Bye and that fresh Peter who hails from Hamburg." Paddy and Biddy Bye were well behaved. Besides caring for her dogs, Mary was said to ride well, swim well, and pilot her own motor boat.[36]

One of the more delightful requests Mary Lewis fulfilled was as judge at a yodeling contest sponsored by the Children's Welfare Federation. The winner was to appear in a performance of *Heidi*, one of the plays presented for the benefit of the Federation. One contestant was aided by the lack of his two front teeth which allowed the yodel to go round and round without obstruction; one contestant would eat a Swiss cheese sandwich but never saw the Alps; and one was so overcome by stage fright he couldn't produce a sound but entertained with some plain and fancy giggling.[37]

Mary Lewis Hague headed up the women's committee in planning and presenting a benefit on February 19 at the Ritz-Carlton for the Adventure Society, a group formed to stimulate an increasing interest in travel, exploration, and adventure. The benefit was a dinner and a diamond fashion show featuring the "Star of Kimberly" diamond. The program was followed by a preview of the Gaumont-British picture, "Rhodes—The Empire Builder." The picture depicted the life of statesman, businessman, and adventurer Cecil Rhodes, for whom Rhodesia (now Zimbabwe) was named. The country in Africa was the site of the world's greatest diamond fields.[38]

Besides the many benefit performances, the days and evenings were filled with social events with friends and acquaintances whose names were well-known and well-publicized.

One journalist of the period wrote, "Golden best describes Mary...her hair...the sheen of her glowing skin, her generous nature and the voice that pours forth its richness so warmly."[39]

Endnotes Chapter 16 The Rich and The Poor

1. *Arkansas Democrat*, 22 Nov. 1931.
2. Ibid.
3. Ibid.
4. Fitch scrapbooks.
5. Lewis file, New York Public Library. Clipping, n.p., 1933.
6. *Chicago Herald*, 1993, wire from New York, Fitch scrapbooks.
7. Ibid.
8. Ibid.
9. Ibid.
10. Clipping, n.p., n.d., Lewis Papers. Cited by Dougan, *Enigma*, p. 276.
11. Dizikes, John. *Opera In America - A Cultural History*. (New Haven, Connecticut and London: Yale University Press, 1993), p. 334.
12. *New York Times* 17 Dec. 1933, sec. IX, p. 8, 18 Dec. 1933, p. 24.
13. Clipping, n.p., 19 Mar. 1934, Lewis file, New York Public Library.
14. Clipping, n.p., 19 Mar. 1934, Lewis file, New York Public Library. *The Musician*, March 1931.
15. Ibid.
16. Ibid.
17. *New York Times*, 18 March 1934, sec. IX, p. 5, 19 March 1934.
18. Clipping, n.p., 17 Sept. 1935, Fitch scrapbooks.
19. Ibid.
20. Mary Lewis's scrapbooks #3, courtesy Holdridge. Numerous newspaper clippings and typed guest list.
21. Faccio, Franco, (1840-1891), an Italian conductor and composer.
22. Mary Lewis's scrapbooks #3, courtesy Holdridge.
23. Ibid. New York *American*, 10 Nov. 1935 and other clippings from Nebraska, Michigan, Wisconsin, Indiana, Massachusetts, and Washington, and New York.
24. Ibid. *Daily Mirror*, 12 Nov. 1935.
25. Ibid. *New York Times*, 12 Nov. 1935; typed copy of radio script, Bozeman Bugler Post 1955, Veterans of Foreign Ward of the United States, Inc.
26. Ibid. *Brooklyn Daily Eagle*, New York, 12 Nov. 1935.
27. Ibid. Three pages of clippings.
28. Ibid. Clippings.
29. Ibid.

30. La Guardia, Fiorella Henry, (1882-1947), gained national recognition serving as mayor of New York City from 1933-1945. He was a reformer, with a program including park and street development and slum clearance.

31. Mary Lewis's scrapbooks #3, courtesy Holdridge. *New York Sun*, 22 Jan., 1936; *New York World-Telegram*, 22 Jan. 1936; *New York Times*, 23 Jan. 1936.

32. Ibid. Typewritten script.

33. Ibid..

34. Ibid. *Birthday Ball Magazine*; *New York American*, 30 Jan. 1936.

35. Ibid. Clippings.

36. Ibid.

37. Ibid. *New York Times*, 18 Feb. 1936; *New York American*, 19 Feb. 1935.

38. Ibid. *New York Herald Tribune*. 16 Feb. 1936.

39. Ibid., n.d., n.p.

Anna Fitch in her garden at Little Rock, circa 1926. Fitch album.

Mary Lewis returned to Arkansas and is pictured at her alma mater, Little Rock High School. Fitch album.

17

Anna

A grass roots reaction to the Great Depression can be picked up from a series of weekly letters written by Anna to her son. By 1933, Anna was an octogenarian, and her son, Rev. Frank F. Fitch, 60, served as pastor of a small Presbyterian church in Earlville, Illinois.

Anna's letters read like a mini-newspaper—world, national, and local news, a weather and crop report, some human interest, and always, a scathing editorial comment. For her Sunday afternoon publication to her son, she spent the week sifting through more newspapers than most people read in a year. She received, either through subscription or gift, Little Rock's *Arkansas Democrat* and *Arkansas Gazette*, the Pulaski *Free Press*, three papers from Washington, D.C., and later another one, Anna described as an "immense" paper called *United States News*, and a Boston subscription sent by her son. She also scanned the weekly Earlville *Leader* to keep up with her son's activities. He worked for awhile as the *Leader's* editor, but Anna disapproved of his attempt to combine two jobs.[1]

Other publications she depended on were the *Literary Digest*, *The Forum*, *The Pathfinder*, *The Christian Advocate*, *Newsweek*, and one she liked very much, the *Reader's Digest*. Anna kept up with old friends through the Ohio Wesleyan Alumni publication, and the *National Geographic* was an expensive treasure shared by a friend.[2]

Clippings arrived daily, sent by her network of correspondents. Anna was a clipper. Some she sent weekly to her son with the instructions, "Read them or burn them." Anna was a fan of Will Rogers who had appeared in the Ziegfeld *Follies* with Mary. Rogers had become popular as a columnist and lecturer, spewing out his Midwestern down-home interpretation of current events. In 1933 Anna pasted Will's column with her own commentary. Rogers wrote concerning the New Deal's alphabet agencies: "The president just created the F.E.R.A. [Federal

Emergency Relief Association], and the A.A.A. [Agricultural Adjustment Administration], and the P.W.A. [Public Works Administration] so the F.E.R.A., the A.A.A. and the P.W.A. are to work in conjunction with N.R.A. with the financial help of the R.F.C., who will pay the C.O.D.'s of the C.C.C. [Civilian Conservation Corps], and take in return for all money loaned out to all these initials, I.O.U.'s. Never was a country in the throes of more capital letters than the old U.S.A., but we still haven't sent out the S.O.S."[3]

In the summer of 1933 Anna predicted: "When Roosevelt gets the 18th Amendment appealed then there will be war."[4] The repeal of Prohibition had been introduced that February and was proclaimed in December. Anna thought of the war fought by the Women's Temperance Union and of its brief victory which lasted from January, 1919, to December, 1933. Needless to say, Roosevelt was not a favorite with the pastor's wife.

On the four-year anniversary of the infamous Wall Street crunch, Anna surmised: "I think the whole world is in a mess and things will get worse before they get better.... They are overhauling the public schools of the state. They need it badly.... The children are kept at every thing under the sun except their books...plays, dancing, making pictures and various other things and when they get through they can't spell." Anna was appalled, "The colleges, Delaware Ohio [Ohio Wesleyan University], among them are hiring the best ball players and promising to pay all their expenses if they will come there and join their crowd." She finished by saying, "Revivals are being held all over the city by the different churches, it's needed badly."[5]

Anna explained, "The people here are doing everything possible to help the poor. Last week they had an election and had everyone who voted to bring a can of something. They got over a thousand cans and lots of money and clothing." Another worry for Anna was her savings were tied up in a bank closing. She wrote, "The Paper says the Bank is going to make us another payment before Christmas," and she assured her son, "I eat well." During the winter she wrote, "I am glad you hear the news over the Radio." Thrifty Anna said, "I'm too poor to have a Radio. I have to get it from the newspapers."[6]

The following spring Anna said, "I see by the paper Roosevelt is going to repair all the houses in the U.S.A. that need it, give everybody a Bath tub and so forth, also see to it that everybody is going to have all the milk they can drink at a reduced price. I suppose he will take over all the cows and have them milked by the government," which was followed with, "I want to know what you are going to do with this place in case of my death, you couldn't sell it as times are now, you couldn't rent it and get your rent, and nobody would have it without a bath tub which I shall never put in. The tearing up of the bathroom would cost a lot of money and the hot water appliances would cost more."[7]

As if the problems weren't bad enough, the weather got into the act: "Read a lot of the drought over most of the country. We had a haze of the dust storms over Kansas. I believe it was a sin to destroy any of the crops when thousands were starving and without decent clothing. Roosevelt better read his Bible!" She was convinced he never did. She reported the Arkansas River the lowest ever known! Then later came the flooding![8] Anna followed with interest the birth of the Social Security System. "If you wait long enough Roosevelt will take care of everybody.... I have read a lot about it, one thing I read was you have to spend it as fast as you get it so as to help business and so forth." She commented, "Glad Illinois is going to take care of the worn out preachers. There are hundreds on the relief roll here."[9]

As Anna read her daily publications, glimpses of happy memories of the faraway places and people she had known flashed before her, as Frank asked her to remember these long ago events. Frank was researching and compiling the family's genealogy.

"Helen Gould, I knew her well, have been at her palatial home," Anna wrote in reference to the daughter of Jay Gould, railroad king of the East. Helen Gould was interested in philanthropic activities, through which Anna became acquainted with her...the giant redwood tree she had seen at the Centennial in Philadelphia and the crowd having a dance on it...recollection of Cape Cod and the dunes and when they crossed Lake Pontchartrain and couldn't see the rails on the track...being awakened at Mt. Dora, Florida, in the middle of the night to watch the opening of rare tropical blooms...the shock of Will Rogers' death. "Can't imagine why he would risk his life in a plane made out of old scrap pieces as the papers said", Anna wrote. She relived the story of Thomas Edison's electric light bulb demonstration...and the gold she carried back to Little Rock to buy the home for William, Mary, and herself... clippings of Mary Lewis... she noted Otto Kahn's death saying, "He helped Mary Lewis get in to the Metropolitan Opera." Anna never said much about Mary.[10]

Along with the fears and bad times, Anna's letters are rich with stories of the charity of Americans, sharing and caring for each other. The elderly widow was never lonely. Her garden abundance was generously distributed. The yard and garden were tended daily by Norah, Anna's colored gardener. As the Depression ate deeper, Anna gave everything she could to "poor starving Norah."[11]

The seasonal changes could be followed by Anna's commentary of her garden. Never having lived in one place long enough to reap a crop, her two lots were her pride and joy. Reports of tulips, hyacinths, spring beauties, jonquils, lilacs, and dogwood gave way to daisies, sweet peas, pinks, verbenas, scarlet salvias, and zinnias, surrounded by covers of crepe myrtle and white layers of dewberry patch. Fall brought blazing mums and roses along with the last of the summer blooms. She wrote, "Most people's homes have nothing but oak trees, of the poorest kind, but my front has a Red Bud from Florida, a sugar Maple from Michigan, a White Oak native, a Red Oak native, and a Holly from Judsonia, Arkansas. It has taken 26 years to grow them.... Norah has been all over the city and he says there's nothing like it on Pulaski Heights." In the lean years Mary's holly was shared with Anna's poor friends. The red-berried twigs were their Christmas trees.[12]

Special attention was showered on the elderly woman on her special days. In 1935 she wrote, "Of course you know I have passed my 89th birthday yesterday. Wish you were here and could see my presents, the dining room table is filled full—fruit cake, candy, grape juice and numerous other things and the table where I am writing is loaded with letters and boxes, don't know what is in them, won't have time to open them today, as I must write letters. I have birthday letters and greeting cards from people I have never heard of who live here. Beside all this, a big party was given for me last Thursday—a long way from here. It was the finest party I ever attended. The table was set in silverware with four large candles about two feet high burning in the center. The dinner had three courses winding up with ice cream and angel cake."[13]

In the spring of 1935, as she was writing to her son, Anna was surprised by "—a rap at the door and I have just received a box nearly four feet long filled with Easter lilies and fern from Mary Lewis. I imagine telegraphed from New York as the flowers came from a florist here. Quite a surprise though she never forgets me at Christmas." Two weeks later she said, "Mary Lewis' lilies are still blooming in the window, the immense bunch was full of buds and they continue to bloom in the water."[14]

That fall she reported, "You will be astounded to know that I have a Radio, haven't got much out of it yet that I cared to hear, will get some sermons today... the neighbors are so worried about me being here alone, they thought the Radio would be company."[15]

And a whole new world opened up for Anna! "This is a wonderful day and age we are living in!" she wrote. The first week she heard sermons over the radio, one by a returned missionary from China, and she was amazed at the collection they received from people who weren't even there! That night she wrote, "This kept me from going to bed at my usual time, which I do not like." She heard the Hallie Sallassie band and a vivid description of a volcano erupting in Hawaii. Her enthusiasm mounted until she discovered the radio was adding to her electric bill and to the heat she must use to keep warm in the living room. She then cut back on her listening until warmer days. Anna's monthly light bill was 90 cents compared to her neighbor's $8 bill. The neighbors were being foreclosed upon as they couldn't collect the rentals due them to pay their own debts.[16] Some sprigs of Mary's holly were sent to Anna's son as a holiday gift. Anna told her son she had received a check from Mary at Christmas and the "usual picture" from her husband.[17]

A clipping concerning Mary was sent to Frank in January, 1936. Anna explained that she had received the clipping from someone she didn't know from St. Louis. She wrote, "I guess everyone who has heard of Mary Lewis has heard of me." Mary was pictured at the piano accompanying a young man on crutches. Joseph Lapima, nineteen, was the son of a poor Brooklyn tailor, and was a victim of infantile paralysis. He was "singing the blues away" because, sponsored by Mary Lewis, he was to realize a life-time ambition to sing at the birthday ball in honor of President Roosevelt. The article explained that thousands of other crippled children would benefit by this and other parties for the president on his January 30th birthday.[18]

The National Broadcasting Company in New York announced on March 3, 1936, "Mary Lewis, Metropolitan Opera star who retired from public life shortly after her marriage to Robert L. Hague, vice president of the Standard Oil Company, in 1931, will return to the world of music as guest soloist with Ben Bernie and All the Lads on the American Can Company program Tuesday, March 10 at 9:00 p.m. E.S.T. over an NBC-WJZ network."[19]

The release reported that the prima donna had been busy "unlearning her operatic technique to be heard in an unusual combination of modern rhythm and classic musicianship." Mary was to sing "I'm Shooting High" and "If I Should Lose You" from *Rose of the Rancho*. Also on the program was a sports round table discussion conducted by Ben Bernie, with the group sitting in the shade of the Miami palms.[20]

For Mary's trip down to Miami, she chose an unusual mode of travel. Lockheed Aircraft Corporation had just built the first pressurized cabin planes, and Mary chartered the Eastern Airliner *Florida Flyer* in an attempt to break the flight record between Newark, New Jersey, and Miami, Florida. The standing transport record stood at six hours and thirty-four minutes.[21]

If Mary's idea was to break the speed record, she was unsuccessful; if it was a publicity stunt, it succeeded. The only occupants of the sixteen-passenger airliner were Mary Lewis, Pilot Dick Merrill, and Co-pilot H.O. Hudges (or Hudgins). They arrived after eight hours of flying time, fighting bitter headwinds much of the trip, and Merrill was forced to fly "blind" as far as Savannah, Georgia. It did clip twenty minutes off the scheduled flight time.[22]

A Miami gossip columnist said, "Mary Lewis, who sang at the Metropolitan Opera House, flew down from New York yesterday in eight hours and was annoyed because it took so long. Passenger cabins supercharged as airplane engines are now, planes flying 30 to 40,000 feet up, will bring real air travel." The columnist predicted soon that people could take weekend vacations anywhere in the United States.[23]

Anna wrote to Frank, "I heard Mary Lewis sing." Then she reported, "Mary Lewis and her husband's mother, have sailed on the *Hindenburg*."[24]

Endnotes Chapter 17 Anna

1. Anna Fitch, letters to her son, 1934-36.
2. Ibid.
3. Ibid.
4. Ibid.
5. Ibid.
6. Ibid.
7. Ibid.
8. Ibid.
9. Ibid.
10. Ibid.
11. Ibid. No further information is available concerning Norah.
12. Ibid.
13. Ibid.
14. Ibid.
15. Ibid.
16. Ibid.
17. Ibid.
18. *St. Louis Daily Globe-Democrat*, 27 Jan. 1936., Fitch scrapbooks.
19. National Broadcasting Company release 3 Mar. 1936, Lewis file, New York Public Library.
20. Ibid.
21. Ibid.
22. Ibid.
23. Clipping, n.p., n.d., Fitch scrapbooks.
24. Anna Fitch letters to her son, 1934-36.

Mary Lewis was the only passenger on a 16-passenger plane she chartered in an attempt to break the flight record between Newark, New Jersey, and Miami, Florida. She is pictured with Co-Pilot H.O. Hudges. *Arkansas Democrat*, Little Rock.

18

Up, Ship!

The launching of the *LZ 129 Hindenburg* airship began a new era in world history. The airship announced to the world that Germany had emerged from its confinement following defeat in World War I. No other country possessed the craftsmanship to put together such an engineering marvel. After the *LZ 127 Graf Zeppelin* meandered successfully back and forth over the Atlantic, plans for the next step, the *LZ 128*, were scrapped and the plans for the *LZ 129* drawn up.[1]

At the helm of the model luxury liner was Dr. Hugo Eckener.[2] Mary and Bohnen were among those who had invoked his displeasure by entertaining the *Graf Zeppelin* stowaway. Eckener was devoted to pursuit of airship transportation, but Third Reich disciple, Dr. Joseph Goebbels, then in power as Minister of Nazi Propaganda, thought its value lay in advertising German supremacy.[3]

On the trial run, while flying over Munich, Doctor Eckener was asked, via radio, the ship's name, to which he replied "*Hindenburg*" to honor Germany's former president. Goebbels promptly called Eckener on the carpet and snapped, "I have given orders today that in Germany, at least, your *Hindenburg* ship will be referred to only by its number *LZ 129*. What the foreign press calls it is not my concern." The name of Eckener was also to be stricken from the records, and Berlin's Eckener Avenue was renamed in Hitler's honor.[4]

The airship was used in a pre-election campaign over the Rhineland; the area had been declared a neutral buffer zone in the Versailles Peace Treaty. In March 1936, Hitler had sent in his troops to repossess the strip, and then gave residents the opportunity to vote to re-annex to Germany. Leaflets and radio messages from the *Hindenburg* bombarded the populace below with instructions on how to vote.[5]

On May 6, 1936, the *Hindenburg* began to float toward the United States. The new Mercedes-Benz diesel motors churned quietly as the ship glided smoothly through the starlit sky. The Americans, struggling to emerge from the Depression, loved it, and reporters were assigned to cover its every aspect. Most were interested only in the glamour aspects of the cruise, and few noticed the giant black swastika, enclosed in a circle of white against a background of blood red, emblazoned on the huge tail fins, announcing Nazi Germany was staking out territory on land and sea, and in this case, in the air.[6]

At 4:55 a.m. the *Hindenburg* was sighted over New York City, as thousands of New Yorkers waited through the night scanning the sky to catch a glimpse of the marvel. Coming in over the Bronx, the ship swung south over Queens and Brooklyn, circled to pass directly over the Times Building, and cheers went up again and again as the ship's searchlight was beamed into the throng gathered in Times Square. Then, quietly, the cruiser droned toward the Lakehurst Naval Air Station.[7]

On May 9, after a sixty-hour trip, the crossing ended. Traffic was jammed on the little New Jersey roads, as more than 100,000 people jostled for position.[8] They loved it! They had followed its adventure by radio and front page headlines.

After the welcoming ceremonies the ship's officers, Captain Lehmann and Doctor Eckener, were flown to Washington to be presented to President Franklin Roosevelt. The Germans pleaded for sale of helium to be used to lift the newest airship, the *LZ 130*, which was being designed.[9] The Americans were the only ones who had helium, an expensive non-flammable gas. It had less lift than the hydrogen being used, but it was safe. Since the Americans were not sure of Germany's peaceful intentions, they promised to provide helium only for the maiden flight of the new blimp on the drawing board.[10] Two days later, the officers returned to prepare the ship for the return journey. Supplies were stocked and the engines refueled. The food was mostly delicacies for Yankee tastes: lobsters, apples, and one hundred boxes of ice cream; the Germans were interested in the fifty quarts of beer which replenished the ship's supply for the two-day journey.[11]

Doctor Eckener studied the weather maps and detected no electrical storms in sight. The storms were regarded as the most serious menace, as the 803-cubic-foot bag was inflated with the inflammable hydrogen from the Standard Oil Company of New Jersey plant. Eight Navy-owned railway tank cars, each holding 200,000 cubic feet, transported the gas to the station, where it was piped underground into the sixteen gas cells. Fuel oil for the ship's four propelling diesel engines was also provided by Standard Oil Company of New Jersey.[12]

With Captain Lehmann at the helm, the blimp was towed out of the hangar with the help of the landing crew of ninety sailors and 150 civilians. The operating company, the Deutsche Zeppelin Reederie, was granted permission to use the naval hangar as long as it represented no cost to the U.S. taxpayer.[13]

The world's largest airship was handled with precision, complicated somewhat by an erratic wind. At 10:45 a.m. the riding car was secured and the passenger gangplank attached. The wind played some tricks as the first passenger, Mrs. Mary Lewis Hague, opera singer and wife of a Standard Oil official, climbed aboard. The breeze veered and the gangplank had to be shifted with Mary standing atop! As Mary was welcomed aboard, an enterprising reporter made an attempt to smuggle aboard, but the American representative of the ship's operating company grabbed the reporter by the ankle and retrieved him after a scuffle.[14]

This opera bouffe interlude was barely concluded when Mrs. Harriet Hague (Mary's rapscallion mother-in-law) was carried in to join the opera singer. She laughed with delight, but fell to her knees as she got inside. Rising, she waved a farewell and shouted, "I'm glad to go. I always wanted a thrill like this. Don't forget—I live at 27 Elk Street, Worcester, Massachusetts."[15] It was her first trip abroad.[16]

The rest of the human cargo, totaling one hundred and four, scrambled on board. Eight of the scheduled fifty-six passengers were "no-shows;" the remaining fifty-six were crew.[17] The last bags of mail and freight were tossed aboard, and a searchlight beamed on the nose of the ship as it was unleashed at 10:20 p.m. The ground crew, clutching the reins, walked the ship back 200 feet. The water ballast rained below as the captain commanded, "Up, ship!" Mary complained that she was not allowed to take any of her fourteen miniature dachshunds along. Hague had put his foot down on the sausage-dogs, saying, "Taking a dachshund to Germany would be like taking coals to Newcastle." Mary retorted, "All done up in blue ribbons they don't weigh much more than a fat gnat."[18]

As Mary and her mother-in-law prepared for bed in the tiny cubicle, the crew was silhouetted overhead as they scampered along the catwalks checking the gauges and inflated bulges. Instead of the passengers housed in a gondola slung below the ship, as on the *Graf Zeppelin*, the new ship contained two decks up inside the hull.[19]

Chief Steward Heinrich Kubis supervised a crew of six stewards; there was also a stewardess for helping the ladies attend to feminine needs. Kubis had made catering to the elite his business and had served as "cruise director" aboard the *Graf Zeppelin* before being tapped for the new honor.[20]

Kubis had learned his trade well. Charming, with impeccable manners, he knew just the right touch, the perfect wine, the most tasty sauce, and the right temperature for serving—hot or cold. Kubis had an eye for quality and catered to it. He avidly read the society columns and kept a notebook of his clientele.[21] Mary, with her fluent German and contagious charm, must have been a favorite with the officers.

The Germans, chafing under the confines of the Versailles Treaty, had been subdued to making pots and pans in their crack aluminum factories, and they perfected the art. The ribs of the giant whale were fashioned of aluminum as was the comfortable furniture, so light it could be lifted with a finger. In the lounge was even an aluminum piano; this was in deference to the passengers of the *Graf Zeppelin*, who said that was the one thing that ship lacked.[22]

On the long, almost boring journey, Mary entertained the guests, accompanying herself on the metallic harp—like an angel she sang on her gray floating cloud. When interviewed at her glittering suite in the Ritz Towers before the trip, Mary explained she was taking about 35 pounds of sheet music which would almost fill the 50-pound quota of baggage for each passenger. "Not much room left for clothes," she sighed.[23]

It was also reported, "When not hitting high C for the high-flying Zep, she'll be flashing dispatches to the Universal News Service." Mary said, "I did some reporting on my non-stop flight to Miami last year and I like it almost better than singing."[24]

When not in the lounge, Mary might have sat around the promenade, leaning over to see the white-capped waves reaching up. The finest fare was served in the dining room, and there was also a library and writing room. Service was just a bell-tone away.[25]

There was practically no vibration, no movement or sound. It was so quiet that on arrival in Germany, the eighty-five-year-old Harriet Hague told reporters she was through with Zeppelins because they were too safe to be much fun. "It was too boring," she said, "You can't even feel seasick."[26]

It was just a year later, on May 6, 1937, the next season's first voyage, that the *Hindenburg* ended Germany's supremacy in blimps when it burst into flames on landing at Lakehurst Air Station.

Endnotes Chapter 18 Up, Ship!

1. Michael Macdonald Mooney, *The Hindenburg*. (New York: Dodd, Mead & Co., 1972), p. 75.
2. A.A. Hoeling, *Who Destroyed the Hindenburg?* (Little, Brown & Co., 1962), p. 88.
3. Hoeling, *Hindenburg?*, p. 8.
4. Ibid., p. 77. Mooney, *The Hindenburg*, p. 87.
5. Hoeling, *Hindenburg?*, p. 88.
6. Ibid.
7. Ibid., p. 90.
8. Ibid., p. 91.
9. Ibid., pp. 91-92.
10. Little Rock *Arkansas Gazette*, May 1936, Fitch scrapbooks.
11. Ibid.
12. Ibid.
13. Mooney, *The Hindenburg*, p. 129.
14. *Arkansas Gazette*, May 1936, Fitch scrapbooks.
15. Ibid.
16. Clipping, Museum of the City of New York.
17. *Arkansas Gazette*, May 1936, Fitch scrapbooks.
18. Clipping, Museum of the City of New York.
19. Hoeling, *Hindenburg?*, p. 71.
20. Ibid., pp. 41, 45.
21. Ibid.
22. Mooney, *The Hindenburg*, pp. 42, 67.
23. Clipping, Museum of the City of New York.
24. Ibid.
25. Mooney, *The Hindenburg*, p. 71.
26. Ibid., p. 94.

Mary Lewis, Diva to Be Zep Reporter

Mary Lewis was the first to board the *Hindenburg's* maiden flight from New Jersey to Germany. With husband, Hague, Mary Lewis models one of her hats she bought in the U.S. to aid trade recovery. Fitch album.

19

Retribution

In the summer of 1936 Anna wrote to her son that Mary's husband had received notice in the "Week in Business" report, which credited Hague, representing the marine division of Standard Oil Company, as having signed contracts for eight new oil tankers. This was recognized as being the largest shipbuilding order ever to be given by a private U.S. corporation. The cost of the new vessels was to exceed 13 million dollars, and the bonus would be 5 million hours of shipyard labor and 2 million hours for the steel plants and factories.[1]

The contracts were divided, with four ships to be built by Federal Shipbuilding and Dry Dock Company and Bethlehem Shipbuilding Corporation Limited, and Sun Shipbuilding and Dry Dock Company to produce two each.[2] Struggling to regain economic stability amid the Great Depression, the labor units eagerly welcomed the contracts.

Mary accepted an invitation to sing at the Saline County Centennial celebration September 19, 1936, at the invitation of the Saline County Centennial Committee and Arkansas Governor Junius M. Futrell. She was scheduled to sing at a 7 a.m. morning open air religious service Saturday at Benton. A Little Rock paper reported:[3]

> Five years have passed since Mary Lewis gave up a career to become the wife of Robert L. Hague, president of the Marine Department of the Standard Oil Company of New Jersey. During that time, she has kept almost strictly to the role of wife—spending the majority of her time traveling to all parts of the globe with her husband. But music throughout this time occupied Mary Lewis. She has sung for charities and various benefits only for five years. But never once has she given up watching that golden voice which made an Arkansas girl arise to meteoric heights in the operatic world. She has studied

relentlessly, and today, Mary Lewis herself is the proud authority for unhesitatingly pronouncing that voice far better than it was in the heyday when a career came first. The past four years have been given over to unceasing study and today the former lyric soprano has a range of nearly four octaves. Her health is better than in several years. Rigid dieting and walks of seven and eight miles daily the past several months have the former star down to almost the weight Mary Lewis was when she left Little Rock years ago to take up a stage career. The same quick smile that brings a couple of dimples into play, and the same wealth of golden hair are all the Mary Lewis of five years ago. Mary laughed at predictions she 'was through' emphatically declaring she was not through and planned on combining her marriage with a new career saying her husband was her greatest booster in plans for her future as a 'good thing to do to occupy my time and keep me out of mischief.' Mary was also busy with her family, her two nephews who were living with her while she provided for their education, Lewis Kidd, 14, and Jack Kidd, 18. Now that she has made up her mind, and understanding from a husband who has great pride in her voice and is modern enough to back her up in it, [are factors that] will bring Mary back to the spotlight again. But Mary contended the contracts she was preparing to sign must permit freedom to be with her husband at her home in New York. The plans were not revealed, although Mary did say announcements would be forthcoming before many more weeks and indicated she planned a weekly radio hour and concert work and possible appearance in motion pictures. 'And while the old Met still is alluring..., opera today isn't quite what it was back in the days of Gatti,' Mary said. 'Nor does it mean quite so much to a singer today as it once did. There isn't the same exactness, though [Edward] Johnson is giving it a chance it deserves and American singers the opportunity to sing as they never before have had [at the Met].'

Of the contemporary singers, Mary declared Lily Pons the greatest of the women and John Charles Thomas and Tibbett the most capable among the men. "Others," she said, "seem rather slipshod—singers whose performances ten years or so ago would not have been tolerated by 'old Gatti.'"[4]

Mary made note that the next morning's appearance would mark the fifth anniversary of her marriage to Hague, and she planned to go direct from the appearance to a telephone somewhere and talk over the event with her husband in New York. Wherever she was, Mary said, she usually has a daily telephone conversation with him.[5]

For sentimental reasons, Mary announced that the performance in her native Arkansas will mark her return to the professional world. She spent the morning, and much of the afternoon, at the studio of Mrs. Alice Henniger, her former vocal instructor.[6]

Mary was pronounced "all graciousness and almost thin, with the bad health she has suffered from during the past four years leaving no traces." No specific information is available concerning the illusive illnesses which Mary suffered. According to Guthrie, The Health Resource, complications of anemia from malnutrition or from radiation can include susceptibility to infections due to decreased resistance along with other possible complications. Mary said, "I feel better than in years. Then, too, I'm really and honestly mighty happy to have a few days here. I like getting back to Arkansas—feeling and smelling its atmosphere. This is the first time I've had opportunity actually to stop here with the feeling of being free and relaxed—and I'm enjoying it. It's after all, home, you know."[7]

Benton welcomed Mary Lewis like a native daughter on her arrival the next morning. Saline County was adjacent to Garland County where Mary was born, close enough to make her a daughter. At sunrise Mary opened the Centennial festivities and almost stole the show. It was "Mary Lewis" day for the little farming community. Mary had arrived in a cloud of dust, the entourage being delayed by car trouble on the twenty-mile trip from Little Rock.[8]

At the daybreak prayer service at the Benton High School stadium, Mary sang "Come Unto Him" from Handel's *Messiah* and Mozart's "Alleluia." The town folk, the farmers and the bauxite miners, were impressed with Mary Lewis as she poured forth vigor and expression and added charm and personality to her performance. Mary had requested her part of the sunrise service be limited to two selections with no encore—but, after her second rendition, the audience continued to applaud. After a questioning glance by the master of ceremonies, Mary nodded her head.[9]

A standing ovation answered his query, "How many of you would like to hear Miss Lewis sing 'Carry Me Back to Old Virginny'?" In the packed stadium, 2,500 fans cheered and rose to their feet and the dignitaries on the stage joined the others in the standing ovation along with the newsmen, journalists, and radio announcers. After the encore, Mary Lewis was swept off her feet with congratulations by friends and strangers who said, "We're glad to have you back again, Mary." The young autograph hunters echoed, "Mary Lewis is home again."[10] Mary loved it!

From the prayer service Mary was hurried to the business district for breakfast before a tour of the city and by 10 a.m. the southern heat was uncomfortable. "I imagine you are getting terribly tired of all of this," a visiting guest asked, but Mary patted her face daintily with her handkerchief and said, "I am tired. I haven't had time to stop for a minute since I reached Arkansas. But I'm not tired of this. I think it is lovely."[11]

Mary viewed the 11:30 a.m. parade from a banner-bedecked stand, after which she left for Hot Springs where she spent the remainder of the day before returning to Little Rock. There she sang at morning services at the Second Baptist church where she formerly sang in the choir and played the organ. She sang "Alleluia" by Mozart and an old hymn, "I'll Go Where You Want Me to Go," to a packed congregation which was reported to be unusually responsive to her singing.[12]

A visit was made to see Anna on Sunday afternoon. In her weekly Sunday letter to her son, Anna said, "We had a nice visit. I can't tell all about it in a letter but I will send some clippings that will explain. She is a handsome woman a head taller than I am." She later wrote, "No, I did not hear Mary sing. I could not go." Anna was nearing her ninetieth birthday. "I'll tell you all about it when I see you." She also told him Mary did not have a German accent, answering his question on that aspect.[13]

Mary then went to Dallas, Texas, for a short visit with her mother before returning to New York.[14]

Much publicity was given to Lewis's singing engagement scheduled at the Versailles, a night club in New York City, on October 29, 1936. The program billed her as the "Golden Girl of the Metropolitan Opera."[15] "She wants so much to please her customers," a reporter noted, and then quoted Lewis: "If it takes hot music to please them," she said, "They're going to get it. I'm from the South, and I've got plenty of rhythm." Mary declared her "program will have everything from soup to nuts. There will be two or three songs highbrow enough for an $8.80 audience at the Metropolitan and perhaps two popular numbers.... Just how hot I shall get depends on how my other songs go over."[16]

"And just how hot can you get, Miss Lewis?" the *World-Telegram* staff reporter queried. Mary patted her blond hair, smiled archly, and replied, "After all, I'm a Southern girl." She explained that her musical tastes were extreme. "I don't like the in between stuff, I either like it low-down or high-up. But in all grades there is good and bad. This idea that only highbrow music is good and the rest is just slush is ridiculous. You know," she added thinking of Anna and the hometown bunch, "there are still some places in the country where they still think night clubs are sinful. The way I figure it—God gave you a voice, and it's there to be used. It's just as good in one spot as another." She refused to include any of the guttural jazz songs that caused the loss of her voice during her vaudeville career.[17]

Mary Lewis was described as still a beauty, although more plump than in her *Follies* days. She still radiated the charm and easygoing ways of the South in her attitude regarding her wealth and fame, and her voice still echoed a Southern twang.[18]

A gossip column reported: "Still another indication of how swank has hit dining-out is symbolized by the recent engagement of Mary Lewis, once of the Metropolitan. She gave the Versailles a couple of operatic arias and wound up with a few popular numbers. Incidentally she was paid more than for her singing to the Horseshoe Circle folk [Metropolitan Opera audiences]."[19]

Back in Arkansas, as Anna approached her ninetieth year, she was no longer sprightly and found it necessary to employ a nurse to care for her. Anna described the nurse as "an unusual jewel," a graduate of two schools of nursing with supplementing training in traditional medicine and rubbing [as Anna called massage therapy] treatments.[20] Frank received a letter from the nurse:

> I have been very anxious to see you and talk with you about certain things but since you have delayed your visit have decided to write to you.
>
> Will say first your mother is about the same. She has severe pain in her back, which is just terrible at times. The Doctor has ordered treatment for her back which I give two or three times a day. It is wonderful how these treatments relieve her. I like to work here but I just cannot pay my bills at $5 per week. That is what she gives me. I have a dear little son 8 years old I am sending to school and he is badly in need of warm clothes and other things, but after paying his board and car fare, I have nothing left. Then the Devil tempts me like this. He says to me 'Just take out more than $5.00 for yourself you know you should get more and besides that is what her pension is sent to her for, to take care of her and she or anybody else will never know a thing about it.' (I might explain she lets me have any amount of money any time to run the house and never counts it.)
>
> Well I had a battle to fight. I went to my friend Jesus and asked him very sincerely to help me to make the right decisions. He answered my prayers and caused me to see that the evil one had almost caused me to commit a great sin. Then since Jesus can't dwell in my life if sin is present I would have been in a terrible fix, because I am depending on Him to care for me and my loved ones. Also there is my boy I am trying to raise up right in this wicked world. It seems almost impossible without the help of the Lord....If I can't get $3.00 per week added to my wages in some way that will be honest I will have to find something else. You know nurses generally get much more but I work as cheap as I can because I must have steady work. I spoke to your mother about giving me more but she refused. I suppose she really can't if she saves for her taxes and etc. Then I spoke to her about your helping and she was afraid you would think she ought to live with you, which she doesn't want to do. She seems very much attached to her home here. But she doesn't seem to think I will ever leave. She believes that providence sent me here

and I suppose providence will keep me here. I hope so, I like to care for your mother, I think she is a wonderful character. She is old and just doesn't realize what all I am doing for her. I do everything. She cannot do anything for herself. I keep house, cook, nurse her, bathe and dress her, everything. If she should get seriously ill I can care for her. Well, I hope you will advise soon. She doesn't know I have written you, but I thought you should know all about it. I have told you some of my Christian experiences. You being a minister of the Gospel, I know you will understand these things which most of us have to face.[21]

Frank responded with encouragement, and sent a check for $12. He explained that his mother's pension was only $40 a month that she had been living on for a long time, and his own salary was small. Anna was unaware that her son was being debilitated by Parkinson's Disease, blaming arthritis for his poor handwriting. Frank added, "My present plans are to start down... so I may be with mother next week. Of course my plans are subject to sudden change here if there are any deaths, or other special church duties that prevent my leaving."[22]

Rev. Frank Fitch spent the week prior to his mother's ninetieth birthday with her in Little Rock. Interested in the family's genealogy, he asked for information Anna could give from her memories. He also was attempting to fathom the strange relationship between his mother and his famous foster sister, whom he didn't know.

Anna was a celebrity on two counts: one for reaching her ninetieth birthday and as the one "who reared Mary Lewis from childhood." The local press mentioned, as usual, the holly tree Mary had planted on the corner of the lot twenty-seven years before. Anna told of the long walks she and Mary had taken through the woods, which were now residential sections. Anna displayed the tattered dress and slip Mary wore when she first became a part of the family, and she reminisced about the first voice and music lessons were given to Mary by Doctor Fitch after they recognized her unusual talent.[23]

But most of all, Anna liked telling of Mary's visits when in the city, and of her faith in her as a "great singer and a good woman."[24]

Anna had witnessed many changes in her ninety years. She lived through several wars and believed we would soon have another.[25] Anna knew about wars—her own grandfather, Jeremiah Kendall,[26] had fought in the Revolutionary War; her teen years were during the Civil War, and her young husband had been a part of its campaigns; and when he was laid to rest by his compatriots, her own two young grandsons, Francis and Finley, were in their Army uniforms as the country became entangled in World War I.

Anna expressed an interest in modern women with "no complaints of what they do, providing their homes come first." She regarded women in politics with a shake of her head, but declared the "liquor question would have been much worse if it hadn't been for them."[27] She thought of the signatures of Carry A. Nation and Frances E. Willard penned in her book many years before when the prohibition fight was in its infancy.

But Anna considered herself a "modern woman" in her day as a college graduate during a period of time when higher education was almost unthinkable for women. She was recognized as one of the oldest alumnae of her school, which made her realize she was the sole survivor of her class of 1869. She displayed, with pride, her many paintings which reflected her love of nature.[28]

On the afternoon of her ninetieth birthday, Anna, in an unusual emotional outpouring, divulged to her son stories that hitherto she had kept secret. Not typical of her usual writings, this letter dealt with only one subject—Mary:

> As you ask about Mary Lewis, I'll write that part now as I have just about got through answering 25 or 30 cards and messages that I received. One came from Germany, one from Delaware Ohio Alumni Office and so forth. Mary Lewis has never failed to send me a check for $50 every Christmas since she began earning money. She got in a hurry this time and sent the check for my birthday so I don't expect any at Christmas time but the greatest surprise was a box five feet long one foot deep and a foot and a half wide filled with flowers from one of the finest florists in the city.... They were delivered to me here by messenger so was the check. I wish you could see the flowers. I can't tell you of them in a letter. The box was lined with the most beautiful ferns then filled with great big mums, carnations, sweet peas, great big bunches of different snapdragons and so

> forth. She knows she would have died when a very little girl had it not been for me. A knock at the door. Another check from Mary Lewis and a note Thanksgiving greetings and $20, so I'll hardly get any at Christmas time.

Mary had seen how Anna, once so robust, was fading into her golden years. Anna continued:

> Now I'll tell you why I have never written any thing about what Mary has done for me. If it was noised abroad it might make a cut in my Conference check and I am sure if you had known you would have told the whole thing to that horrid news reporter that was here when you were here so it's best to keep some things to myself. I hope you will never tell what I have written you this morning. Mary loves me as if I were her own mother. She sends me big boxes of white lilies at Easter time.... The neighbors who saw the recent box of flowers said it cost 15 or 20 dollars.... I have learned it's best to keep my own secrets.[29] The nurse added, 'She had a grand time on her birthday.... It made her very happy for Mary to remember her as she did.'

The following week Anna wrote, "I couldn't [write] Sunday because of so many calls...I am rather weak today, so I can't write a long letter. The beautiful fence of iron in front of my window was paid for with Mary Lewis' money. The posts are set in the ground four feet deep holes one foot wide filled with cement guaranteed for one hundred years."[30] The letter is noted: "My mother's last letter." With it was a note from the nurse: "Just after she had finished writing your letter and had started with it to the dining room she fell. I had started with her but she told me to turn out the light, and when I stopped to do that, instead of waiting, she went on and fell...I try to encourage her all I can, I just can't stand to see her discouraged. I wait on her day and night and it is wearing me out. The doctor thinks she will last until the first [of January]."[31]

Anna Lecky Fitch died Dec. 23, 1936. She was laid to her final rest at Christmas in Roselawn Cemetery in Little Rock covered with a huge floral spray wired by Mary Lewis from New York. Mary's holly, bright with red berries, bent beneath the winter winds high on the Arkansas bluff.[32]

Mary Lewis had repaid her debt to the pastor's wife.

Endnotes Chapter 19 Retribution

1. *News-Week*, 25 July 1936, Research by Starved Rock Library System.
2. Ibid.
3. Clipping, n.p., n.d., Fitch scrapbooks.
4. Ibid.
5. Ibid.
6. Ibid.
7. Ibid.
8. Ibid.
9. Ibid.
10. Ibid.
11. Ibid.
12. Ibid.
13. Anna Fitch, letters to her son, 1934-36.
14. Clippings, n.p., n.d., Fitch scrapbooks.
15. Mary Lewis's scrapbooks #3, courtesy Holdridge.
16. Raphael Avellar, New York *World-Telegram*, n.d., Mary Lewis file, New York Public Library.
17. Ibid.
18. Ibid.
19. Clipping, n.p., n.d., Fitch scrapbooks.
20. Anna Fitch, letters to her son, 1934-36.
21. Fitch collection.
22. Ibid.
23. Clipping, n.p., 25 Nov. 1936, Fitch scrapbooks.
24. Ibid.
25. Ibid.
26. Sergeant Jeremiah Kendall, 1758-1843, 3rd Virginia Regiment., United States Pension Department No. S-23743, Certificate No. 11466 issued 2 May 1822, rate $80 per annum.
27. Clipping, n.p., 25 Nov. 1936, Fitch scrapbooks.
28. Ibid.
29. Anna Fitch, letters to her son, 1934-36.
30. Ibid.
31. Ibid.
32. Oral interviews, Mildred Fitch, Finley and Blanche Fitch. Attending the funeral were Anna's son, Rev. Frank F. Fitch, and his wife, Mildred, of Earlville, Illinois; Anna's grandson, Finley Fitch, and his wife, Blanche; and great grandchildren, Clark, 7, and Alice, 5, of Yorkville. Alice Fitch Zeman is the author of the Mary Lewis biography.

Anna Fitch wrote to her son, "The beautiful fence of iron in front of my window was paid for with Mary Lewis's money. The posts are set in the ground four-feet deep holes one-foot wide filled with cement guaranteed for one hundred years." Mary's holly bush can be seen in the front yard. Fitch album.

Mary Lewis shows she can vary her career from opera and classical to singing the latest hit songs at the Versailles night club in New York. Mary Lewis's scrapbooks #3, courtesy Holdridge.

20

Nova

On New Year's Day, 1937, Mary sang "The Star Spangled Banner" in Albany, New York, at the third-term inauguration of the New York governor, Herbert Lehman, who had taken over the helm when Roosevelt moved to the White House in 1933. Mary Lewis also concluded the ceremony with the singing of "America."[1]

About this same time Mary Lewis made a substantial number of recordings for the Thesaurus series. This series was intended for radio broadcast at the convenience of local stations. The discs were produced for NBC by RCA. Originally developed to produce sound-tracks to accompany films, the recording process was found to be useful in the developing radio broadcasting industry. The discs were 16 inches in diameter and played at 33⅓ rpm. The large discs could be used to make recordings of live broadcasts, which could be re-broadcast later. It was then possible to provide an enormous variety of recorded material for use, not only by the originating broadcaster, but also by radio stations all over the world. The "transcription discs" were generally not sold, but their use was controlled by a rental contract. In 1977 a treasure-trove of Mary Lewis material was discovered in Australia.[2]

Robert B. Stone, who was a writer-producer for the NBC Radio-Recording operation under the name, Thesarus, met with Mary Lewis in her ornate Park Avenue apartment, along with her agent Bernie Foyer for the purpose of an audition for Thesaurus. Mary ordered up highballs for the two men, but drank tea herself on that occasion.[3]

Stone remembered, "She was then 37 [actually she was 40]...her voice was badly worn at the top, and she would have been well advised to omit the high Cs and even Ds which she insisted on singing. But the voice was still good in the middle register."[4]

Two of the recording sessions at the Victor studios on West 24th Street went off without incident. Mary recorded fifteen sides, most with three songs to a side. The repertoire ranged from German Lieder and French art songs to ballads, with only a few operatic arias included. Fittingly, one of these harkened back to her earliest days in the studio. The *Thaïs* aria, "L'amour est une vertu rare," at last was down for posterity.[5]

But on the third session, at 9 a.m. Mary arrived highly intoxicated. They started rehearsing the aria "Care Selve" ("Come, Beloved") from Handel's *Atalanta*. Mary was unable to sing and kept breaking off to insult the musicians, who were playing faultlessly.[6]

Stone said, "Finally I opened my mike in the control room and said that Lucien Schmidt (the cellist from the New York Philharmonic) was wanted on the phone. Outside the studio, I told Lucien we would get one 'take' and then call the session off—the 'take' being for evidence."[7]

Bernie Foyer wept real tears as he told Mary, "You can't do this to me!"—meaning he would not get his 15 percent commission. Stone later said, "She walked out of the studio and out of my life—no word of regret or farewell; she just walked out."[8]

On January 30, Mary Lewis was invited to sing "The Star Spangled Banner" at the inauguration of the 1937 Saturday Afternoon Forum Course conducted by the National Democratic Club. Broadcast over a nation-wide hook-up at 2 p.m., Mary was assured that: "our beloved President [Roosevelt] will be an interested listener, as well as all the leading figures of the nation."[9]

The year of 1937 brought a separation between Mary and her husband, Robert Hague. Mary returned to Europe to resume her singing career.[10] She sang in concert in Hamburg, Germany on May 2, in Berlin on May 6, and on June 3 in Paris at Maison Gaveau. Following the Paris concert she received a complimentary letter from a friend, "I enjoyed your programme...and of course you looked wonderful, such a beautiful gown—it was an eyeful even for Paris!"

On June 15, 1937, Mary Lewis presented a concert in Queen's Hall, London, accompanied by the esteemed Gerald Moore, who for half a century was ranked foremost in his field. From the time Moore made his first important London appearances in 1926, he accompanied virtually every eminent solo singer and instrumentalist in recitals, abroad as well as in Britain.

Although Mary Lewis said when she left that she was not returning to the United States,[11] her beloved Europe, where she so often had sought refuge in study, was being ensnared by Hitler's tentacles. By this time Germany, under the leadership of Hitler, had broken the Versailles Treaty and moved into the demilitarized zone to bring German troops next to the border of France. Beginning in 1938 German troops were marching into Austria and Czechoslovakia. The policy of giving in to keep peace had failed. It is not clear when Mary returned home, but the ominous warning signs were clear that war in Europe was imminent.

While Mary Lewis was busy in Europe, her estranged husband was active on other fronts. On January 3, 1939, Hague had arranged with Joseph P. Kennedy, America's Ambassador to Great Britain as well as chairman of the Maritime Commission, one of the largest shipbuilding contracts to take place up to that time. The contract called for the construction by the Standard Oil of New Jersey to build twelve high-speed national defense auxiliary tankers. Hague suffered a severe attack of influenza while on the business trip to London. On his return, he visited Arizona to recuperate and then went on to Palm Springs, California. Hearing of trouble in his fleet, Hague flew from Palm Springs to personally direct the maneuver. The Esso *Baytown*, one of his tankers, had announced they were answering an S.O.S. call from the flying boat, *Cavalier*. While back East, he officiated in the launching of two new Navy tankers, one at Kearny, New Jersey, and the other at Chester, Pennsylvania. Both ships had been built by Standard Oil Company of New Jersey according to government specifications. The world was gearing up for war pulling the end of the Depression with it.[12]

Still legally married to Mary, Hague died on March 8, 1939. Death for Hague came in his Ritz Tower apartment, with the cause given as cirrhosis of the liver. His last visitor was New York's ex-mayor Jimmy Walker. Hague was fifty-nine years of age.[13]

In obituary credits acknowledgment of Hague's tributes to the stage and theatrical performers were given. Hague was a life-time member of "The Lambs" since 1919. A eulogy written in *The Lambs Script* read: "He built a monument of love in the hearts of all who knew him."[14] He was cited as manager of the largest privately owned fleet in the world, that of the Standard Oil Company; as a lieutenant commander in the U.S. Naval Reserve; a Grande Officiale of the Crown of Italy; director of the American Bureau of Shipping; and trustee of the Webb Institute of Naval Architecture. He also was known for originating and directing the annual international lifeboat races. The United States Lines extended sympathy and announced that out of respect for Hague as a friend of the American merchant marine, flags on all ships of the United States Lines would be flown at half-mast.[15]

Hague's mother, Harriet, now 90, raced by plane from Arizona, in a futile effort to be at his bedside when the end arrived. Asked by reporters if she was not afraid of the strain of flying, she retorted, "Young man, I've been flying ever since I was eighty!" Unlike some of Hague's other women, Harriet profited as recipient of a large life insurance policy payable to her.[16]

Mary Lewis interrupted a vacation visit to Hot Springs to fly to New York when she heard of her husband's illness. Along with stage stars and industrial leaders, Mary attended the funeral, as well as Hague's former wife, Edith "Just Call Me Princess" Bobe.[17] In the obituaries there were almost as many photos of Mary Lewis as Hague's widow than there were of Hague himself.

In a separation agreement, Mary had been endowed with a liberal provision and was named to receive a life-interest in one-half of Hague's estate. She had been remembered in his will. In fact, Broadway Bob's punch line when he permanently parted from his feminine friends was, "I'll remember you in my will!" Bob had made the promise often, much to the amusement of his cohorts, and distributed more than $5,000,000 in remembrances in his last testament. His will directed to twenty-one pals checks for $1,000 each "to buy something to remember me by."[18] But when executors overhauled the estate, the debts were found to exceed the assets. Three of Bob's girls found themselves big losers of their own funds, Mary included. One tally estimated $718,129 in debts with claims arriving daily.[19]

Mary filed a claim for $22,000, which she asserted was the value of a block of stock which Hague had given to her, but he had neglected to deliver the certificates or even to transfer the shares to her name.

Ex-wives Edith Bobe Hague and Alba Kneeland Hague did not file claims, but Stella Ritchie Hague gave an outcry, "He promised to remember me in his will with $50,000—if I did not remarry." Having fulfilled her vow of celibacy, she appeared to reap her reward. As a compromise, she filed a claim for $16,297.[20]

The largest and loudest claimant was an actress who made an assertion that she was to be the fifth Hague spouse, and in prospect of this, the couple had purchased a $50,000 house for their honeymoon residence. Christine Fischer (known in the arts as Christine Forrest) was a neighbor to Hague and lived at 280 Park Avenue. Christine claimed, "Bob and I were deeply in love. He had been legally separated from his wife and there is no question but that he intended to marry me. Just a month before he died, I gave an agent my own check for $35,000 in return for a bond and mortgage on the house at 127 East 80th Street. I also gave an assignment of the mortgage in blank." After the death of Hague, the hapless bride-to-be found his name had been inserted in the blank space.[21]

In the ensuing trial, the Supreme Court (Surrogate Court) ruled that Hague's own money lifted the mortgage, and his attorneys moved for foreclosure. Checks were introduced which gave evidence that Hague had given the actress $67,000 in the eighteen months prior to his death. Private detectives also testified that more than $16,000 was found in her apartment, hidden under rugs, in flower pots, and in mattresses. Then the deluge of debts rained down on her. Suits and claims showered down on the actress and against the Hague estate. Furniture, interior decorators, contractors, cabinetmakers, plumbers, and Oriental art dealers, all came forward. A swank furrier claimed $5,000 for a sable coat; $5,000 for a mink coat; $2,500 for a silver fox coat; $1,600 for a Russian ermine coat. The total bill was $14,100 with $8,565 unpaid.[22]

Christine said, "I knew Bob for three years. He was a magnificent fellow. At first we were good friends, then friendship ripened into love and we talked of marriage. Of course, nothing could be done until Mary Lewis gave him a divorce. But Bob told me all that had been arranged. It was in anticipation of our marriage that I purchased the house and obtained the mortgage and assigned it in blank. I gave the assignment to Bob in return for a loan he was to arrange for me." The honeymoon house was then placed on the auction block in an effort to reclaim some cash to pay creditors. Salvage operations were sunk when another claimant, the U.S. government, put in a bill for $500,000 in back income taxes.[23]

Hague had given Mary life-use of half of an estate worth less than nothing. Back to providing for herself again, Mary arranged a concert tour of Puerto Rico in the summer of 1939. Ellmer Zoller, faithfully still at her side as accompanist, said she was making the tour "because she was an artist" and not because she needed the money. Mary succumbed to illness, a swelling of her throat, while attempting the tour. A silver tube was inserted down her throat so she could breathe, but she never regained her health.[24]

When her mother died in Little Rock the following year, March 11, 1940, Mary could not attend the funeral. Hattie Maynard had been living at the home of Mrs. Bruno Haustein, 1600 West Eighteenth Street, North Little Rock. She was buried in Pinecrest Memorial Park in Alexander, Arkansas. She was aged seventy-five when she died.[25]

Her health, spirit, and bank account broken, Mary survived until New Year's Eve, 1941. She died at Roy Sanitarium, a general hospital in New York, after four months of illness.[26] The world's attention was diverted to the Pacific, where Japan had just unleashed its hostility on Pearl Harbor. In December 1941, after declaring war on Japan, President Roosevelt announced the country was also at war with Germany and its allies, as they were threatening to take over the globe.

Mass was celebrated for Mary Lewis at a 10 a.m. service on January 2, 1942, at St. Matthew's Roman Catholic Church at 215 West 67th Street in New York. Mary had reverted to her early Catholicism. Soloist William Aubin was accompanied on the organ by the faithful Ellmer Zoller. Funeral music included "Panis Angelicus," "Ave Maria," "Agnus Dei," and "Goin' Home."[27] A second service was held at the Second Baptist Church in Little Rock on January 5, with only relatives and close friends in attendance. Mary was laid to rest beside her mother. Her business manager and nephew had accompanied the body from New York.[28]

Mary's estate, worth more than $10,000, was left to her mother, already deceased. Her brother, Joe Kidd of Chicago, survived.[29]

No one seemed sure of the facts when Mary came into the world and no one seemed any more sure of the facts when she left. Her age was listed as 41; she was actually three years older. In some reports the cause of death was attributed to a gall bladder ailment or, in other reports, a bladder ailment.[30] Her own letters testify to her belief that she had suffered from anemia every since childhood, but that diagnosis may have been a misreading of the symptoms of radiation poisoning dating back to the radium-treated dress she wore in the *Ziegfeld Follies*. At least one tumor, that in a dangerous location, had earlier been removed.

The *Metropolitan Opera News* said she was born and educated in Hot Springs; born, yes—educated, no. They remembered her for the vivid personality she brought to the roles of Mimi, Marguerite, Nedda, Giulietta, and Antonia.[31] The United Press labeled her one of the most publicized singers in America in the 1920s.[32] An unidentified New York clipping listed her as the daughter of Joseph Lewis and Hattie Lewis Kidd, but was confused about the 1930 announcement of Osborne [sic] O'Hagan as her father.[33]

One obituary reported she left Little Rock to go to Chicago where she made a rapid rise and was considered a leading opera star there for nearly twenty years. Wrong.[34] Little Rock knew it was somebody they ought to know, but they weren't quite sure who. Little Rock's *Arkansas Democrat* and *Arkansas Gazette* hastily sent someone to contact voice teacher Mrs. Henniger. The *Gazette* said she made her home with H.F. Auten and her parent's name was Maynard.[35]

Whoever she was, Mary Kidd Maynard O'Hagan Fitch Auten Lewis Bohnen Hague, the little waif had made a name for herself—"the golden haired beauty with the golden voice."

Chapter 20 Nova

1. New York Times, 23 Dec., 1936, p. 26.
2. Michael Quinn. "Mary Lewis—The Radio Discs," The Record Collector, XLII, Sept. 1997, 188-194.
3. Robert B. Stone, n.p., to Michael B. Dougan, 9 Sept. 1977.
4. Ibid.
5. Dougan, notes to author, Sept. 1998.
6. Stone, n.p., to Dougan, 9 Sept. 1977.
7. Ibid.

8. Ibid. Stone admitted he enjoyed seeing Foyer in tears. In 1977 Foyer still owed Stone $20.
9. Letter from the National Democratic Club, 233 Madison Ave., New York. Mary Lewis's scrapbooks #3, courtesy Holdridge.
10. Mary Lewis's scrapbooks #3, courtesy Holdridge. *Daily Mirror*, n.p., 9 March 1939.
11. Mary Lewis's scrapbooks #3, courtesy Holdridge.
12. Ibid.
13. *New York Times*, 9 Mar. 1939, Lewis file, New York Public Library.
14. The Lambs *Script*, April 1939, Vol. 4, p. 8. Mary Lewis's scrapbooks #3, courtesy Holdridge.
15. *New York Times*, 9 Mar. 1939, Lewis file, New York Public Library.
16. Roberts, n.p., n.d., Fitch scrapbooks.
17. Mary Lewis's scrapbooks #3, *Daily Mirror*, n.p., 9 March 1939.
18. Clipping, n.p., n.d., Fitch scrapbooks.
19. Roberts, n.p., n.d., Fitch scrapbooks.
20. Ibid.
21. Ibid.
22. Ibid.
23. Ibid.
24. Clipping, n.p., n.d., Lewis file, Arkansas Historical Commission. According to Guthrie, The Health Resource, radiation, such as Mary Lewis received when she wore the famous "radium dress" in the *Ziegfeld Follies*, can cause later effects by altering the "information system" of proliferating somatic and germ cells causing nonspecific shortening of life. Guthrie concluded that not enough medical records were available to make an accurate diagnosis of the exact cause of Mary Lewis's death.
25. Obituary, Hattie Maynard, file Pinecrest Memorial Park.
26. Clipping, n.p., 2 Jan. 1942, Fitch scrapbooks.
27. Clipping, n.p., 2 Jan. 1942, Lewis file, New York Public Library. No biographical information concerning Ellmer Zoller is given.
28. Clipping, n.p., 2 Jan. 1942, Lewis file, Little Rock Public Library.
29. Clipping, n.p., 6 Jan. 1942, Lewis file, New York Public Library.
30. Clippings, Lewis files, Little Rock & New York Public Libraries, Fitch scrapbooks.
31. *Metropolitan Opera News*, 22 Jan. 1942, Lewis file, New York Public Library.
32. Clipping, n.p., 2 Jan. 1942, Fitch scrapbooks.
33. New York *Herald Tribune*. 1 Jan. 1942, Lewis file, New York Public Library.
34. Little Rock *Arkansas Gazette*, 5 Jan. 1942, Lewis file, Little Rock Public Library.
35. Little Rock *Arkansas Democrat*, 1 Jan. 1942, p. 15. *Arkansas Gazette*, 1 Jan. 1942, p. 2.

Epilogue

The story of Mary Lewis—the very essence was captured by Michael B. Dougan, associate professor of history at Arkansas State University at Jonesboro, Arkansas. In a paper, "A Touching Enigma: The Opera Career of Mary Lewis," delivered in 1975, Dougan says, "Yet the wonder is not that Mary failed to reach the highest pinnacle but that she even came close."

Mary had many problems with which to deal—including alcoholism. Current research into the nature of alcoholism attributes the disease to a number of factors. Physiological causes may be partially responsible for the excessive use of alcohol by some people. In other words, a person may have a biochemical makeup that causes his or her initial experiences to be more euphoric than a "normal" person's would be. Genetic factors also seem to play a part in making some people more prone to alcoholism than others.[1] Not enough is known about what roles might have been played by Mary Lewis's heredity, which apparently included an Irish/German ancestry.

Until recently understanding of addictive behavior has been both unsophisticated and moralistic. Thinking which held that drugs and alcohol were themselves somehow "evil" or "demonic" lay behind the 18th Amendment to the U.S. Constitution. The amendment sought to eliminate the consumption of alcohol entirely by making its production, sale, and use illegal. It took effect in 1920 and was known as Prohibition. The early view that the afflicted were suffering from moral weakness or character disorders did little to promote treating and curing addictive behavior. Enlightened opinion today holds that people do not become addicts because they are "sinful" or "bad" to begin with and that overcoming addiction is not a simple matter of moral fortitude or willpower. By the end of the Prohibition era, American society realized how misguided it had been to attempt to eliminate alcohol problems by prohibiting alcohol entirely. There is some evidence that the number of people who developed problems with alcohol [such as Mary Lewis] actually increased during the 13 years of Prohibition.[2]

It is now realized alcoholism is a complex phenomenon, and many factors contribute to its development. In addition to biological factors, there are environmental factors such as peer pressure Sociocultural forces and psychological factors help decide a person's expectation about the effects that drinking will have on them. An individual might be affected to varying degrees by any or all of these contributing causes of alcoholism.[3] According to the psychoanalytic theory, psychological disturbances can be traced to events that occurred during early childhood.[4] Today, some drugs are prescribed by a physician to relieve the underlying causes of depression which contribute to alcoholism.

In review of what is known about Mary Lewis, many of these factors could have influenced how and why she became an alcoholic. It seemed at times she was in control of the habit, but at other times, it controlled her. Once addiction to alcohol or other drugs has set in, the victims are trapped in a vicious cycle of depression, anxiety, and low self-esteem which they futilely and self-destructively attempt to manage by using ever-increasing amounts of the substance that caused so many problems in the first place.[5]

The social scene and company in which Mary Lewis was involved with were factors which influenced the use of alcohol. Dougan wrote, "Despite a varied career, Mary Lewis never became an American institution like Geraldine Farrar, Mary Garden, or Grace Moore.... Mary belonged to the Roaring Twenties, to fast cars, snapping cameras, Mayor Jimmy Walker, and bathtub gin. For a time her life made good copy which was the basis for much of her success. Irrelevant publicity obscured her real merits and may have contributed to the tragedy behind her personal life."[6] Jessica Dragonette, in her autobiography, contrasted Grace and Mary: "Grace Moore—beautiful, yet not as beautiful as Mary Lewis—went dauntlessly on, as she vowed she would, while Mary—the perfect type for opera—lacked the indispensable drive; she was a touching enigma, evidently bent on destroying herself, in spite of excelling gifts."[7]

Mary was driven by a powerful motivation to overcome her rather wretched beginnings. The pieces of the puzzle begin to fit together with the discovery of the intense training Mary received in the home of the pastor and his wife. Their elderly ages and diversity of background makes this aspect even more intriguing. From their home, she stepped easily into the family of one Arkansas's leading citizens. From there, she reached for the stars. She was beautiful, talented, and had a vivacious personality.

She was compared to Cinderella, but unlike Cinderella, she didn't live happily ever after—but that was a fairy tale—and the Mary Lewis story is true.

Endnotes Epilogue

1. W. Miles Cox, Ph. D. University of Minnesota. *The Encyclopedia of Psychoactive Drugs: The Addictive Personality*. (New York, New Haven, Philadelphia: Chelsea House Publishers) 1986. pp. 20-21.
2. Ibid. pp. 38-41.
3. Ibid. pp. 48-49.
4. Ibid. p. 42.
5. Ibid. p. 83.
6. Dougan., "Enigma," p. 278
7. Jessica Dragonette, *Faith is a Song*. (New York: David McKay Company, Inc.) 1951. p. 78.

Mary Lewis, Ex-Star Of Met, Is Dead at 41

New York, Jan. 2.—(UP)—Funeral services will be held today for Mary Lewis, 41, former star soprano of the Metropolitan Opera and one of the most publicized singers in America in the 1920's, who died at the Le Roy Sanitarium after a four-month illness.

Miss Lewis had lived in virtual retirement since the death in 1939 of her husband, Robert L. Hague, former vice-president of the Standard Oil Company. She rose to stardom in the Ziegfeld "Follies," and made her debut at the Metropolitan in January, 1926, singing the role of Mimi in "La Boheme."

Fitch family scrapbooks, n.d., n.p.

"She has come home like a bird to its nest,
Home, at last, for a long, long rest."
- an Arkansas poet

A painting by A.L. Halmi captures the wistful quality which made Mary Lewis so endearing to her fans. Reproduction from Fitch album. The original art work is in the collections of the Little Rock Public Library, a donation from the late Robert Doyle of Little Rock.

The Recordings Of Mary Lewis

1. His Master's Voice

HUGH THE DROVER, Selections. Text by Harold Child; Music by Ralph Vaughan Williams. First produced (privately) at the Royal College of Music, London, 30 June 1924. First public performance, His Majesty's Theater, London, 14 July 1924.The acoustic recordings made during September 1924 (specific details not available), with original cast:

Mary (the Constable's Daughter) . . . . Mary Lewis
Constable's Sister) . . . . Constance Willis
Hugh the Drover . . . . Tudor Davies
John the Butcher . . . . Frederic Collier
The Constable . . . . William Anderson
A Showman . . . . William Michael
Conductor: Malcolm Sargent

(In addition to the above members of the original cast, the following singers are heard in the recordings: Peter Dawson, Keith Falkner, Robert Gwynne, Trefor Jones, Janet Powell, William Waite, and Nellie Walker). All records play at 78.00 r.p.m.

Side No. Cat. No. Mtx-take Title.

1. 2-04529 D922 Cc 038-5 "The Fair" Pt. 1: The Showman
Singers--Michael, Gwynne, Falkner, Powell, & Chorus

1) 2. 2-04530 D922 Cc 039-2 "The Fair" Pt. 2:
Tuesday Morning: John the Butcher boasts of his Strength
Singers--Lewis, Collier, Anderson, Jones, Gwynne, & Chorus

2) 3. 04377 D923 Cc 039-2 "The Morris Men"
Aunt Jane's song; Entrance of Hugh
Singers--Lewis, Willis, Davies, & Chorus.

3) 4. 04378 D923 Cc 5054-4 The Song of Hugh the Drover
Singers--Lewis, Walker, Davies

5. 04379 D924 Cc 5041-2 The Love Duet
Singers--Lewis, Davies

5) 6. 2-04531 D924 Cc 5058-4 The Challenge and the Fight
Singers--Lewis, Walker, Davies, Collier, Anderson, Michael, & Chorus.

7. 04380 D925 Cc 5059-2 "May Morning": Hugh in the Stocks
Singers--Davies, Collier, & Chorus

6) 8. 04381 D925 Cc 5042-1 Mary sets Hugh free
Singers--Lewis, Davies

7) 9. 2-04532 D926 Cc 5053-4 Mary joins Hugh in the Stocks
Singers--Lewis, Walker, Davies, Collier, Anderson, & Chorus

8) 10. 2-04533 D926 Cc 5040-2 The Sergeant releases Hugh— Finale
Singers--Lewis, Willis, Davies, Dawson, Anderson, Waite, & Chorus

The preceding work is now available on one long play 33 r.p.m disc Gem 128.

*9) *FAUST: Il était un roi de Thulé* (Gounod)(F)(Or.)
Cc 5156-1, -2, **-3** 1 Oct. '24 (2-033092) . . . . Unpublished
Cc 5156-3 was assigned a single faced part number and was thus presumably scheduled for release.

*10) *FAUST: Ah! je ris de me voir (Air des bijoux)*(Gounod)(F)(Or.)
Cc 5155-1, -2 1 Oct. '24 . . . . Unpublished
-3 6 Oct. '24 . . . . Unpublished

*11) *MANON: Je suis encore tout étourdie* (Massenet)(F)(Or.)
Cc 5181-1,-2 6 Oct. '24 (2-033093) DB800 78.00

*12) *MANON: Allons! Il le faut!.... Adieu, notre petite table*
(Massenet)(F)(Or.)
Cc 5182-1, -2, **-3** 6 Oct. '24 (2-0330944) DB800 78.00

*13) *MANON: Suis-je gentille...Obéissons quand leur voix appelle*
(Massenet)(F)(OR.Goosens)
Cc 5550-1, **-2** 7 Jan. '25 (2-0330955) .... Unpublished

Cc 5550-2 was assigned a single faced part number and was thus presumably scheduled for release.

*14) *THAÏS: (Ah! Je suis seule ...)*
Dis-moi que suis belle (Massenet)(F)(Or.Goosens)
Cc 5552-**1**, -2 7 Jan. '25 (2-033097) DB810 78.00

*15) *THAÏS: Te souvient-il du lumineux voyage* (Massenet)(F)(Or.Goosens)
Cc 5551-1, **-2**, -3 7 Jan. '25 (2-033096) DB810 78.00

+16) *LOUISE: Depuis le jour* (Charpentier)(F)(Or. Sargent)
Cc 6574-1, -2 26 Aug. '25 .... Unpublished
Cc 6575-1, -2 26 Aug. '25 .... Unpublished
Bb 6620-1 1 Sept. '25 .... Unpublished
Cc 6620-1 1 Sept. '25 .... Unpublished

+17) *MANON: Je marche sur tous les chemins* (Massenet)(F)(Or. Sargent)
Bb6583-1, -2 27 Aug. ' 25 .... Unpublished
Bb6585-1 27 Aug. ' 25 .... Unpublished
Bb6619-1, -2, -3, -4 1 Sept. '25 .... Unpublished

+18) *MANON: Obéissons quand leur voix appelle* (Massenet)(F)(Or. Sargent)
Bb6582-1, -2 27 Aug. '25 .... Unpublished
-3, -4 1 Sept. '25 .... Unpublished

+19) *THAÏS: L'amour est une vertu rare* (Massenet)(F)(Or. Sargent)
Cc 6573-1, -2 26 Aug. ' 25 .... Unpublished
Cc 6584-1, -2 27 Aug. ' 25 .... Unpublished
Cc 6618-1, **-2**, -3, -4, -5 1 Sept. '25 (2-033111) .... Unpublished

Cc 6618-2 was assigned a single faced part number and was thus presumably scheduled for release.

20) From the Land of the Sky-Blue Water
(Eberhart-Cadman)(E) (Or. Pasternack; Flute, Barone)
BVE-34250-1, -2, -3, -4 24 Dec. '25
-5, **-6**, -7 4 Jan. '26 1140 74.23

21) Little Grey Home in the West
(D. Eardley Wilmot-Hermann Löhr)(E)(Or. Pasternack)
BVE-34349-1, -2, -3, -4, -5 24 Dec. '25 .... Unpublished
-6, **-7**, -8 4 Jan. '26 1140 74.23
-9, -10 13 Jan '26. .... Unpublished

22) *I PAGLIACCI: Qual fiamma avea nel guardo!... Che volo d'augeli*
(Leoncavallo) (I) (Or. Pasternack)
CVE-3341661-1, -2, -3 4 Jan. '26 .... Unpublished
-4, -5, -6 13 Jan. '26 .... Unpublished
-7, -8, **-9**, -10 20 Jan. '26 6578 (2-053258) 74.24

CVE-34161-9 was apparently scheduled for release in Europe as a part number was assigned.

23) *THAÏS: Te souvient-il du lumineux voyage* (Massenet)(F)(Or. Pasternack)
CVE-34255-1, -2, -3 4 Jan. '26 6578 (2-033109) 74.23

CVE-34255-1 was apparently scheduled for release in Europe as a part number was assigned.

-4, -5, -6 13 Jan. '26 .... Unpublished
-7, -8, -9, -10, -11 20 Jan. '26 .... Unpublished

24) *MANON: Je marche sur tous les chemins* (Massenet)(F)(Or. Bourdon)
BVE-35434-1, -2, -3 28 Apr. '26 .... Unpublished

25) *MANON: Obéissons quand leur voix appelle* (Massenet)(F)(Or. Bourdon)
BVE-35435-1, -2, -3, -4 28 Apr. '26 .... Unpublished

26) O Little Town of Bethlehem
(Phillips Brooks-Lewis H. Redner) (E) (Or. Pasternack)
BVE-35881-1, -2, -3, 24 Sept. '26 .... Unpublished

27) *LOUISE: Depuis le jour* (Charpentier)(F)(Or. Bourdon)
CVE-35433-1, -2, -3, -4, -5 28 Apr. '26 .... Unpublished

Recordings # 24-27 carry a note in the Victor books "Made for the Gramophone Company."

28) The Holy Child
(The Martin Luther Hymn)(E)(Or. Pasternack, except 4 Apr. Shilkret)
BVE-35880-1, -2, -3, -4 24 Sept. '26 .... Unpublished
-5, -6, -7 7 Mar. '27 .... Unpublished
-8, -9, -10 4 Apr. '27 .... Unpublished

Victor Talking Machine Co.

29) The Hand of You
(Carrie Jacobs Bond)(E)(Or. Bourdon; 'Cello, Lennartz;4 Apr. Shilkret)
BVE-38209-1, -2, -3, -4 7 Mar. '27 .... Unpublished
-5, -6, -7, -8 4 Apr. '27 .... Unpublished

30) *Stille Nacht, Heilige Nacht*
(Franz Gruber)(w. Paul Reimers) (G) (Or. Shilkret)
BVE-38341-1, -2, -3 12 Apr.'27 .... Unpublished
-4 13 Apr.'27 .... Unpublished

31) *Der Tannenbaum*
(Traditional, arr. Zarnack)(w. Paul Reimers) (G) (Or. Shilkret)
BVE-38342-1, -2, -3 12 Apr.'27 .... Unpublished

32) *Ach, wie ist's Moglich Dann*
(Thuringian Folk Song, arr. Kucken) (w. Paul Reimers)(G)(Or. Shilkret)
BVE-38344-1, -2, -3 13 Apr. '27 .... Unpublished

33) *Du, Du, Liegst mir im Herzen*
(Traditional, arr. Pax)(w. Paul Reimers) (G)(Or. Shilkret)
BVE 38343-1, -2, -3 13 Apr. '27 .... Unpublished

34) The Old Folks at Home (Swanee River)
(Stephen C. Foster)(E)(Or. Bourdon)
BVE-40007-1, -2, -3 12 Sept. '27 1345 DA 1022 76.60

35) Love's Old Sweet Song
(G. Clifton Bingham-J.L. Molloy)(E)(Or. Bourdon, pf. Linton)
BVE-40005-1, -2, -3 12 Sept. '27 .... Unpublished
-4, -5, -6 11 Oct. '27 .... Unpublished

36) Blue Danube Waltz ("On the Beautiful Blue Danube")
(J. Strauss II, Op. 314)(Or. Bourdon)
CVE-40232-1, -2 23 Sept. '27 .... Unpublished
-3, -4, -5 11 Oct. '27 .... Unpublished
-6, -7 -8, -9 20 Dec. '27 .... Unpublished

37) *FAUST: Ah! Je ris de me voir (Air des bijoux)*(Gounod)(F)(Or. Bourdon)
BVE-40006-1, -2, -3 12 Sept. '27 .... Unpublished
-4, -5, -6 11 Oct. '27 .... Unpublished
-7, -8, -9 20 Dec. '27 .... Unpublished
-10, -11 26 Mar. '28 .... Unpublished

38) The House that Jack Built
(Homer)/The Night Wind (Field-Farley?) (pf. Elmer Zoller)
BVE-test-1 23 Sept. '27 .... Unpublished

Composers for this test are not specified in the recording books. A check with Lewis concert programs established the fact that the Homer selection was frequently used. It has not been established that Lewis used the Roland Farley setting for the Field poem.

39) The Second Minuet (Audrey Dowdon-Maurice Besley)(pf. Elmer Zoller)
BVE-test-1 23 Sept. '27 .... Unpublished

40) *Voci di Primavera (Frühingsstimmen)*
(J. Strauss II, Op. 410)(I)(Or. Bourdon)
CVE-40297-1, -2, -3 11 Oct. '27 .... Unpublished

41) *La Danza* (Pepoli-Rossini)(I)(Or. Bourdon)
CVE-42564-1, -2, -3 26 Mar. '28 6878 76.60

42) Dixie (Dan D. Emmett)(E)(Or. Bourdon)
BVE-42565-1, -2 26 Mar. '28 1345 DA 1022 76.60

43) *Les Filles de Cadix* (A. De Musset-L. Delibes)(F)(Or. Bourdon)
CVE-42563-1, -2, -3 26 Mar. '28 6867 .... Unpublished

44) Little Bit of a Fellow (Norris): The Nightingales of Lincoln's Inn
(Oliver)(pf. Bourdon)
CVE-test-1 26 Mar. '28 .... Unpublished

This un-numbered 12" test is listed in the recording books with a note that the recording was made at the request of Mr. Clifford Cairns, then Victor Director of Artists and repertory. The Nightingales of Lincoln's Inn (from "Songs of Old London," Edward Teschemacher-Herbert Oliver).

45) Little Bit of a Fellow (Norris)(pf. Elmer Zoller; Violin, Raderman)
BVE-43583-1, -2, -3 18 Apr. '28 .... Unpublished

46) The Second Minuet
(Audrey Dowdon-Maurice Besley)(pf. Elmer Zoller; violin Raderman)
BVE-43584-1, -2, -3 18 Apr. '28 .... Unpublished

Notes: Titles marked * HMV were acoustic, Titles marked + and all VE VICTOR were electrical recordings. Take number in bold indicates that take issue or assigned catalog number.

Acknowledgments

Data from the HMV files was kindly supplied by Messrs. Alan Kelly, John F. Perkins and John Ward. Information with respect to the Victor records has been obtained from the files of the Victor Project, with special thanks to my associate, Ted Fagan.

Philip L. Miller checked programs in the New York Public Library to verify composers on some unpublished items.

Speed determinations have been made from copies in the author's collection.

W. R. Moran
La Cañada, California
March 13, 1976

Above information appeared in The Record Collector Vol. 23. Nos. 7 & 8. Issue Dec. 1976. Used by permission.

The Mary Lewis Records: An Appreciation

by Michael B. Dougan

Mary Lewis's recording career began in September 1924 when His Master's Voice assembled members of the original cast of Ralph Vaughan Williams' *Hugh the Drover*, threw in extras of the stature of Peter Dawson, and under Malcolm Sargent's direction, proceeded to record ten sides. A ballad-opera based on folk tunes, *Hugh the Drover* lacks a formal aria for the heroine. However, Mary, the role Mary Lewis sang, does have an extended love duet with Hugh in the first act and plays a pivotal role in the opera's second act. In all, Mary Lewis appeared in eight of the ten recorded sides.

The acoustic recording process then in use was not unkind to Lewis's voice, but HMV's habit of issuing its English records on some kind of recycled shellac resulted in the very opposite of silent surfaces. These defects are much in evidence on Pearl Records (GEM 138) otherwise exemplary 1975 reissue on a long playing record. A modern reconstruction might well go far to remove the singers from contending with a background of battle noise.

Even so, Lewis's contribution is valuable. Her voice, heard here at its freshest and lightest, nevertheless holds up against the competition of the noted sometime-Wagnerian tenor, Tudor Davies. Supplying both silvery tone and drama, she easily out-pointed the work done by Sheila Armstrong on EMI's 1979 complete stereo recording. Listeners should note that the 1924 version presents the original Act II ending the composer later revised.

Mary Lewis's next venture in the studio resulted in two unpublished arias from *Faust* and two published arias from *Manon*. The *Faust* ballad, "Il etait un roi de Thulé," was approved for publication and a number assigned to it for single-side issue. Apparently Lewis had problems with the coloratura on the intended second side, the Jewel Song, "Ah! je ris de me voir." Since single-side records were becoming extinct, the company presumably decided not to publish the approved aria separately.

Lewis had better success with *Manon*. The entrance aria, "Je suis encore toute etourdie," cannot be conveyed properly by those with mushy pronunciation, and Lewis does not disappoint. The contrasting aria from the second act, "Adieu, notre petite table," is sung with proper pathos. A second pairing failed, apparently for the same reasons that doomed the *Faust* sides. "Obeissons quand leur voix appelle" was approved but never issued, but "Je marche sur tous les chemins" failed to pass. In addition, Lewis was caught by the changeover from the acoustic to the electric recording method, which rendered this first "Obeissons" obsolete shortly after it was recorded.

Lewis's best work came in the arias from *Thaïs*, "Dis-moi que suis belle," and "Te souvient-il du lumineux voyage," the later the so-called "Meditation" so popular for violinists and actually a duet (Dorothy Kirsten and Robert Merrill recorded it correctly in the late 1940s).

Lewis's success in the *Manon* and *Thaïs* arias shows what a tragedy it was that she was not around to record the complete *Manon* issued by Columbia with Germaine Feraldy in the early days of the electric process. Feraldy's *coloratura* was superior to Lewis's, but the American soprano had other compensating strength. We also lament that Lewis was not the soprano chosen to make those wonderful duets from *Manon* with French tenor Georges Thill. Interestingly, the soprano with Thill was also an Arkansas girl who sang under the name of Mary McCormic. Despite being a Mary Garden protégée, she was much inferior vocally to Lewis.

Lewis's recording career in the United States began in December 1925 with the Victor Talking Machine Company (later RCA Victor). Sessions in December 1925 and January 1926 produced "From the land of the Sky-Blue Water" (Cadman) and "Little Grey Home in the West" (Lohr). Both were well sung if hardly challenging material. Apparently since the *La Bohème* arias were already spoken for by Lucrezia Bori in Victor's catalogue, company officials were reluctant to assign major arias to Lewis. Of her 26 Victor titles, only six were published, and of these only two were arias.

The songs may be disposed of briefly. "Dixie" (Emmett) was successful on its second take on March 26, 1928, and was one of her most effective records. Her clear pronunciation is much in evidence. She sings the song "straight," and with a sufficient but not excessive Southern accent. The same session also produced on first tries Rossini's "La Danza," and Delibes' "Les Filles de Cadix." "The Old Folks at Home" (Foster), recorded in 1927, neatly balanced the "Dixie" and was issued in England. A number of interesting song titles never left the studio, among them two duets with veteran Paul Reimers. Two separate attempts were made on "The Second Minuet" (Besley), and Lewis's delightful version of this rarity for radio later makes one wonder why it failed.

For nearly twenty years Lewis was best remembered for a twelve-inch 78 with Nedda's aria from *I Pagliacci* on one side and *Thaïs* "Meditation" on the other. It was this record that first introduced me to her art, and it was kept in the catalogue for some years. In contrast to her songs and some of her acoustics, these takes did not come easily. There were ten tries on the *I Pagliacci* aria before the ninth take was approved; eleven attempts were made on the *Thaïs*, although it was the first one that ultimately received approval. The electric recordings seem to show that her voice had strengthened at the expense of some of her earlier sweetness.

For a long time only some home recordings taken from radio broadcasts hinted at Lewis's extensive exposure on this medium. Her obituary in the *New York Times* mentioned the existence of these transcriptions, and a private letter from one of the musicians provided poignant details. Then came the discovery in Australia by Michael Quinn.

These radio transcription discs were made in New York City. In the absence of recording logs, it is impossible to say how many takes were made, but probably the number was limited. The voice is well forward, too much so at times, but the registers are well equalized and the breath support is really quite good. There is some swooping, but her diction was admirable, especially in the French and English songs. For some odd reason, she really never sounded at home in German. The series ended when she arrived at the studio too drunk to sing.

As to the quality of her work, I share Mr. Quinn's preferences [see radio recordings p. 212]. The "Eli, Eli" is truly extraordinary for the lower register Lewis employed, all without any hint of forcing. Mr. Quinn compared it to the famous rendition by Rosa Raisa, but she was a soprano who had grown up in the cantorial tradition. No good reasons explain Lewis's decision to record this piece or the power of her performance unless it was her way of getting back at Bohnen and her unhappy German years. American public opinion had not really turned against Hitler at the time of the recording, but her total identification with the text suggests some deep reason for its recording.

On the other end of the scale is the well-known popular song, "Wien, du Stadt Meiner Träume" (Siecznski). Here the standard was set by Richard Tauber, but many others have recorded it successfully. Lewis's version must surely rank as one of the worst on record, the vocal line being considerably altered for no good reason.

It is easy in the light of the Mozart tradition that was being established during the last years of Lewis's life to criticize her singing of "Deh vieni, non tardar" with its rewritten ending. However, listeners are to be reminded that a similar ending was used by Toti Dal Monte in her earlier acoustic version (HMV DB 831) and was probably common in the nineteenth century. In order to offset what discomfort an added high note might produce, listeners should pay attention to Lewis's effective handling of the recitative.

Lewis was set a consistently high standard in her French songs. There the voice appears to be in its natural element. The Strauss Lieder are good, and the salon orchestra is less offensive than in some of the other orchestrated versions on record.

Lewis appeared in concerts at times with John McCormack, and his influence can be heard "The Kerry Dance" (Molloy) and other popular parlor songs. However, if one song defined Mary Lewis's appeal and should be used as a sample of her mastery of English, it is "The Second Minuet" (Besley). In life, Lewis did not attain the longevity of the song's characters, and that tragedy makes these rescued recordings all the more valuable. While Lewis did not reach into the realms once occupied by Adelina Patti or Nellie Melba, she was vocally and dramatically gifted. Seen through the totality of her recorded art, she deserves to be mentioned in the company of Dorothy Kirsten, Grace Moore, Eleanor Steber, and other important American artists.

The Radio Transcription Discs Of Mary Lewis

by Michael Quinn

Brisbane, Queensland, Australia, published in *The Record Collector*, Vol. 42 No. 3, September 1997. A Quarterly Journal of Recorded Vocal Art, Larry Lustig, England, editor.

Like many another fine singer the American soprano Mary Lewis seems destined to be forgotten by all but a few record collectors. She has no entry in the Grove Dictionary of Opera and is unknown to the Metropolitan Opera Encyclopedia. My discography covers the recordings made by RCA for use in radio broadcasts both on their own NBC network and internationally by radio stations who purchased the rights to use them.[1]

Until optical recording of sound-on-film became a practical and reliable reality early sound films relied on a cumbersome system of synchronizing the film with a sound-track on disc. To contain the roughly 10 minutes of sound required to accompany a full 1,000 foot reel of 35mm film the discs were 16 inches in diameter and played at 33⅓ rpm. Though the sound-track discs were soon superseded by the rapid improvements in sound-on-film technology they found a particularly important use in the developing radio broadcasting industry. The large discs could be used to make recordings of live broadcasts which could be re-broadcast at a later date and also permanent recordings could be made in the studio and used for broadcast at will. It thus became possible to provide an enormous variety of recorded material for use not simply by the originating broadcaster but also by radio stations all over the world. These so called "transcription discs" were generally not sold but, instead, their use was controlled by a rental contract. Theoretically, that after use, the discs had to be returned to the owner or rendered unplayable after the contract period had expired.[2]

Among the discs imported by a local Brisbane radio station 4BK in the late 1930s was a group of 100 "transcriptions" in the NBC Thesaurus series. This was a long-lasting series produced in the United States between 1935 and 1957. The discs were recorded and pressed by RCA and contained an extraordinary variety of musical material, ranging from jazz and dance bands to classical vocalists and instrumentalists. The singers include soprano Vivien della Chiesa and the baritone Thomas L. Thomas and the soprano Mary Lewis, who made a substantial number of these radio discs, which greatly augment her all too slender legacy of commercial recordings. I have been fortunate in obtaining all the Mary Lewis discs once in the possession of Station 4BK. They were saved from destruction by the Brisbane poet and music critic, Ernest Briggs, who is fondly remembered by many both for his own tremendous enthusiasm for record collecting and his unfailing generosity to fellow record collectors.[3]

It is hard to give a fair appraisal of a career that for the most part promised more than it actually produced. Yet all is not disappointment, for Mary Lewis achieved much in the face of the considerable odds against her. I doubt whether many other slum kids sang leads at the Metropolitan, the Opéra Comique, and the Volksoper. For us there are also the records, which hold an enduring trace of the individual charm and beauty of voice of a pretty Irish-American girl from Hot Springs, Arkansas.[4]

16-INCH RED LABEL NBC THESAURUS SERIES—U.S.A.

Circa 1937 33⅓ r.p.m. Outside-start.
Accompaniment: small salon type orchestra

RECORD NO. 334

9. *Sortita* (It.) MS 03539 A
10. *Les Filles de Cadix* (Fr.)(de Musset-Delibes) MS 03539 B
11. *Wien, du Stadt Meiner Träume* (Ger.)(Sieczynski) MS 03539 C
12. The Golden Cockerel: *Hymn au Soleil* Act 2 (Fr.)(Rimsky-Korsakov) MS 03540 E
13. *Ay, ay, ay* (Sp.)(Perez-Freire) MS 03540 F
14. *Wohin*? (D.795) *Die Schöne Müllerin* No. 2 (Ger.)(Müller-Schubert) MS 03540 G

RECORD NO. 337

15. *Eli, Eli* (Heb.)(Psalms; Sandler arranged by Schalit) MS 03542 E
16. Danny Boy (E.)(Weatherly to Trad. Melody) MS 03542 F
17. Carry Me Back to Old Virginny (E.)(Bland) MS 03542 G

The other side of Record No. 337 features the Xavier Cugat Orchestra.

RECORD NO. 363

18. *Si mes vers avaient des ailes* (Fr.)(Hugo-Hahn) MS 03543 A
19. From the Land of the Sky-Blue Water (E.)(Eberhardt-Cadman) MS 03543 B
20. *Exsultate jubilate: Alleluia* - K.165 (Lat.)(Mozart) MS 03543 C

The other side of Record No. 363 features Richard Liebert (organist).

RECORD NO. 339

21. *Ave Maria* (Lat.)(Bach/Gounod) MS 03544 E
22. The Last Rose of Summer (E.)(Moore) MS 03544 F
23. The Kerry Dance (E.)(Molloy) MS 03544 G

The other side of Record No. 339 features Betsy White (contralto).

RECORD NO. 430

24. *Le Nozze di Figaro: Giunse alfin il momento....Deh vieni, non tardar* Act 4 (It.)(Mozart) MS 033572 A
25. *Du bist wie eine Blume* (Ger.)(Heine-Liszt) MS 03572 B
26. My Old Kentucky Home (E.)(Foster) MS 03572 C

RECORD NO. 355

27. The Slumber Boat (E.)(Alice C.D. Riley-Jessie Gaynor) MS 03573 E
28. Old Folks at Home (E.)(Foster) MS 03573
29. Annie Laurie (E.)(Douglas-Scott) MS 03573 G

RECORD No. 604

30. *Die Lorelei* (Ger.)(Liszt) MS 03574 A
31. The Holy Child (Away in a Manger)(E.)(Easthope Martin) MS 03574 B

The other side of Record No. 604 features The Dreamers

RECORD NO. 385
32. The Merry Widow: Vilia (?E.)(Lehár) MS 03576 F
33. Deep River (E.)(Negro spiritual) MS 03576 G
34. The Nightingales of Lincoln's Inn (from Songs of Old London)(E.) MS 03576 F (Teschemacher-Oliver)

The other side of Record No. 385 features Artie Shaw Rhythmakers.

RECORD NO. 357
35. *Panis Angelicus* (Lat.)(Aquinas-Franck) MS 03865 E
36. Morgen - Op. 27 No. 4 (Ger.)(Mackay-R. Strauss) MS 03865 F
37. My Lovely Celia (E.)(arranged by Henry Lane Wilson) MS 03865 G

The other side of Record No. 357 features Joey and Chuck.

RECORD NO. 414
38. *Still wie die Nacht* - Op. 326 No. 27 (Ger.)(C. Böhm) MS 03866 A
39. *Carmela* (Sp.) - Spanish-Californian folk-song (Hague-Ross) MS 03866 B
40. Last Night (E.)(C. Winter)(Eng. Trans...Theo Marzials-Halfdan Kjerulf) MS 03866 C

The other side of Record No. 414 features Nathaniel Shilkret's Orchestra.

RECORD NO. 561
41. *Star Vicino* (It.)(Salvator Rose) MS 011552 E
42. *Im Abendrot* D.799 (Ger.)(Lappe-Schubert) MS 011552 F
43. *Thaïs: L'amour est une vertu rare* - Act 2 (Fr.)(Massenet) MS 011552 G

The other side of Record No. 561 features The Dreamers

RECORD NO. 522
44. *Les Deux Sérénades* (Fr.)(Leoncavallo) MS 011554 E
45. Rain (E.)(Eugene Ford) MS 011554 F
46. Little Boy Blue (E.)(Field-Nevin) MS 011554 G

The other side of Record No. 552 features the Robert Hood Bowers Band.

RECORD NO. 462
47. La Colomba (E.)(arranged by Schindler) MS 011630 A
48. *L'Adieu du Matin* (Fr.)(Roche-Pessard) MS 011630 B
49. The Second Minuet (E.)(Audrey Dowden-Maurice Besley) MS 011630 C

The other side of Record No. 462 features the Robert Hood Bowers Band.

RECORD No. 494
50. *Wiegenlied* - Op. 41 No. 1 (Ger.)(Dehinel-R.Strauss) MS 011634 E
51. *Ständchen* - Op. 17 No. 2 (Ger.)(Schack-R.Strauss) MS 011634 F
52. *Clair de Lune* (Fr.)(Verlaine-Szulc) MS 011634 G

The other side of Record No. 494 features the Xavier Cugat Orchestra.

DISC - The discs are made of a flexible but rather brittle form of black vinyl which I presume to be Vitrolac.

LABEL - All the Mary Lewis "Thesaurus" discs I have examined bear a dark red label, which is the same color as the standard commercial RCA label of the 1930s.

DATING - It has not been possible to ascertain precise dates of recording or issue of these discs. However the corporate style for the company name as it appears on the label (RCA MANUFACTURING CO., INC.) dates the discs to 1935 or later. Comparison of these discs with the "Thesaurus" discs for which a recording date is known suggests that the Mary Lewis titles were probably cut during 1937.

MATRIX NUMBERS - The quoted numbers which appear both on the printed label and embossed on the land area between the recording groove and the label have an MS prefix followed by a five or six-digit number sequence. The added capital letter which is given after the numbers is the track identification that appears both on the label and inscribed between the tracks.

TRACKS - Thesaurus transcription discs usually have two or three tracks per side, which completely separate from each other to prevent the inadvertent playing on from one track to the next. The tracks are designated by capital letters, which follow in sequence through the tracks on both sides of the disc, with the exception that the letter "D" is used so as to avoid confusion with "B."

THE TITLES - which appear on the labels are completely inadequate to identify the items properly. Apart from the lack of any composer credit the titles themselves are often quite vague and misleading. As an example the title "Arioso" conceals an aria from *Thaïs*. Thus it requires the playing of each track to find out whose "Wiegenlied" or "Städchen" is actually being sung. Apparently the reason for this seeming carelessness in titling is that, originally, each disc was accompanied by a program card which gave details of the items being sung. Alas, cards are now lost.

THE RECORDINGS - This group of discs offers a fascinating glimpse of Mary Lewis as a concert artist. They greatly amplify the impression given by her commercial recordings, which display an attractive, if rather limited, picture of the singer's repertoire.

It would seem that the "Thesaurus" discs are the result of studio sessions rather than live "off air" recordings. Accompaniments are most provided by a small salon-type orchestra or simply harp in item 42 and piano and harp in items 43 and 44.

My own favorites are the Liszt songs "Du bist wie eine Blume" and "Die Lorelei," which are sung with lovely tone and considerable interpretative power.

Many of the other Lieder and art songs are performed with great distinction, memorable for their skilled use of tonal color and dynamic shading.

The French songs, particularly "Clair de Lune" and "Si mes vers," are poised and delightful performances.

In such ballads as "Little Boy Blue" and "The Slumber Boat" there is a gently lyrical quality with an engaging hint of her Arkansas accent to give them a thoroughly personal touch.

She brings a surprising intensity of expression to "Eli Eli" and in my opinion easily matches the fine version by Rosa Raisa.

It must be admitted that there are some misfires, such as "Wohin," and that the Mozart pieces do sound a little awkward. These comparative failures are very much in the minority and there are many pleasures to be had from these discs. They are undeniable an important addition to the Mary Lewis discography and worthy of being far better known than they are at present.

Acknowledgments - The information on Record No. 385 (items 24, 25, and 26) is gratefully credited to the only published listing of the Thesaurus series discs. Working Draft Thesaurus Transcription Listing, Volume 1 by Charles Garrod, Ken Crawford, and Dave Kressley (1992) published by the Joyce Record Club, Box 1687, Zephyrhills, Florida, 33539, U.S.A. Thanks are also due to John Simpson for his help and advice in preparing the discography.[5]

Endnotes The Mary Lewis Radio Discs

1. Lustig, Larry. *The Record Collector* Vol. 42 No. 3 September 1977, England. Article by Michael Quinn, "The Mary Lewis Radio Discs," p. 188.
2. Ibid.
3. Ibid.
4. Ibid, p. 190.
5. Ibid., the above information from pp. 190-194.

Chronology

Chronological record of Mary Lewis during the years of her career, 1920-1941.

NOTE: This list is a guide to Mary Lewis's appearances designed to give some idea of her basic repertory. New material and major arias are emphasized. As best as can be determined the term recital is used when Mary Lewis was the only performer with an accompanist and the term concert is used when she sang with others. In the interests of saving space, the first listing will provide the aria title, the opera from which it is taken, and the composer. Subsequent entries will consist only of the aria title. Aria titles are enclosed in quotation marks. Exceptions are those opera arias which have no title; in those cases the aria is identified by first line with foreign words italicized. The first listing of songs include full information (if known) and subsequent entries will be of title only. Readers should note that in the case of opera arias the German press in particular used the German titles, although Mary Lewis sang in the original language, as well as in German.

(+) indicates from Mary Lewis's scrapbook #1; (*) #2; (#) #3

August 30, 1920 - New York: *Greenwich Village Follies of 1920* at Shubert Theater, opening and 7 month season followed by tour in Philadelphia, Boston, and Pittsburgh. Mary Lewis appeared as The Singer in the skit, "The Village Pawn Shop"; "I'll be Your Valentine"; skit, "Come to Bohemia"; "Snap Your Fingers at Care" with Frank Crummit, Mary Lewis, and Harriet Gimbel; the singer in the skit, "Tsin"; and Mary Lewis appeared in the numbers in which the entire cast appeared. Music by A. Baldwin Sloane. Lyrics by John Murray Anderson and Arthur Swanstrom. Dialogue by Thomas J. Gray.

June 21, 1921 - New York: Globe Theater, opening and 119 performances of Ziegfeld's *Follies of 1921*. Mary Lewis was the Pink Rose in "The Rose Bower"; duet "Now I Know" with Margery Chapin; and she introduced "Kiss in the Dark," music by Victor Herbert. Mary Lewis left the *Follies* on the road to return to New York for Ziegfeld's nightclub show on the reopening of the New Amsterdam Roof in mid-December, 1921. The show ran 3 months. Music for the 15th annual production was by Jerome Kern, Rudolph Friml, Victor Herbert, and B.G. DeSylva. Book by Willard Mack, Channing Pollock, and others. 119 performances.

June 5, 1922 - New York: New Amsterdam Theater opening and 67 weeks in New York, 40 weeks on the road, Zeigfeld's *Follies of 1922*. Mary Lewis was "Miss Take" in "Blunderland"; Duet, "Radio" sung by Mary Lewis and Alexander Gray; "Weaving" in the "Lace-Land" spectacle (Mary Lewis wore a dress with the lace dipped in radium, which glowed when the lights were out); "Sweet Adeline" in the skit "Songs I Can't Forget." Mary Lewis subsequently became ill after her nightly radiation "treatment." [Program resource incomplete]. Music for the 16th annual production by Victor Herbert, Louis A. Hirsch, and Dave Stamper. Lyrics by Gene Buck. Book by Ring Lardner and Ralph Spence. A record run of 67 weeks in New York and 40 weeks on the road.

1923 - Mary Lewis auditioned for Giulio Gatti-Casazza, general manager of the Metropolitan Opera. She was encouraged to study in Europe for training and experience. Mary Lewis was released from the 3rd year of her contract by Florenz Zeigfeld and went to Europe.

July 13, 1923 - Paris, France: Audition for Raoul Gunsbourg and Auturo Serrano - "Caro Nome" ("Dearest Name") from *Rigoletto* (Giuseppe Verdi), "Ah! Je veux vivre" ("Oh! I want to live") from *Roméo et Juliette* (Charles Gounod).

October 19, 1923 - Vienna, Austria: Debut at Volksoper, played the role of Marguerite in *Faust* (Gounod). Others in cast were some of Vienna's best artists including Trajan Gosavescu, Emmanuel List, and Viorica Ursuleac. Conductor, Felix Weingartner.

October 26, 1923 - Vienna: Appeared as Mimi in *La Bohème* (Giacomo Puccini). Conductor, Weingartner. Rest of cast unavailable.

October 29, 1923 - Vienna: Appeared as Micaela in *Carmen* (Georges Bizet). Conductor, Weingartner. Rest of cast unavailable.

November & December, 1923 - Bratislava, Czechoslovakia: Staadtheatre, as Marguerite in *Faust*, Gilda in *Rigoletto*, Micaela in *Carmen*. Conductors and rest of casts not available.

January, 1924 - Monte Carlo, Monaco: Theater of Monte Carlo debut, Musetta in *La Bohème*. Continued through rest of operatic season, number of performances not available. Conductor and rest of cast not available.

*April 6, 1924 - Monte Carlo: Recital at Casa Del Mare, guest of Osbourne O'Hagan. [Mary Lewis later referred to O'Hagan as her "adopted father" and to Casa Del Mare as "home."] She sang "Caro Nome"; "Ah! Je veux vivre"; air from *Manon* (Jules Massenet); "Depuis le jour" ("Since the Day") from *Louise* (Gustave Charpentier); "Mandolines et Guitares" by Camille Saint-Saëns; "Hindoo Song" by Nicholas Rimsky-Korsakoff; "Tes Yeux" ("Your Eyes") by R. Rabey; "Air de Mimi" and "Air de Musetta" from *La Bohème*; "Vissi d'arte" ("Love and Music") from *La Tosca* (Puccini); "Down in the Forest" by Landon Ronald; "Valgovind's Boat Song" and "All for You" by Easthope Martin. Pianist, Easthope Martin. [Martin was a well known song writer.]

June 12, 1924 - London, England: British National Opera Company, first night of the season, substituted for Maggie Teyte as Antonia in *The Tales of Hoffman* (*Les Contes d'Hoffmann*) (Jacques Offenbach). Sylvia Nelis, Gladys Ancrum, May Blyth, Eda Bennie, Tudor Davies, Sidney Russell, Frederick Davies, William Michael, Frederic Collier, and Philip Bertram. Conductor, Eugene Goosens.

June 18, 1924 - London, England: B.N.O.C., Mary Lewis sang in a matinee performance as Musetta in *La Bohème*, with Miriam Licette, Browning Mummery, Percy Heming, Russell, William Anderson, and Frederic Collier. In the evening Mary Lewis appeared as Antonia in *The Tales of Hoffman*.

June, July, 1924 - London: B.N.O.C., as Musetta in *La Bohème* (three performances), and Antonia in *The Tales of Hoffman* (thirteen performances).

June 30, 1924 - London: Private premiere performance, Royal College of Music, B.N.O.C., Mary Lewis as Mary in *Hugh the Drover* (Ralph Vaughan Williams).

*July 14, 1924 - London: Public premiere performance, His Majesty's Theater, *Hugh the Drover*, season followed by tour of provinces and special performance at Number 10 Downing street for the Prime Minister. Played 5 weeks in London and 3½ months tour. Date of special performance not known.

+July, 1924 - Deauville, France: Mimi in *La Bohème*. Cast included Merky [as listed], Mathieu Rodoux, Jacques Borel, Parpignal [as listed], Roga Rogatchewsky, Maurice Gariette, André Pernet, and André Philippe. Conductor, Nestor Leblanc.

+Fall, 1924 - Nice and Deauville, France: Mimi in *La Bohème*, Micaela in *Carmen*. Director, casts, dates unknown. In Monte Carlo Mary Lewis performed 3 recitals at Casa Del Mare.

September (dates unknown) and October 1, 3, & 6, 1924 - London: Recording for His Master's Voice.

January 7, 1925 - London: Recording for His Master's Voice.

+/*February 15, 1925 - Monte Carlo: Recital at Casa Del Mare. "Voi Che Sapete" (What Is This Feeling?") and "Air de Suzanne" (Giunse alfin il momento....Deh vieni, non tardar) from *Le Nozze di Figaro* (Wolfgang Amadeus Mozart); "Air de Lauretta" ("O Mio Babbino Caro" or "Oh, My Beloved Daddy") from *Gianni Schicchi* (Puccini); "The Early Morning" by Graham Peel; "Solveig's Song" by Edvard Grieg; "Valgovind's Boat Song"; "Hymn au Soleil" from *The Golden Cockerel* (Rimsky-Korsakov); "Depuis le jour"; "Gavotte" ("Obeissons quand leur voix appelle" or "List to the Voice of Youth") from *Manon* (Massenet); "O Lovely Night" by Ronald; "The Holy Child" (Luther's "Cradle Hymn") by Martin; and "One Fine Day" ("Un bel di") from *Madama Butterfly* (Puccini). Martin, pianist.

+/*March 7, 1925 - Monte Carlo: Concert at Casa Del Mare. "Le Nil" ("The Nile") by X. Leroux; "The Holy Child" (by request); "Ave Maria" (Johann Sebastian Bach-Gounod) with violin obligato by Henry Wagemans. Martin, pianist. Also appearing was the Monte Carlo String Quartet.

+April 16, 1925 and season - Paris: Apollo Theatre, *La Veuve Joyeuse* (*The Merry Widow*)(Franz Lehár) with Henri Defreyn as Danilo. Defreyn played the role in the original French production 20 years previous and appeared in the role 1,000 times.

+June 27, 1925 - Paris: Recital at Theatre Edouard VII. "Care Selve" ("Come Beloved") by Handel; "Lass with the Delicate Air" by Thomas Arne; "Bergerette" by Jean Baptiste Wecerlin; "Caro Nome"; "Le tempe a laissé son manteau" ("Time has left its coat") and "Fantoches" ("Marionettes") by Claude Debussy; "Clair de Lune" by Szulc; "Notre Amour" by Gabriel Fauré; "I Came with a Song" by Frank La Forge; "An Astronomer" by Seneca Pierce; "Valgovind's Boat Song"; "To a Messenger"; and "Depuis le jour." Pierce, pianist.

Unknown location in Europe: Audition Mr & Mrs. Herbert Johnson, Chicago (Illinois) Opera Company, approved for 1925-26 or 1926-27 season. Mary did not accept the offer.

August 26, 27, & September 1, 1925 - London: Recording for His Master's Voice.

*October 26, 1925 - New York: State Symphony Concert, Carnegie Hall, sponsored by Gaelic Musical Society. With the Symphony Mary Lewis sang "Je marche sur les chemins" ("I walk on all the roads") from *Manon* (Massenet). Director, Ernst von Dohnany. Mary Lewis sang, accompanied by Ellmer Zoller, "Depuis le jour"; "Rain" by Curran; "The Answer" by J. Huntington Terry; "My Lovely Celia"; "The Holy Child"; a Hebridean love-lilt; "Ye Banks and Braes of Bonnie Dune" by James Miller; and "The Kerry Dance" by Molloy. Encore was "The Last Rose of Summer."

November 1, 1925 - New York: Concert with Harlem Philharmonic and radio broadcast over WEAF network.

November 5, 1925 - New York: Contract signed following audition for the Metropolitan Opera Company, New York City, New York. Guilio Gatti-Casazza, director.

*November 29, 1925 - New York: solo at The Pleiades Club, Hotel Brevoort.

*December 3, 1925 - New York: 3rd Artistic Morning, Ballroom of Plaza Hotel.

December 24, 1925 - Camden, New Jersey: Recording for Victor Talking Machine Co.

January 4, 13, & 20, 1926 - Camden: Recording for Victor Talking Machine Co.

*January 7, 1926 - New York: State Charities Aid Association, ballroom of Mr. and Mrs. Vincent Astor, 840 Fifth Ave. Mary Lewis sang selections from George Frideric Handel, Arne, and Puccini; "Depuis le jour"; "The Waltz Song" from *Roméo et Juliette*; and selections from Fauré and Curran. Zoller, pianist.

*January 20, 1926 - New York: Soloist, Scottish Rite Hall.

January 28, 1926 - Debut at Metropolitan Opera Company, Mimi in *La Bohème* with Edward Johnson, Antonio Scotti, Leon Rothier, Elizabeth Kandt, Millo Picco, Paolo Ananian, Max Altglass, Pompilio Malatesta, Vincenzo Reschiglian. Conductor, Gennaro Papi.

*February 6, 1926 - New York: 7th annual Biltmore Musicale. Duet with Armand Tokatyan from *I Pagliacci* (Ruggiero Leoncavallo), and solo "The Waltz Song."

February 19, 1926 - New York: Metropolitan Opera Company, Nedda in *I Pagliacci* with Vittorio Fullin, Scotti, Giordano Paltrinieri, and Lawrence Tibbett. Conductor, Papi.

February 26, 1926 - New York: Guest artist at reception sponsored by William Matheus Sullivan. Mary Lewis sang selections from Maurice Ravel and Debussy. Mary Lewis and Edward Johnson sang duet from the first act of *La Bohème*.

*February 28, 1926 - New York: Carnegie Hall. "Care Selve" by Handel; "Danza" ("Dance") by Durante; "Deh vieni, non tardar"; "Le Tempe a laisse son manteau" and "Fantoches" by Debussy; "Air de l'Enfant" by Ravel; "Clair de Lune" by Fauré; "Depuis le jour"; "June Morning" by Willeby; "Down in the Forest"; "I Will Walk With My Love" by Hughes; "La Colomba" by Schindler; and "The Holy Child."

March 12, 1926 - New York: Metropolitan Opera Company, Giulietta in *Les Contes d'Hoffmann* with Marion Talley, Lucrezia Bori, Kathleen Howard, Merle Alcock, Ralph Errolle, Giuseppe DeLuca, Ananian, Tibbett, James Wolfe, Louis D'Angelo, Angelo Bada, Altglass, William Gustafson, and Picco. Conductor, Louis Hasselmans.

*March 13, 1926 - New York: Honored with American Debutantes of the Metropolitan Opera Company at The Biltmore.

March 17, 1926 - Little Rock, Arkansas: Recital at Little Rock High School, old auditorium, sponsored by Little Rock Musical Coterie.

*March 22, 1926 - Memphis, Tennessee: Recital at Auditorium. Myron Jacobson, pianist.

April 1, 1926 - New York: Metropolitan Opera Company, Mimì in *La Bohème* with Giacomo Lauri-Volpi, Adamo Didur, Scotti, Rothier, Ananian, Altglass, Malatesta, Louise Hunter, and Reschiglian. Conductor, Papi.

*April 8, 1926 - New York: Guest soloist at dedication of the Sun Club, rooms for employees of the Sun Printing and Publishing Company. Speaker, Mayor Jimmy Walker.

April 12, 1926 - New York: Metropolitan Opera Company, Giulietta in *Les Contes d'Hoffmann* with Talley, Bori, Howard, Henrietta Wakefield, Armand Tokatyan, Didur, DeLuca, Ananian, Reschiglian, Wolfe, D'Angelo, Bada, Altglass, Gustafson, and Picco. Conductor, Hasselmans. Benefit for the Free Milk Fund for Babies, Mrs. William Randolph Hearst, chairman.

*April 11, 1926 - Boston, Massachusetts: Symphony Hall, recital with People's Symphony Orchestra. Conductor, Stuart Mason.

*April 13, 1926 - Washington, D.C.: Washington Auditorium recital for the benefit of the Hebrew Home for the Aged.

April 21, 1926 - Atlanta, Georgia: Metropolitan Opera Company, on tour, as Nedda in *I Pagliacci.*

April 28, 1926 - Camden: Recording for Victor Talking Machine Co.

*April 28, 1926 - New York: Guest artist at supper dance at home of William Randolph Hearst, Other artists were Efrem Zimbalist, violinist, and Rafaelo Diaz, tenor.

*May 3, 1926 - Columbus, Ohio: Recital at Memorial Hall.

*May 7, 1926 - Newark, New Jersey: Concert at 12th annual Newark Music Festival. Also appearing Lawrence Tibbett. Conductor, C. Mortimer Wiske.

*May 11, 1926 - Norfolk, West Virginia: Recital at Academy of Music sponsored by the Norfolk Teachers' Association. Zoller, pianist.

*May 14, 1926 - Springfield, Massachusetts: Springfield Bay Music Festival concert, Mary Lewis sang Marguerite from *Faust*. Others in the cast were Rothier, Emily Roosevelt, Anna Harris, Ernest Davis, Eugene Frey. Boston Festival Orchestra conducted by Emil Mollenhauser. Chorus of 350 voices directed by John J. Bishop.

July 1, 1926 - Paris, France: Opéra Comique, Mimi in *La Bohème*. Conductor and rest of cast not available.

*September 15, 1926 - New York: Radio Industries banquet, Hotel Astor. It was estimated 15 million listeners would hear Mary Lewis over the 35 radio station hook-up broadcast. Mary Lewis and Reinald Werrenrath, both Victor artists, sang a duet, "Barcarolle," from *Tales*. Mary Lewis sang an aria from *Louise*; "From the Land of the Sky-Blue Water" by Eberhart-Cadman; "Ay-ay-ay," a Spanish song by Osman Terez Sreire; and "The Answer."

September 23 & 24, 1926 - Camden: Recording Victor Talking Machine Co.

#Wolfsohn Music Bureau tour - Seattle, Spokane, and Moscow, Oregon; Chico, Oakland, San Francisco, Stockton, and Bakersfield, Los Angeles, California; Denver, Colorado; Kansas City, Missouri; Chicago and Peoria, Illinois; Little Rock and Hot Springs, Arkansas; Memphis and Nashville, Tennessee; Louisville, Kentucky; Atlanta, Georgia; New Orleans, Louisiana; Deland, Tampa, and Miami, Florida; Dayton, Columbus, Detroit, and Akron, Ohio; Buffalo, Syracuse, and Auburn, New York; Pittsburgh and Philadelphia, Pennsylvania; Roanoke and Norfolk, Virginia; Washington, D.C.; Trenton and Montclair, New Jersey; Waterbury, Hartford, New Haven, and New Britain, Connecticut; Poughkeepsie and Worchester, New York; Providence, Rhode Island; Boston, Fitchberg, and Northhampton, Massachusetts; booking for the 1927-28 season Wolfsohn.

Identified appearances on the tour:

*October 19, 1926 - Dayton, Ohio: Recital, Memorial Hall.

*October 27, 1926 - Nashville, Tennessee: Recital.

*November 10, 1926 - San Francisco, California: Recital at Exposition Auditorium, 4,000 attended.

*November 4, 1926 - Los Angeles, California: Recital with Philharmonic Symphony.

December 13, 1926 - New York: Recital, Carnegie Hall.

February 18, 1927 - New York: Metropolitan Opera Company, Giulietta in *Les Contes d'Hoffmann* with Talley, Bori, Howard, Wakefield, Mario Chamlee, Didur, DeLuca, Rothier, George Meader, Reschiglian, Wolfe, D'Anglelo, Bada, Altglass, Gustafson, and Picco. Conductor, Hasselmans.

March 7, 1927 - Camden: Recording for RCA Victor.

March 15, 1927 - Brooklyn, New York: Metropolitan Opera Company on tour, Giulietta in *Les Contes d'Hoffmann*.

March 17, 1927 - New York: Metropolitan Opera Company, Nedda in *I Pagliacci* with Johnson, DeLuca, Bada, and Tibbett. Conductor, Vincenzo Bellezza.

March 21, 1927 - New York: Metropolitan Opera Company, Giulietta in *Les Contes d'Hoffmann* with Talley, Queena Mario, Howard, Wakefield, Chamlee, Didur, DeLuca, Rothier, Ananian, George Cehanovsky, Wolfe, D'Anglelo, Bada, Altglass, Gustafson, and Picco. Conductor, Hasselmans.

March 22, 1927 - New York: Metropolitan Opera Company, Marguerite in *Faust* with Tokatyan, Feodor Chaliapin, DeLuca, Wolfe, Ellen Dalossy, and Howard. Conductor, Hasselmans.

*April 3, 1927 - New York: Atwater Kent radio program WEAF, Beniamino Gigli, the evening's scheduled performer, was ill and could not appear. Presenting the program were Mary Lewis and Allen McQuhae. Further information not available.

April 4, 12, & 13, 1927 - Camden: Recording for RCA Victor.

April 14, 1927 - New York: Marriage to Michael Bohnen, bass-baritone at the Metropolitan Opera Company.

April 15, 1927 - New York: Metropolitan Opera Company, Giulietta in *Les Contes d'Hoffmann* with Nina Morgana, Bori, Howard, Wakefield, Tokatyan, Didur, Tibbett, Rothier, Ananian, Cehanovsky, Wolfe, D'Anglelo, Paltrinieri, Altglass, Gustafson, and Picco. Conductor, Hasselmans.

April 1927 - New York: Filming Vitaphone picture, abridged version of *The Tales of Hoffman*, one of the first talkies, not completed. The producers said the filming was not usable because Mary Lewis was inebriated. Mary presented affidavits this was not true. This was the first indication alcoholism could be a problem.

May 10, 1927 - Contracted to appear as Giulietta in *Les Contes d'Hoffmann* at Rochester, New York, Metropolitan Opera Company. Mary sailed for Europe with Bohnen, the role was played by Bori.

*May 15, 1927 - Monte Carlo: Recital at Casa Del Mare. "Deh Vieni, non tardar"; "Ariett" from *Manon*; "Wohin" ("Where are you going?") from *Die Schöne Müllerin* (The Pretty Miller) by Franz Schubert; "Die Mainacht" ("May Night") by Johannes Brahms; "Ständchen" ("Little Song") by Richard Strauss; "Depuis le jour"; Musetta's "Waltz Song"; "Down in the Forest"; "Valgovind's Boat Song"; "The Holy Child"; and "Voices of Children" by Rummel. Pierce, pianist.

Summer 1927 - Concert tour of European capitals. Berlin, Germany, Marguerite in *Faust* with Bohnen, Tauber, and Heinrich Schlusnus. Dates and appearances not available.

August 10, 1927 - Chicago, Illinois: Ravinia Festival. Giulietta, *Les Contes d'Hoffmann* with Helen Freund as Olympia, Florence Macbeth as Antonia. Rest of cast: Chamlee, Ina Bourskaya, Rothier, Danise, Désiré Defrère, D'Angelo, Cehanovsky, José Mojica, and Philine Falco. Conductor, Hasselmans.

August 14, 1927 - Chicago, Illinois; Ravinia Festival. Mimì in *La Bohème* with Margery Maxwell, Johnson, Basiola, Rothier, Defrere, Ananian, and Paltrinieri. Conductor, Papi.

*September 4, 1927 - Chicago, Illinois, Ravinia Festival: Orchestra Program with soloists Mary Lewis, Alfred Wallenstein, Walter Hancock. Conductor, Eric DeLamarter. Mary Lewis sang "Portrait of a Young Girl" and "Festivals" by Felix Borowski; "The Waltz Song" (*Roméo et Juliette*); "The Answer"; "Iris" by Ware; "The House that Jack Built" by Sidney Homer; "Rain"; and "One Golden Day" by Fay Foster. This was a 3 p.m. performance with American compositions.

September 12 & 23, October 11, 1927 - Camden: Recording for RCA Victor.

October 31, 1927 - Little Rock: Recital at Little Rock High School new auditorium, Civic Music Course, Musical Coterie.

November 21 - 1927 - New York: Scheduled for radio broadcast at Capitol Theater. Performance not broadcast.

December 20, 1927 - Camden: Recording for RCA Victor.

February 13, 1928 - New York: Metropolitan Opera Company, Nedda in *I Pagliacci* with Giovanni Martinelli, Bohnen, Alfio Tedesco, and Tibbett. Conductor, Bellezza.

*February 19, 1928 - Miami Beach Garden, Florida: Recital.

*February 28, 1928 - San Francisco, California: Recital, Civic Auditorium. Zoller, pianist.

*March 8, 1928 - Waterbury, Connecticut: Recital at Buckingham Hall, Paul Prentzel Course. Lester Hodges, pianist.

*March 8, 1928 - East Stroudsburg, Pennsylvania: Recital for dedication of new auditorium at State Teacher's College.

March 11, 1928 - New York: Carnegie Hall, 4th annual Wolfsohn Concert Course, Italian songs by Lotti, Paisello, and Faccio; Lieder by R. Strauss, Brahms, and Joseph Marx; French songs by Reynaldo Hahn, Debussy, Erik Satie, and Léo Delibes; English numbers "Symphony in Yellow," by Charles Griffes, "The House that Jack Built," and "The Nightingales of Lincoln's Inn" by Herbert Oliver; and "Tarantella Napoletani" (Rossini). Encores included: "Carry Me Back to Old Virginny," "The Song of India" from *Sadko* (Rimsky-Korsakov); and Rossini's "La Danza."

*March 14, 1928 - Toronto, Canada: Recital sponsored by Eaton Choral Society at Mossey Hall.

March 15, 1928 - New York: Metropolitan Opera Company, Giulietta in *Les Contes d'Hoffmann* with Morgana, Mario, Howard, Wakefield, Tokatyan, Pavel Ludikar, DeLuca, Rothier, Meader, Cehanovsky, Wolfe, D'Angelo, Paltrinieri, Tedesco, Arnold Gabor, and Gustafson. Conductor, Hasselmans.

*March 16, 1928 - Haddonfield, New Jersey: Recital.

March 20, 1928 - New York: Metropolitan Opera Company, Marguerite in *Faust* with Chamlee, Chaliapin, DeLuca, D'Angelo, Dalossy, and Howard. Conductor, Hasselmans.

March 21, 1928 - New York: Metropolitan Opera Company, Nedda in *I Pagliacci* with Johnson, Mario Basiola, Tedesco, and Tibbett. Conductor, Bellezza.

*March 23 - Philadelphia, Pennsylvania: Recital at the Forum.

*March 24, 1928 - Atlantic City, New Jersey: Recital in Chalfonte-Haddon Hall. Zoller, pianist.

March 26, 1928 - Camden: Recording for RCA Victor.

*March 31, 1928 - Shreveport, Louisiana: Recital. Zoller, pianist.

*April 8, 1928 - Lindsborg, Kansas: Afternoon recital, a feature of the annual Messiah festival. Zoller, pianist.

*April 13, 1928 - Goldsboro, North Carolina: Recital at the Eastern Carolina Exposition.

April 18, 1928 - Camden: Recording for RCA Victor.

May 14, 1928 - Appearance at Newark Music Festival, canceled. Mary Lewis sailed for Europe.

+June 5, 1928 - Berlin: Joint Concert with Bohnen. Mary Lewis-Bohnen sang "Du bist die Ruh" ("You are the silence") and "Wohin," "Mainacht" by Brahms; "Ständchen"; and "From the land of the sky-blue water"; "To a massenger"; "Endlich naht sich die Stunde" ("Finally the hour comes"); "Rezitativ und Arie aus" from *Figaros Hochzeit* by Mozart; "Man nennt mich jetzt Mimi" ("My Name is Mimi") from *La Bohème*; and "Wie flammte auf sein Auge" ("How did his eye start to flame") from *Bajazzo* by Leoncavello. [Spellings as appeared. Although the titles are in German, Mary sang in English, French, and Italian, as well as German.]

+October 11, 1928 - Berlin: Concert, four language program, Mary Lewis sang "Pur Dicesti" by Lotti; "Chi vuol la zingarella" (Who wants this lady without a home") by Paisifello; "Sortita d'Ofelia" (*Amleto*, 1865, a little known 19th century opera by Franco Faccio based on Shakespeare's *Hamlet*); "Alleluja" by Mozart; "Hat dich die Liebe berührt" ("How did love touch you"), "Der bescheidene Schäfer" ("The modest shepherd") and "Nocturne" ("Night") by Marx; "Schlechtes Wetter" ("Bad weather") and "Ständchen"; "Recueillement" ("Meditation") and "Fantoches" by Debussy; "Hymn au soleil" by Alex Georges; and "Les filles de Cadix" by Delibes. Five encores: "From the land of the sky-blue water" (*indianisch*); "The Kerry dance" (*irländisch*); "Carry me back to old Virginny" and "The house that Jack built" (*amerikanisch*); and "La danza." Coenraad V. Bos, pianist. [Language descriptions as given in programs.]

+October 26, 1928 - Budapest, Hungary: Concert.

*December 2, 1928 - Monte Carlo: Recital at Casa Del Mare. "Pur dicesti" by Antonio Lotti; "Addio" ("Final Good-bye")(*La Bohème*); "Alleluja"; "Der bescheidene Schäfer" and "Nocturne"; "Schlechtes Wetter" and "Ständchen"; "Hymne au soleil" by Georges; "Si mes vers avaient des ailes" by Hahn; "Depuis le jour"; aria from *Manon*; "The Holy Child"; "The Nightingales of Lincoln's Inn"; "The Kerry Dance"; and "The House that Jack Built." Emmeline Brook, pianist.

#December 25, 1928 - Arrives from Europe on White Star liner *Majestic*. Although Bohnen's name was not listed among the 8 celebrities noted among the 1,000 passengers on board, it is assumed he returned with Mary Lewis.

*January 1, 1929 - Rochester, New York: Recital, Columbus Auditorium.

*January 11, 1929 - Des Moines, Iowa: Recital, Shrine Temple Auditorium. Fred Bristol, pianist.

*January 15, 1929 - Lincoln, Nebraska: Recital at St. Paul Church. Bristol, pianist.

*January 21, 1929 - Baltimore, Maryland: Concert at The Belvedere Hotel. Zoller, pianist.

Mary Lewis

*January 27, 1929 - New York: WEAF Atwater Kent radio concert 9:15 p.m.. Included some little known Spanish Folk Songs of California. "Un Pagarito," Spanish love lyric; "Ballatella" from *I Paglicacci*; "Serenade Francaise"; "An Oriental Romance"; "Serenade" (Gounod); "The House That Jack Built"; "Nocturne"; "Little Bit of Fellow" with violin obligato; and "Blue Danube Waltz" (On the Beautiful Blue Danube) by Johann Strauss. Supported by Symphonic Orchestra directed by Josef Pasternack. Telegram from Chicago from Hattie Maynard, "Program coming in fine give Mary Lewis my love from her mother" to National Broadcasting Company, WEAF 5th Ave. 10 p.m. Other telegrams received from Iowa, Kansas, Arkansas, Connecticut, California.

*January 31, 1929 - Rochester, New York: Recital, Columbus Auditorium. Zoller, pianist.

*February 5, 1929 - Paterson, New Jersey: Recital, Eastside High School for the benefit of Paterson State Normal School. Zoller, pianist.

*February 11, 1929 - Joplin, Missouri: Concert at Memorial Hall. Zoller, pianist. Also appearing was Renée Chemet, French violinist.

#March 4, 1929 - Scranton, Pennsylvania: Recital at Central High School Auditorium. Zoller, pianist.

#March 8, 1929 - New York: Metropolitan Opera Company, Marguerite in *Faust* with Lauri-Volpi, Chaliapin, Basiola, Ananian, Pearl Besuner, and Wakefield. Conductor, Bellezza. Benefit for Sir Wilfred Grenfell's Medical Mission in Labrador. Proceeds of $7,500 to be used to help rebuild an orphanage and build a new hospital.

#March 11, 1929 - York, Pennsylvania: Recital at William Penn High School. Zoller, pianist.

March 17, 1929 - New York: Metropolitan Opera Company, Concert. "Ah je ris," (*Faust*) and excerpts the Garden Scene with quartet consisting of Lewis, Falco, Tedesco, and Ludikar. Bohnen did not perform as scheduled.

March 20, 1929 - New York: Metropolitan Opera Company, Marguerite in *Faust* with Lauri-Volpi, Chaliapin, Tibbett, Wolfe, Dalossy, and Wakefield. Conductor, Hasselmans.

March 30, 1929 - New York: Metropolitan Opera Company, Marguerite in *Faust* with Lauri-Volpi, Bohnen, Basiola, Ananian, Dalossy, and Wakefield. Conductor, Hasselmans.

April 12, 1929 - New York: Metropolitan Opera Company, Micaela in *Carmen* with Bourskaya, Aida Doninelli, Dorothea Flexer, Antonin Trantoul, Ezio Pinza, Picco, Bada, D'Angelo, and Cehanovsky. Conductor, Artur Bodanzky.

NOTE: No information concerning Mary Lewis is available until the following year. In 1929 the stock market of the United States collapsed, leading to a world-wide economic depression.

April 13, 1930 - New York: Metropolitan Opera Company, Concert, "Deh vieni, non tardar" (*Le Nozze di Figaro*), and "Les filles de Cadix."

April 20, 1930 - New York: Metropolitan Opera Company, Concert, "Ah! Je vieux vivre." (*Roméo et Juliette*).

May 4, 1930 - New York: Collapsed after singing 2 numbers over nation-wide radio hook-up, following receiving word her "adopted" father Osbourne O'Hagan in Monte Carlo was critically ill.

Summer 1930 - Los Angeles: Concert at Hollywood Bowl, California.

August 1930 - Hollywood: Divorce from Bohnen.

Week of November 22, 1930 - New York: RKO-Keith Palace Theater, vaudeville appearance.

January 29, 1931 - New York: Town Hall concert. Zoller, pianist.

May 9, 1931 - Paris: *La Comtesse Maritza* (Emmerich Kálmán's *Grafin Maritza* or *Countess Maritza*). The operetta was sung in French at Theatre Ambassadeur in Paris, and followed by season, length unknown.

September, 19, 1931 - Marriage to Robert Hague, Standard Oil executive.

June 7, 1933 - New York: Radio broadcast station WMCA, completed before Mary Lewis was rushed to hospital for an emergency appendectomy.

December 17, 1933 - New York: Majestic Theater, fund-raising concert with John McCormack for Church of St. Benedict the Moor. Mary sang selections by Faccio, Handel, and Mozart; "Bird Song" (by Edwin Schneider, McCormack's accompanist); "The Nightingales of Lincoln's Inn"; and "Blue Danube Waltz." Benefit sponsored by Hague.

May 18, 1934 - New York: Re-debut recital Town Hall, New York. Selections in French by Henri Duparc, Satie, Debussy, and Saint-Saëns; German Lieder by Brahms, Hugo Wolf, and R. Strauss; "The Sleep That Flits on Baby's Eyes" by John Alden Carpenter; Frédéric Chopin's "Lithuanian Song"; and "Romance" from *Preciosa* (Karl von Weber).

September 17, 1935 - Visit to Little Rock, press report Mary Lewis has shown a violent dislike to the publicity spotlight. Mary Lewis and Hague had recently returned from their second trip to Europe since Christmas of 1934.

#October 16, 1935 - New York: Hosts dinner for artists cooperating in the interest of the Brooklyn Academy of Music at Ritz Tower, 465 Park Ave. For the benefit Mary Lewis sang "Sortita d'Ofelia" (*Amleto)*.

#November 8, 1935 - New York: Rehearsal for November 17 broadcast, held at the Hague's apartment, Ritz Tower, invitation only.

#November 10, 1935 - Rumor Mary Lewis has husband's permission to resume her career and is interested in radio, information sent out by wire service.

#November 10, 1935 - New York: Attended Rafaelo Diaz concert at Waldorf-Astoria. Mary was persuaded to sing and was very favorably received.

#November 11, 1935 - New York: Radio broadcast WYNC, Joyce Kilmer Memorial Program. Kilmer was a poet and newspaper man killed in battle in World War I. Mary Lewis sang "Trees," a poem written by Kilmer set to music.

#November 13, 1935 - New York: Musicale sponsored by Verdi Club at Hotel Plaza. Mary Lewis replaced the singer who was ill. Zoller, pianist.

#November 15, 1935 - New York: Dinner in honor of 85th birthday of Harriet Hague, Mary's mother-in-law.

#November 17, 1935 - New York: Radio broadcast WMCA for the 11th annual dinner and ball for the Brooklyn Federation of Jewish Charities at Hotel St. George. Mary Lewis sang "Blue Danube Waltz," "Les Filles de Cadix," and "Eli, Eli" (Hebrew). Comedian Milton Berle was also on the billing. Two thousand attended.

#November 17, 1935 - New York: Starlight Roof, Waldorf-Astoria. Reception and dance sponsored by American Merchant Marine Conference Committee.

#November 18, 1935 - New York: Reception and ball, invitation of Board of Directors of Radio Personalities, Park Central Hotel.

#November 22, 1935 - New York: Benefit Bridge, Supper, and Dance for Catholic Actors Guild at the Plaza, Mary Lewis vice-chairman.

#November 24, 1935 - New York: Thanksgiving Eve, American Christmas Fund and Relief benefit at Fabian's Fox Theater.

#December 9, 1935 - New York: Evening at the Metropolitan Opera with former Mayor Jimmy Walker, and his wife, and Zoe Atkins, playwright/poet.

#January 8, 1936 - New York: Mary Lewis and Hague were hosts for reception for Atkins, author of "O Evening Star" which had premiered at Empire Theater. Guests included Grand Duchess Marie, Ina Claire of the Metropolitan Opera, Dorothy Parker, Elsa Maxwell, columnists.

#January 19, 1936 - New York: Majestic Theater, benefit performance for Church of St. Benedict The Moor. Mary Lewis Hague was listed as a box holder, as well as one of the artists.

#January 22, 1936 - New York: Played Hurdy-Gurdy organ at Day Nursery with publicity to persuade Mayor Fiorella La Guardia to rescind the ban on the street musicians.

#January 29, 1936 - New York: Radio broadcast interview about Hurdy-Gurdies, WABC. Cable from London from Hague wishing Mary Lewis "Happy Birthday," although he was not sure of the correct date.

#January 30, 1936 - New York: Franklin D. Roosevelt parties for the benefit of those afflicted with infantile paralysis. Mary Lewis helped plan the party sponsored by Diaz. She sang "My Man's Gone Now" from *Porgy and Bess*, composer George Gershwin accompanied.

#January 31, 1936 - New York: 7th annual Press Photographers Association, Grand Ballroom Hotel Commodore.

#February 4, 1936 - New York: Afternoon benefit for United Order of True Sisters at Hotel Biltmore, Cascades Room. Eight hundred attended.

#February 4, 1936 - New York: Guest of honor at "Evening of Celebrities" at the Ambassador. Mary Lewis sang "My Man's Gone Now," accompanied by Vincent Lopez orchestra.

#February 8, 1936 - Kearny, New Jersey: Guest at launching stand for Tanker, "T.C. McCobb," at Federal Shipbuilding and Dry Dock Co.

#February 11, 1936 - New York: Entered half-a-dozen Dachshunds in Westminster Kennel Club show, Madison Square Garden.

#February 16, 1936 - New York: Benefit for The Catholic Actors Guild, Hotel Astor.

#February 18, 1936 - New York: Judge at Yodeling Contest for Children's Welfare Association.

#February 19, 1936 - New York: Benefit for Adventure Society at Ritz-Carlton, Mrs. Robert (Mary Lewis) Hague headed the women's committee.

#March 4, 1936 - New York: Hostess for party prior to radio show with Ben Bernie. This was to announce her return to the professional world.

March 10, 1936 - Miami, Florida: Guest soloist on American Can Company radio broadcast from Miami, Florida, over NBC-WJZ network. "I'm Shooting High" and "If I Should Lose You" from *Rose of the Rancho*.

May 11-13, 1936 - Lakehurst, New Jersey, to Berlin, Germany: Carried 35 pounds of sheet music aboard the *Hindenburg* airship to entertain while en route to Berlin.

September 19, 1936 - Benton, Arkansas: Saline County Centennial celebration. 7 a.m. morning open air religious service. Mary Lewis, soloist. Henry Sanderson, accompanist.

September 20, 1936 - Little Rock: Second Baptist Church, "Alleluia" and "I'll Go Where You Want Me to Go."

October 29, 1936 - New York: Versailles night club engagement.

January 1, 1937 - New York: Inauguration of Gov. Herbert Lehman, Mary Lewis sang "The Star Spangled Banner" immediately after the governor took the oath of office, and concluded the ceremony with singing "America."

#January 30, 1937 - New York: Inauguration of Saturday Afternoon Forum Course, conducted by National Democratic Club broadcast over nation-wide radio hook-up.

#February 26, 1937 - Philadelphia, Pennsylvania: Vaudeville/Concert at Fox Theater.

February, 1937 - New York: Recording for Thesaurus series, RCA label.

#Spring, 1937 - Mary Lewis separated from Hague and sailed to Europe. She stated that she was not returning.

+#May 2, 1937 - Hamburg, Germany: Recital, "Sortita d'Ofelia"; "Deh vieni, non tardar" ("Oh Come, Do Not Delay")(*Figaro*) and "Alleluja" ("Exultate"); "Die Mainacht," "Das Mädchen spricht" (The girl speaking), "Alte Liebe" (Old love), and

"Gang zur Liebsten" (The walk to the beloved) by Brahms; aria from "*Der goldene Hahn*" (*The Golden Cockerel*) by Rimsky-Korsakov; "Verschwiegene Liebe" (Discreet Love) and "Auf dem grünen Balkon" (On the green balcony) by Wolf; "Nocturne," "Der bescheidene Schäfer" by Marx; "Du bist wie eine Blume" (You are like a flower) and "Die Lorelei" by Franz Liszt; "Carmela" by Gertrude Ross; "One golden Day"; "Wiegenlied" (Lullaby) and "Kling" by R. Strauss. Prof. Michael Raucheisen, pianist. [Language descriptions as given in programs.]

+#May 6, 1937 - Berlin: Concert, *Aire der Ofelia aus „Amleto*"; *Arie aus „Figaros Hochzeit*" and "Alleluja"; Die Mainacht, Das Mädchen, Alte Liebe, Der Gang zum Liebchen; Sonnenhymne aus „*Der goldene Hahn*"; Verschwiegene Liebe; Auf dem grünen Balkon; Nocturne, Der bescheidene Schäfer; Du bist wie eine Blume; Die Lorelei; Carmela; One Golden Day; Wiegenlied; and Kling. Raucheisen, pianist. [Language descriptions as given in programs.]

+#June 3, 1937 - Paris: Concert at *Maison Gaveau*. "Sortita d'Ofelia"; "Deh vieni, non tardar" (*Figaro*); "Alleluja"; "Air de l'Enfant"; "Le Chapelier" by Satie; "Recueillement"; "Les filles de Cadix"; Aria from "*Le Coq d'Or*" by Rimsky-Korsakov; "Lithuania Song" by Chopin; "Cuckoo Clock" by Young; "Symphony in Yellow"; "In the Garden where the Praties grow" by Liddle; "One golden day"; "Verschwiegene Liebe"; "Der bescheidene Schäfer"; "Nocturne"; "Wiegenlied" and "Kling." Gerald Moore, pianist.

+#June 15, 1937 - London: Recital in Queen's Hall. "Sortita d'Ofelia"; "Deh vieni, non tardar"; "Alleluja!"; "Air de l'Enfant"; "Mai" by Saint-Saëns; "Recueillement"; "Les filles de Cadix"; "Sweet was the Morning" (Lithuanian Song) by Chopin; "Pierrot" by Cornelius Rybner; "Symphony in Yellow"; "In the Garden where the Praties grow"; "One golden day"; "Verschwiegene Liebe"; "Der bescheidene Schäfer"; "Nocturne"; "Wiegenlied"; and "Kling." Moore, pianist.

In March, 1938, German troops marched into Austria, a preliminary to World War II. Date unknown when Mary Lewis returns from Europe.

March 8, 1939 - New York: Hague dead. Mary Lewis flew from Arkansas to attend funeral service. Although the couple had been separated, Mary Lewis was still married to Hague.

#April 19, 1939 - New York: Soloist at Hotel Astor benefit for the Detective's Endowment Association Incorporated, Police Department of City of New York.

#April 22, 1939 - New York: Ziegfeld Memories at the Starlight Roof, Waldorf-Astoria. Mary sang "The Star Spangled Banner" to open the program and she also sang "Les Filles de Cadix."

#June 25, 1939 - New York: Soloist at dedication of sign for Wethered J. Boyd Council Knights of Columbus.

Summer - 1939 - Final concert tour, Puerto Rico. Zoller, pianist. Mary Lewis became ill on tour.

March 11, 1940 - Mother of Mary Lewis, Hattie Maynard dead.

December 31, 1941 - Mary Lewis dead.

Index

G

H

I

J

K

L

M

N

O

S

T

U

V

W

Z

Selected Bibliography

Baral, Robert. *Revue - The Great Broadway Period.* New York and London: Fleet Press Corporation, 1962.

Blum, Daniel. *A Pictorial History of the Silent Screen.* New York: G. B. Putnam's Sons, 1953.

Bohnen file, clipping, n.p., n.d., New York Public Library.

Calhoun, Frances. "Snaring a Song Bird With Sound," n.p., May 1930.

Carter, Randolph. *The World of Flo Ziegfeld.* New York: Praeger Publishers, 1974.

Cox, W. Miles, Ph. D. University of Minnesota. *The Encyclopedia of Psychoactive Drugs: The Addictive Personality.* New York, New Haven, Philadelphia: Cheslsea House Publishers, 1986.

Daughters of the American Revolution Magazine. Washington, D.C., May 1974.

Day, Donald. *Will Rogers—a Biography.* New York: David McKay Co., 1962.

Dennis, James F.E. *The Record Collector.* Ipswich, England, Vol. 23, Nos. 7 & 8, Dec. 1976.

Dennis, James F.E. "Michael Bohnen," *The Record Collector.* Ipswich, England, Vol. 27, Nos. 9 & 10, 27 Jan. 1983.

Dillard, Tom W. "H.F. Auten: A Man Who Could Not Stand Still," (Arkansas) *Pulaski County Historical Review XXIX* (Spring, 1981).

Dizikes, John. *Opera In America - A Cultural History.* New Haven, Connecticut and London: Yale University Press, 1993.

Dougan, Michael B. "An American Tragedy." *Opera News,* July 1984.

Dougan, Michael B. "A Touching Enigma, The Opera Career of Mary Lewis," delivered at the 1975 meeting of the Arkansas History Association at Jonesboro, Arkansas.

Dougan, Michael B. "Mary Lewis, An Arkansas Girl in Grand Opera."

Dougan, Michael B., Jonesboro, Arkansas. Notes to author, September, 1998.

Dragonette, Jessica. *Faith Is a Song - The Odyssey Of An American Artist.* New York: David McKay Company, Inc., 1951.

Drinkow, John. *The Operetta Book.* New York: Drake Publishers, 1973.

Eaton, Quaintance. *Opera Caravan: Adventures of the Metropolitan on Tour 1883-1956.* New York: Farrar, Straus and Cudahy, sponsored by Metropolitan Opera Guild.

Ewen, David. *Great Composers 1300-1900 - A Biographical and Critical Guide.* New York: The H.W. Wilson Company, 1966.

Ewen, David. *Composers Since 1900 - A Biographical and Critical Guide.* New York: The H.W. Wilson Company, 1969.

Fitch family file: Knight, Mary, n.p. 10 May 1931; clipping, n.p., 17 Sept. 1935; *St. Louis Daily Globe-Democrat,* 27 Jan. 1936; Little Rock *Arkansas Gazette,* May 1936; clipping, n.p., 2 Jan. 1942; *Arkansas Democrat,* n.d.; Roberts, Rob. n.p., n.d.; Moore, Edward, n.p., n.d.

Fitch, Anna Lecky, personal letters written to her son, Rev. Frank Fitch, 1934-36.

Focus #38. Delaware, Ohio: Ohio Wesleyan University, Nov. 1977.

Gilman, Lawrence, New York *Herald Tribune.* 29 May 1932, Bohnen file, New York Public Library.

Guthrie, Janice. The Health Resource, 209 Katherine Drive, Conway, Arkansas.

Green, Stanley. *Broadway Musicals Show by Show.* Milwaukee, Wisconsin: Hal Leonard, 1985.

Hall, Gladys, "She Obeyed That Impulse," *Motion Picture,* n.p., n.d.

Hoeling, A.A. *Who Destroyed the Hindenburg?* Little, Brown & Co., 1962.

Hughes, Rupert. *The Biographical Dictionary of Musicians.* Revised & edited by Deems Taylor and Russell Kerr. New York: Blue Ribbon Books, Inc. 1940.

Jones, Harry Earl by K.J. Kutsch and Leo Riemens, translated from German by Jones. *A Concise Biographical Dictionary of Singers - From the Beginning of Recorded Sound to the Present.* Philadelphia, New York, London: Chilton Book Company, 1969.

Katkov, Norman. *The Fabulous Fanny, the Story of Fanny Brice.* New York: Alfred A. Knopf, 1953.

Kolodin, Irving. *The Metropolitan Opera 1883-1966: A Candid History.* New York: Alfred A. Knopf, 1967.

"The Lambs," *Notable Names in the American Theatre.* James T. White & Co., 1976. Research by New York Public Library.

Lewis, Mary. "From the Slums, to the Follies, to Grand Opera." *Ladies' Home Journal,* (May, June, July 1927).

Mary Lewis

Lewis, Mary. File, Little Rock, Arkansas: Arkansas Room, Music and Musicians.

Lewis, Mary. File, Metropolitan Opera Company, New York.

Lewis, Mary. File, New York Public Library: clipping, n.p., 1926; clipping, n.p., 1933; clipping, n.p., 19 March 1934.

Lewis, Mary. Scrapbooks (3), courtesy of Lawrence Holdridge, Amityville, New York, Oct. 1998.

Lewis, Mary Woodward. Letters to author from 3rd wife of J. Keene Lewis.

Marsh, Leo A. New York *Telegraph*, 31 Aug. 1920, New York Public Library Theater Collection.

Metropolitan Opera News, 22 Jan. 1942, Lewis file, New York Public Library.

Miller, William H. *The First Great Ocean Liners in Photographs, 1897-1927*. New York: Dover Publications, Inc., 1984. Courtesy of Charles F. Martin.

Mooney, Michael Macdonald. *The Hindenburg*. New York: Dodd, Mead & Co., 1972.

Moran, W.R., "The Recordings of Mary Lewis," *The Record Collector*. Vol. 23, Dec. 1976.

The Musician. March 1931.

National Broadcasting Company release 3 Mar. 1936, Lewis file, New York Public Library.

National Consumers League, Workers Protected Due to Early League Efforts, http://www.natl-consumersleague.org/radium.htm.

Nelson, E.T. *Fifty Years ofHistory of the Ohio Wesleyan University, 1844-1894*. Cleveland, Ohio: The Cleveland Printing & Publishing Co., 1895.

News-Week. 25 July 1936. Research by Starved Rock Library System.

Norwood, Paul. *New York Telegraph*, 11 Sept. 1926.

O'Brien, P.J. *Will Rogers—Ambassador of Good Will, Prince of Wit and Wisdom*. n.p., 1935.

O'Connell, Charles. *Victor Book of the Opera*. RCA Manufacturing Co, 1936.

Oral interview, 1983, Mildred McCausland Fitch, (1896-1992), second wife of Rev. Francis F. Fitch, (1873-1952), son of Rev. William and Anna Fitch.

Oral interview, 1983, F.T. Fitch, (1900-1992), son ofRev. Frank F. Fitch, and with Blanche Fitch, (1899-1983), wife of Finley T. Fitch. Blanche and Finley were parents of the author.

Orr, W.E. *That's Judsonia*. Judsonia: White Company Printing, 1957.

Pinecrest Memorial Park, Alexander, Arkansas. File, Hattie Maynard, Mary Lewis Hague.

Phillips, Julien. *Stars of the Ziegfeld Follies*. Minneapolis, Minnesota: Lerner Publications Co., 1972.

Program *Greenwich Village Follies 1920*, New York Public Library.

Program *Ziegfeld Follies 1921* and *1922*.

Prosser, David E. "Unruly Giant," *Opera News*, 31 Jan. 1970.

Quinn, Michael, "Mary Lewis—The Radio Discs," *The Record Collector*, XLII, Sept. 1977, pp. 188-194.

Ravinia program, Fitch scrapbooks.

RKO-Keith Palace Theatre Magazine of Vaudeville, 22 Nov. 1930.

Seltsam, William H. *Metropolitan Opera Annals*. New York: The H.W. Wilson Company in Association with The Metropolitan Opera Guild, Inc., 1947.

Stone, Robert B., n.p., to Michael B. Dougan, 9 Sept. 1977.

Talbot, Nellie. *Praises*. E.O. Excell, n.p., n.d..

Tallquist, Kay. *Arkansas Democrat*, 28 March 1926.

Taylor, Robert Lewis. *W.C. Fields—His Follies and Fortunes*. New York: The New American Library, 1967.

The Cage, Little Rock High School yearbook, fifth edition, 1911.

The Encyclopedia Americana, 1968, 1984, Grolier Incorporated, Danbury, Connecticut.

Vaeth, J. Gordon. *Graf Zeppelin*. New York: Harper & Bros., 1958.

Variety, 6 Jan. 1960. New York Public Library Theater Collection.

Wentworth, Myrene. "Who's An Ugly Duckling?" *Screenland*, July 1930.

Who's Who in America, 1932-33.

The World Book Encyclopedia, 1961 ed. S.v., Field Enterprises Educational Corporation, Merchandise Mart Plaza, Chicago, Illinois.